Single Black Mother

PHILOSOPHY OF RACE

Series Editors
Linda Martín Alcoff, Hunter College and the Graduate Center CUNY
Chike Jeffers, Dalhousie University

Socially Undocumented: Identity and Immigration Justice
Amy Reed-Sandoval

Unruly Women: Race, Neocolonialism, and the Hijab
Falguni A. Sheth

Reconsidering Reparations
Olúfẹ́mi O. Táíwò

A Realistic Blacktopia: Why We Must Unite to Fight
Derrick Darby

Critical Philosophy of Race: Essays
Robert Bernasconi

Beauvoir and Belle: A Black Feminist Critique of *The Second Sex*
Kathryn Sophia Belle

Race, Time, and Utopia: Critical Theory and the Process of Emancipation
William Paris

Single Black Mother: Queer Reflections on Marriage and Racial Justice
Anika Maaza Simpson

Single Black Mother

Queer Reflections on Marriage and Racial Justice

ANIKA MAAZA SIMPSON

OXFORD
UNIVERSITY PRESS

Oxford University Press is a department of the University of Oxford.
It furthers the University's objective of excellence in research, scholarship,
and education by publishing worldwide. Oxford is a registered trade mark of
Oxford University Press in the UK and in certain other countries.

Published in the United States of America by Oxford University Press
198 Madison Avenue, New York, NY 10016, United States of America.

© Oxford University Press 2025

All rights reserved. No part of this publication may be reproduced, stored in a retrieval system, transmitted, used for text and data mining, or used for training artificial intelligence, in any form or by any means, without the prior permission in writing of Oxford University Press, or as expressly permitted by law, by license or under terms agreed with the appropriate reprographics rights organization. Inquiries concerning reproduction outside the scope of the above should be sent to the Rights Department, Oxford University Press, at the address above.

You must not circulate this work in any other form
and you must impose this same condition on any acquirer

CIP data is on file at the Library of Congress

ISBN 9780197555934 (pbk)
ISBN 9780197555927 (hbk)

DOI: 10.1093/9780197555965.001.0001

Paperback printed by Integrated Books International, United States of America
Hardback printed by Bridgeport National Bindery, Inc., United States of America

To Basil and Sabine
Souls of my soul

Contents

Acknowledgments ix

1. Introduction 1
2. Canaries in the Mine 25
3. Black Liberation and Deviant Moralities 53
4. Corrupted Intimacies 83
5. An Abolitionist Invitation 110

Notes 137
Index 167

Acknowledgments

I must first thank those who inspired me to bring pen to page.

To A. J. Verdelle, I am ever grateful to you for receiving my daily checkmarks. This small act renewed my commitment to the craft of writing and to myself as a writer.

Inspiration must give way to consistent practice. For this, I must thank the incredible, brilliant, hilarious, and generous Daily Writing Crew. To Eve Dunbar, Crystal Donker, Jessica Rofé, and Jennifer Williams, thank you for supporting me during this journey. I could not have finished this book without each of you.

I am eternally grateful to Kristie Dotson, Denise James, and Paul Taylor for your sharp and insightful critiques at the start of this project. Without mincing words or sparing laughter, you helped me forge the path that ultimately led to this final destination. Thank you once more for participating in the book incubator process (we survived the Mansion at O!). I must especially thank Paul for lending research support through Vanderbilt University. Your wise counsel and steadfast friendship has been a rare light in this profession of ours.

I would like to thank Angela Davis, Gina Dent, and Seneca for generously sharing your majestic mountainside home with me. Your scholarship has had a profound impact on my intellectual and political commitments. I continue to cherish the experience of conjuring Black feminist abolition dreams in your California haven.

I must thank Linda Alcoff and Charles Mills for the invitation to present my work at the Black Women Philosophers Conference at the CUNY Graduate Center. The feedback that I received from my sister scholars was instrumental to the completion of this project. I remain deeply saddened by the untimely loss of Charles. His scholarship and encouragement are still quite meaningful to me.

Ellen Feder, thank you for inviting me to serve as the McDowell Fellow at American University. This book would not exist in its present form with this publisher had you not invested in my scholarship with such generosity. I would also like to thank Matt Ferguson and Adeline Guitierrez for their vital work as research assistants during my tenure at American University.

Bashon Mann, thank you for your unwavering friendship and support as we raise two amazing wonders of the world.

Finally, I would like to express my gratitude for the constructive feedback provided by my copy editor Sara Street and this project's external reviewers. I am also grateful for the funding support provided by the Quarles Institute at Morgan State University.

1
Introduction

The inspiration for this book began the moment I knew with certainty that my marriage was over. The break was deep and clean. Stark in its clarity, the rupture was too absolute to ignore or sweep under a rug. While coming to terms with the impending disintegration of my relationship, I was awestruck by the realization that the world as I knew it would never be the same. I would no longer be a wife. My life and my identity were to begin anew. While divorced mothers are common in the United States, I understood at that moment that I would be joining a particularly castigated category: I was to become a single Black mother.

I was familiar with the statistic that almost half of Black children in the United States are being raised by unmarried Black women.[1] The prevalence of this familial configuration tempered neither the teasing nor worried remarks uttered by family and friends. On the contrary, the weight of the statistic elevated the community's concern about our fracturing union. We were good stewards of the race: the Spelman alum married to the Naval officer with two beautiful daughters. What would a divorce mean for our community? Another broken family? Two more Black children raised without a father in the home? The questions pulled at the vestiges of worn, familiar tropes of expectations for Black families like ours.

I found comfort and strength during this difficult time in the words of Black women. Words sung to me by Sade, Michelle N'degecello, Betty Carter, and Dianne Reeves lifted my spirits. The words of sister scholars, who so poetically distill our life experiences into thought-provoking prose, lit a fire within me. These women helped me to put the pieces of my broken heart back together again. I emerged from this dark period as a confident and openly queer, Black, single mama. The healing powers of Black feminism also filled me with a deep and abiding love for my fellow unmarried Black mothers. The kinship of maternal sisterhood fueled my desire to counter the harmful impact of stigmatization endured by single Black mothers.

According to the Pew Research Center, overall marriage rates in the country have been decreasing precipitously since the 1990s.[2] This decline is most pronounced within the Black population. In 2020, the percentage of never-married Black men was 51.4 and never-married Black women was 47.5.[3] By comparison, in the overall population, the percentages are 35.8 and 30, for men and women, respectively.[4] These statistics encourage the preponderance of negative judgments within scholarly and popular discourses concerning the precarity of unmarried Black mothers. Deficit model discourses illuminate the vulnerabilities particular to unmarried Black mothers, who are routinely blamed for their diminished life conditions. It is my contention, however, that single Black mothers are not parasitic problems in need of eradication. On the contrary, it is the institution of marriage itself that is the problem.

Black women have been at the forefront of liberation movements since our earliest battles against enslavement. One prominent contribution to the cause of freedom offered by Black feminism is the expansion of our understanding of the significance of love, interpersonal relationships, gender, and sexuality to Black liberation movements. This contribution persists despite the competing interests and disparate goals found within Black feminist thought on our most intimate relationships. Responses to the consequences of anti-Black racism upon our intimate selves range from liberal feminists seeking equitable inclusion within state institutions to abolition feminists striving toward the creation of a world anew. While this literature reflects different views about the meaning and importance of marriage and participation in marriage, Black feminists across the ideological spectrum share a tacit acceptance of the marital institution.

One can begin to recognize the enduring acceptance of the state-regulated marriage by revisiting the pervasive trope of the Black matriarch, which haunts Black intimate relations in the United States. The Black matriarch, within which inhabits the specter of the single Black mother, is characterized as a dangerously overbearing, emasculating female head of household that undermines the formation of proper heteronormative nuclear families. In her seminal essay "Reflections on the Black Woman's Role in the Community of Slaves," Angela Davis asserts that the ascription of matriarch to Black women is a "cruel misnomer" because it falsely implies that enslaved women enjoyed stable familial lives and enjoyed authority and/or power.[5] Enslaved Black women had neither authority nor power, as evidenced by their experience of forced childbearing through sexual assault, routine separation from their children, and relentless physical, sexual, and psychological violence. Nevertheless, the false symbol of the Black matriarch continues to negatively impact Black women. Half a century ago, Davis addressed the insidiousness of the "controlling images" of Black women and noted that we must "assume the responsibility of shattering them."[6] Black feminists have done important work on gender roles, patriarchy, and heteronormativity in an attempt to dislodge the historical underpinnings that sustain tropes of Black motherhood.[7] But to date, this work has not been sufficient to attend to the specific needs of single Black mothers, who exist outside of the moral, political, and economic protection of the state-regulated marital institution.

This insufficiency is evident in the work of those who champion liberal reform. For those aligned with liberalism, marriage serves not only as a nexus for romantic love and familial belonging but also as a necessary component of racial uplift, a marker of personhood, and a sign of sexual heteronormativity. These enduring significations have historically informed troubling assumptions regarding the nuclear family structure and gender norms, which motivate the uncritical acceptance of, and advocacy for, the marital institution. Indeed, the prevailing narrative in recent academic and popular literature focused on single Black mothers, authored by those wedded to racial uplift and assimilation, remains aligned with the problematic trope of the Black matriarch. This stance reinforces the familiar, anxiety-ridden refrain within Black communities to protect "The Black Family."[8]

The predilection among contemporary Black liberal reformers toward idealizing the nuclear family model can be traced back to the racial uplift era of the late 19th and early 20th centuries. This period is marked by the efforts of the Black bourgeoisie to link racial progress to the institution of marriage. Middle-class reformists believed that Christian, monogamous marriages would aid in the pursuit of racial equality and Black respectability. The campaign for these purportedly moral homes is evident in the words and deeds of the Black women's club movement and W. E. B. Du Bois, for example.[9] I will address the influence of the Black women's club movement in Chapter 3. At present, I will consider briefly Du Bois's unwavering sentiments regarding the value of the marital institution in contrast to his evolving theoretical assessment of Black liberation.

Paul C. Taylor notes that Du Bois "became one of the foremost shapers of opinion in the Afro-US community," during his tenure as editor of *The Crisis* from 1910 to 1934, a journal published by the National Association for the Advancement of Colored People (NAACP).[10] Du Bois's early work reflects his alignment with the champions of liberal reform and the virtues of the Black elite. His writings, including *The Philadelphia Negro* (1899) and *The Negro American Family* (1908), a comprehensive study conducted under his leadership, profoundly influenced our understanding of the social and ethical mores of Black family life, including the prevailing opinions of unmarried Black mothers.[11] While we can certainly contextualize Du Bois's views within the pervading social and moral codes of the day, it is telling that the crux of his beliefs persists in much the same form in 21st-century Black thought.

In *The Philadelphia Negro*, for example, Du Bois concludes, "The result of this large number of homes without husbands is to increase the burden of charity and benevolence, and also on account of their poor home life to increase crime."[12] He writes further, "The great weakness of the Negro family is still lack of respect for the marriage bond."[13] The continuity of this judgment is evidenced over a century later in the aftermath of the murder of Tyre Nichols, who was beaten to death by five Memphis police officers in January 2023. Black commentator Jason Whitlock appeared on Fox News to speak about the incident and said, "It was a group of young Black men, five on one. It looked like gang violence to me. It looked like what young Black men do when they're supervised by a single Black woman."[14] The blame placed upon single Black mothers for raising criminals and draining state benefits is consistent across time and space. In the aftermath of the 2019 murder of 14-year-old Jayden Moodie in London, journalist Rod Liddle penned an op-ed titled "Half of Black children do not live with their father. And we wonder why they're dying."[15] These criticisms leveled against single Black mothers cannot be dismissed as the views of a few extremists. The negative portrayal of female-headed households is promulgated routinely within mainstream literature, academic scholarship, and state institutions.[16]

Although it can be argued that Du Bois did not explicitly promote the vilified Black matriarch trope in his early writings, we cannot dismiss his considerable anxiety concerning unmarried Black mothers. In her analysis of Du Bois's 1920 article "Damnation of Women," literary scholar Farah Jasmine Griffin writes, "Interestingly, where others have found the seeds of an emasculating Black matriarchy, Du Bois applauds the emergence of economically independent Black women."[17] In addition, she notes that "he asserts the necessity of women's control over their reproduction."[18] While I agree with Griffin's assessment, I remain troubled by Du Bois's lamentation over the consequences he associates with Black women's maternal capacities coupled with their economic prowess in opposition to Black men, who earn considerably less than their white male counterparts. The financial discrepancy, according to Du Bois, leads to an increased dissolution of Black families and a steady number of children born out of wedlock. In response to the "mighty dilemma" of "the unhusbanded woman," Du Bois implores God to "send us a world with woman's freedom and married motherhood inextricably wed."[19] Black freedom is inseparably, nay divinely, tied to the marital institution in Du Bois's influential estimation. Du Bois may have indeed supported the economic independence of women, but their financial gains needed to be subsumed within the marital bond.

Du Bois's stance persisted through his increasing discontent with "the 'respectable' Black leadership in the US," including those associated with the NAACP, who were becoming "increasingly bourgeois and liberal."[20] Du Bois began to consider the interconnectedness of anticolonialist and anticapitalist ideologies in the pursuit of racial justice in the United States. However, his critique of settler colonialism did not impact his perspective concerning unmarried Black motherhood, which remained consistent from his early liberal works to his 1935 study *Black Reconstruction in America*. In this study's assessment of the success of Reconstruction in Mississippi, for example, Du Bois writes, "The advance of the masses of the people was shown in the increase of marriage licenses."[21] Du Bois's consideration of anti-Blackness and colonialism did not deem the foundational institution of marriage as a component of US settler colonialism. Du Bois and his ilk continued to encourage Black people to form families that reflected the nuclear, heteronormative, patriarchal ideal. For middle-class Black people according to historian Anastasia Curwood, "morality within the family was a cornerstone to morality in public life."[22] Sexual conservatism and married motherhood were essential facets of Black lives mattering. Single Black mothers, therefore, undermine our public worth and dignity. While Du Bois can be deemed progressive owing to his insightful arguments regarding colonialism, Pan-Africanism, and capitalism, he remained wedded to the sexual and familial mores of the very colonialists he fought against.

The strong attachment to the marital institution for Black liberationists is rooted within the legacy of chattel slavery. One of the most egregious components of slavery for those committed to Black uplift, according to historian Tera Hunter, was "the destruction of Black families."[23] Prior to emancipation, the variety of family structures, gender expressions, and sexual behaviors present within Black communities could be attributed to the ravages of slavery. In the wake of slavery's end, Black people were considered personally responsible for their alleged and actual misalignments with the tenets of settler sexual citizenship. Proponents of a revisionist view of slavery's history were eager to counter portraits of broken Black families with emasculated men and overbearing matriarchs by touting the presence of nuclear family models during slavery and in its aftermath. However, their revisioning served to erase the agency of Black women who did not wish to marry. According to sociologist Shirley Hill, slavery "negated ideas of female dependency among Black women, and showed them that love, sexuality, childbearing, and family life need not unfold in the context of marriage."[24] This agency is reflected, for example, by enslaved Black women who refused marriage in an effort to prevent bringing enslaved children into the world. Historian Frances Foster recounts the work of Elizabeth Keckley's *Behind the Scenes* (1868) as evidence that "refusing to marry was a form of birth control."[25] Keckley did not accept her love's marriage proposal because she could not endure the thought of bearing enslaved children.

Black women's negation of settler sexual citizenship, in practice, reflects a nuanced valuation of marriage, such that some refused matrimony in favor of fashioning intimate relationships of their choosing. The cultivation of sexual and romantic independence prompted a nonmarriage ethos among a substantial number of Black women "who resisted patriarchal relationships and marriage."[26] This ethos is manifest within communities of Black women as a collective memory and has forged "a matrifocal cultural model" that remains prevalent today.[27]

Throughout this book, I use the terms "settler sexuality" and "settler sexual citizenship" interchangeably.[28] My usage is an extension of Scott Lauria Morgensen's conception of the term "settler sexuality," which captures both the historicity of the white settler-colonial regulation of Indigenous sexuality and gender and the contemporary imposition of hegemonic settler definitions of modern sexuality upon Natives and non-Natives alike.[29] I situate these terms within the context of the marital institution's role in maintaining the settler state. Specifically, I explore the manner in which the US marital regime serves as a conduit through which settler sexuality is institutionalized socially and politically. Further, I trace how the marital institution fosters sexual citizenship defined by alignment with racial capitalism, liberal notions of property, and the socioeconomic privileging of heteronormative, nuclear families. My critique of state-regulated marriage is situated in the settler-colonial context for three reasons.

First, the American marital regime is an integral component of the country's emergence "as a racial capitalist settler state through the simultaneous operation of colonialism and anti-blackness."[30] As noted by historian Nancy Cott, the significance of marriage has remained "deeply implanted in public policy" since the country's founding.[31] She writes, "political and legal authorities endorsed and aimed to perpetuate nationally a particular marriage model."[32] The emphasis on lifelong, monogamous commitment; Christian values and mores; and a patriarchal ethos was in contradistinction to the romantic and familial practices of the global majority. In particular, the US marital regime was counter to both the practices of the Indigenous people originally on this land and of the enslaved Africans brought to it. The marital regime imposed by the state was instrumental in defining American citizenship. As a public institution, marriage is a "vehicle through which the apparatus of the state can shape" the order of race, gender, and sexuality.[33] The marital institution provides a site for examining the indivisibility of anti-Blackness and settler colonialism.[34] Marriage, as observed by Native feminist theorists Maile Arvin, Angie Morrill, and Eve Tuck, illuminates the "relentlessness of settler colonialism" through "the hetero-paternal organization of citizens into nuclear families." The expression of a "'proper,' modern sexuality, has been a cornerstone in the production of a citizenry that will support and bolster the nation-state."[35]

Second, the radical Black feminist tradition emphasizes the pursuit of liberation for all. To ignore how our collective histories of sexual, gender, and familial atrocities are entangled through the machinations of anti-Black racism and settler colonialism would be a dangerous "form of colonial unknowing" or "the refusal to see the full scope of slavery and settlement's interconnected history."[36] As a descendant of enslaved Africans forcibly brought to Turtle Island and as a Black feminist seeking liberation in my present homeplace, I must consider the relationships that need to be established with the Indigenous peoples of this same land whose humanity is also compromised.[37] Black liberation scholar-activists who neglect to negotiate a "mutually supportive relationship" with Indigenous people "risk truly becoming 'settlers,' complicit in the extermination of those whose lands they occupy."[38] Importantly, reciprocity is required in the forging of Black-Indigenous revolutionary alliances.[39] In my view, advocacy for state-regulated marriage is a declaration of one's investment in the settler state. Such an investment undermines our collective liberation efforts. While it is beyond the scope of this book to fully explore Black-Indigenous alliances, a commitment to our mutual liberation informs this project.

Finally, by shifting the focus from pursuing equitable state recognition to attending to historical traditions and communal practices of self-determination present within Black and Indigenous queer communities, we attain generative entry points from which to imagine different social orders. Eschewing the purported immutability of the liberal state opens space for the conjuring of radical freedom dreams. For instance, such an opening is evident within Indigenous communities for whom "land constitutes a different ontological position than liberal property regimes. The land is not a place Indigenous subjects occupy or possess: it is a place that says who they are, that they are, through which they exist."[40] This ontological conceptualization of land invokes an open-ended relationality between communities and families. It allows one to consider home places in a different and creative manner. We can begin to imagine thriving families headed by Black single mothers, of all sexual orientations and gender identities. This has clear implications for queer folks. The tacit acceptance of settler sexual citizenship has given rise to Black queer movements that "naturalize settlement and assume a homonormative and national form that may be read specifically as settler homonationalism."[41] Black feminist queer freedom dreams open ways to reject settler sexual citizenship, which relegates land to property, families to individual nuclear monads, and romantic partners to marriageable commodities.[42]

The subversive implications of this matrifocal cultural model continue to cause consternation among those who advocate for racial uplift.[43] Cultural anthropologist Riché J. Daniel Barnes captures modern-day respectability politics in *Raising the Race*, in which she studies married Black mothers who have opted out of the labor market. She focuses on professional, economically advantaged women who are shifting away from "older cultural models of marriage and parenting that privileged matrifocal conceptualizations of family life to a more nuclear model that privileges companionate marriage and biological children."[44] The women in her study enact "strategic mothering" through what Barnes calls the "neo-politics of respectability."[45] Evoking Evelyn Brooks Higginbotham's notion of the "politics of respectability," Barnes considers the motivations of these married mothers, whose choices reflect a response to "current portrayals of all Black women as unmarriageable and incapable of parenting" through the idealization of marriage.[46] These women believe in the "promise of 'respectability'" to inoculate their families against negative stereotypes of Black families.[47] Barnes concludes rightly that adherence to a neopolitics of respectability, which promotes heteronormative, Christian, and Victorian gender norms, does not serve to overcome anti-Black views of Black sexual and familial life. Rather, this cultural model remains complicit in the process that perpetuates the racist ideologies of Black animality and baseness. By reinforcing the narrow, restrictive rules imposed by settler sexuality through embracing a unitary model for acceptable familial life, single Black mothers remain cast as deviant problems to be expunged.

While Barnes focuses on married Black women, who aim to be good stewards of the race by mimicking settler sexual and familial norms, African American studies scholar Dianne M. Stewart trains her research upon unmarried, heterosexual Black women, who represent a "veritable national 'sorority' of disappointed and dismayed Black women."[48] Stewart cites barriers erected by the state that thwart Black women's marital prospects and, in response, calls for the positive application of federally sponsored marriage promotion programs to bolster heterosexual Black marriage rates. While she is critical of programs that cast single Black mothers as morally deficient, she advocates for marriage promotion efforts that ensure "pathways to financial stability and wealth building."[49] Reminiscent of the economic concerns espoused by Du Bois a century ago, Stewart argues that a focus on wealth will increase the number of Black men worthy of matrimony.

Reflecting upon her research topic and methodology, Stewart posits that her "deliberate focus on heterosexual unions" does not "discount sexual diversity as a constant dynamic of the human condition."[50] In addition, she asserts that her research does not promote a particular religious or political agenda. The line of argumentation advanced by Stewart is commonplace and, as has been shown, enjoys a long history within Black communities. However, her suppositions are far from benign. The personal is political. Or, put differently, the lines demarcating the public and private spheres are spurious at best. Stewart explicitly champions a neoliberal political agenda through her embrace of capitalism and her appeal for state intervention upon romantic unions. My characterization of Stewart's approach as neoliberal draws from David Harvey's definition of neoliberalism as a "theory of political economic practices that proposes that human well-being can best be advanced by liberating individual entrepreneurial freedoms and skills within an institutional framework characterized by strong private property rights, free markets, and free trade."[51] I am troubled by the alignment of Stewart's position with the process of neoliberalization, which serves to reduce romantic and familial relationships to contractual relations within the marketplace. Further, to forego consideration of queer women in a book purportedly dedicated to the examination of Black women and marriage is squarely aligned with the predominant heteronormative narratives advanced by mainstream religious and political discourses.

It is understandable that proponents of Black inclusion within the liberal state would frame families led by unmarried Black mothers across the sexuality continuum through a paradigm of lack. Settler sexual citizenship demands adherence to sexual, gender, and familial norms. These norms reward nuclear families bound by a marital contract through the accordance of over 1,000 federal rights, benefits, and privileges.[52] The existence of matrilineal kinship within the homes of unmarried Black mothers is antithetical to the normative strictures of settler sexual citizenship. The violation committed by these women produces anxiety and scorn, which provides justification to withhold benefits. While I remain sympathetic to academic and liberatory endeavors that seek to counter notions of Black animality and baseness through the examination of love relationships, I maintain that it is shortsighted to center that work solely upon the valorization of marital unions. By glorifying state-regulated marriage as the ideal family formation, scholars and activists continue to perpetuate problematic notions of family, gender, and sexuality that, ultimately, undermine the moral worthiness of the very Black people they seek to uplift.

In contrast to the Black liberal reform movement, the Black radical tradition reflects a stark departure from the striving for equitable inclusion within settler citizenship. At the heart of this work lies the invocation of freedom dreams that compel the realization of intersubjectivities unencumbered by oppression. Black radical feminists, in particular, have historically forged movement strategies and goals with intentional focus on the broad range of identities and experiences of Black-embodied people. As noted by Robin D. G. Kelley, Black radical feminists provide "one of the most comprehensive visions" of human freedom.[53] Their conception of liberation is steeped within the recognition of "the deep interconnectedness of struggles around race, gender, sexuality, culture, class, and spirituality."[54] Thus, radical Black feminists speak to the heart of our intimate familial and sexual relations beyond the confines of settler sexuality. Yet, even within the richness of these visions of liberated human possibilities, the merit of state-regulated marriage remains largely unquestioned.

The absence of a body of literature on marriage abolition reveals more about the deep entanglement of settler sexuality with the radical tradition than silence on the part of our Black feminist foremothers. For instance, in 1970, Linda La Rue spoke to the "unique contradiction" in the Black radical liberation movement between the "renunciation of capitalistic competition and the acceptance of sexual colonialism."[55] In her estimation, the contradiction lies within the "Black adoption of the white values of women," which engenders an acceptance of the Black matriarch myth.[56] Further, E. Frances White critiques the paradox within Black nationalist ideology that is both "radical and progressive in relation to white racism" and simultaneously "conservative and repressive in relation to the internal organization of the Black community."[57] She asserts that the conservatism of Black nationalism is present within its advocacy for familial formations that "construct sexist and heterosexist ideal models for appropriate behavior."[58] The 20th century is replete with influential interventions by Black feminists striving to counter settler sexuality embedded within the radical tradition, as evidenced in the work of Audre Lorde, Cheryl Clarke, and June Jordan, to name a few. This seminal work on intimacy has advanced our understanding of the centrality of sexuality and gender to the achievement of Black liberation.

For instance, Jordan offers an incisive critique of those who denounce the comparison of the oppression of LGBTQ+ people with that of Black people. She writes,

> If you can finally go to the bathroom wherever you find one, if you can finally order a cup of coffee and drink it wherever coffee is available, but you cannot follow your heart—you cannot respect the response of your own honest body in the world—then how much of what kind of freedom does anyone of us possess? Or conversely, if your heart and your honest body can be controlled by the state, or controlled by community taboo, are you not then, and in that case, no more than a slave ruled by outside force?[59]

Jordan resists the excising of sexually and gender-diverse people from the struggle for Black freedom. Excision is a negation of freedom itself, which cannot be selective in its manifestation. Thereby, the radical Black activist who rails against settler logics without attending to settler sexuality only serves to perpetuate Black oppression. The project of Black liberation must encapsulate the totality of Black existence, inclusive of its innumerable expressions of gender and sexuality.

The indispensability of queerness to Black radical politics is captured in the 1977 Combahee River Collective Statement, which brilliantly attends to the complexity of Black women's identity formation. Barbara Smith, cofounder of the Combahee River Collective, explains in an interview that "one of the reasons we were marginalized in the Black movement, besides sexism and misogyny, was also homophobia."[60] The Collective's understanding of marginalization led to their coinage of the term "identity politics."[61] The Collective defines identity politics as the recognition of marginalization, or systemic oppression, as a wellspring of "political radicalization."[62] Black women's multifaceted experiences of oppression, according to the Collective, "made them more open to the possibilities of radical politics and activism."[63] The framework of identity politics is not considered a simple marker of social identification or social location. Rather, as articulated by the Collective, the framework of identity politics references the particularity of anti-Black racism as experienced by Black women, which cultivates the "possibility of radical and revolutionary politics."[64]

The legacy of radical and revolutionary politics developed by our feminist foremothers is evident within contemporary movements for Black lives that champion abolitionism. Radical Black feminism in the 21st century continues to challenge American institutions that undermine the quality of Black life. This includes interrogating institutions that threaten the stability of Black women's intimate relationships across the spectrum of gender and sexuality. Prison abolitionists, like Andrea J. Ritchie, for example, investigate the gender-specific harms inflicted upon transgender and cisgender women ensnared within the criminal justice system.[65] Black feminists' commitment to the flourishing of intimacy within Black families is also clearly reflected in the work of scholar-activists pursuing reproductive justice.[66]

Among this body of rich and powerful work, however, one does not find a sustained engagement with the marital institution. There is insufficient scholarship and activism directed toward the harms that the marital institution inflicts upon Black women generally, and unmarried Black mothers specifically. This absence of critique is regrettable, given the institution's foundational role in supporting the state's construction of normative gender, sexuality, and family formations. Tacit acceptance of, or mere ambivalence toward, state-regulated marriage, as is present in both the Black liberal and radical traditions, remains a serious impediment to addressing anti-Black racism. I contend that the vantage point of single Black mothers provides an additional resource for the advancement of radical and revolutionary politics. Unmarried motherhood advances the vital work of our radical Black foremothers through the embodiment of nonhegemonic sexual and familial configurations outside the bounds of the state-regulated marital institution. Questioning the assumed necessity of state-regulated marriage allows for the negation of the concomitant hierarchal valuation of familial configurations, which prioritizes the nuclear family. By dispensing with intimate hierarchy, we can begin the radical work of thinking creatively about how communities can support and protect the well-being of all families equitably.

The liberatory potential of disentangling familial and sexual intimacies from marriage is explored in the work of African American Studies scholar L. H. Stallings. In *Funk the Erotic*, Stallings describes how "Black cultural producers have used funk to destroy Western humanist concepts of love and their social contracts and products."[67] One aspect of this cultural production is Stallings's concept of *funky love*. It encapsulates "publically [sic] radical configurations of family, love, and relationships," which decenter marriage and monogamy as "the ideal praxis."[68] Stallings shares the nontraditional sexual and familial practices expressed within her family history as evidentiary counters to "the dispossession and displacement that happens through privatization and politicization of love and intimacy via monogamy and marriage."[69] She also encourages readers to consider marginalized sources of Black women's knowledge production, as they contribute to the fruition of "radical genealogies that thwart capitalist arrangements of family and intimacy."[70] Attending to the affective registers of these marginalized sources of cultural and knowledge production provides a theoretical foothold to begin examining monogamy and Western marriage as sites of oppression and inequality. Despite the phenomenal scholarship and activism dedicated to excavating the nuances of Black women's oppression fueled by the simultaneity of race, gender, and sexuality, it is telling that scholars critical of state-regulated marriage, such as Stallings, remain in the minority of the radical Black canon. The marital regime continues to enjoy an enduring hold on the otherwise diverse Black political imaginary.

Turning to Africana philosophy specifically, one encounters a much more dire situation. It is clear that incisive deliberation regarding freedom and thriving in the wake of colonization is an enduring theme within Africana philosophy.[71] Put differently, the theorization of Black liberation is the core work of Black philosophers.[72] But oddly, at least in my view, Black philosophers have remained conspicuously muted on the topic of Black intimacy.[73] This is unfortunate because, as discussed previously, intimate relations, including our romantic, sexual, and familial relationships, are foundational to Black liberation movements. This absence is deafening when juxtaposed with the voluminous literature on intimate relations authored by white-embodied philosophers. The lack of examination of Black intimacy in relationship to Black oppression and the pursuit of liberation betrays an implicit acceptance of settler sexual citizenship.

A cursory literature review reveals only a handful of articles in the Africana philosophy canon that squarely address marriage.[74] The uncritical affirmation of the marital institution's value is consistent for each author. For instance, Anita L. Allen offers a defense of interracial marriage, in contrast to the prevailing view among many African Americans, who consider it to be problematic both morally and emotionally.[75] Those who morally oppose interracial marriage believe that it indicates a sense of self-loathing or a lack of race loyalty. Others contend that interracial marriage fosters emotional stress and an erosion of well-being.

Offering a different perspective, Allen writes, "For blacks, the ban on interracial marriage had been seen as a powerful symbol of exclusion and inequality, particularly in the South where interracial sex was commonplace despite the ban on interracial marriage."[76] She states that Black women felt shame for having sex with white men outside the confines of marriage and that white men were able to exploit unmarried Black women sexually. She believes these wrongs were addressed by *Loving v. Virginia*, which she considers to be a "legally and morally just" decision by the Supreme Court.[77] She deems *Loving* to be an "important milestone in American's quest for racial equality" as justice was achieved within state-regulated marriage.[78]

While I support Allen's argument that interracial intimacy is not counterproductive to Black solidarity, I am troubled by her advocacy for the marital institution, especially as it pertains to the emotional well-being of Black women. First, I reject the claim that broadening access to state-regulated marriage has advanced racial justice for Black people. Second, the purported shame caused by nonmarital sexual relations is exacerbated by *Loving*, by Allen's very line of reasoning. I challenge the conservative moral view that restricts morally appropriate sexual intimacy to the marital bed while vilifying sexual relations between unmarried, consenting adults. I will address the implicit sexual conservatism of Black scholar-activists aligned with settler sexuality in greater detail in Chapter 3.

The affirmation of state-regulated marriage is also found in the work of social and political philosopher Charles Mills. The argument he presents in "Do Black Men Have a Moral Duty to Marry Black Women?" is puzzling in light of his influential and searing critique of liberal democracy.[79] In the aforementioned article, Mills assumes the moral neutrality of the marital institution and offers a rebuttal to six different arguments provided by his Black women-identified students, who support this particular moral duty. I do not doubt Mills's assertion that this topic generates robust class discussion; indeed, the morality of Black endogamy situated in the context of Black liberation is a provocative ground for inquiry. I do, however, question the absence of a pedagogical intervention that would invite students to also interrogate marriage as a moral good, the heteronormativity of the institution, and the foundations of the question posed in the course.[80]

The arguments offered by his women-identified students are rooted in the desire to attain Black liberation. Their resistance to interracial marriage is informed, in part, by their understanding of an underlying connection between morality, marriage, and Black freedom. For instance, Mills recounts his students' Questionable Racial Motivations argument. He writes, "The more radical version of this accusation is that one is actually trying to achieve some kind of derivative personhood, personhood by proxy, in such marriages, insofar as Black personhood is systematically denied in a racist society."[81] He finds this argument to be the most plausible, but he rejects it as a sufficient reason to regard interracial marriage as immoral. However, I believe Mills misses the most compelling line of inquiry in the Questionable Racial Motivations argument, namely, how is the marital institution structured in such a way as to undermine Black personhood? How could proximity to whiteness through interracial marriage be seen as a step closer to personhood? These questions speak to the whiteliness of the marriage institution and beckon us to question how that institution is connected to anti-Black racism.[82]

Mills published "Non-Cartesian *Sums*: Philosophy and the African-American Experience" in the same year as "Moral Duty." In "Non-Cartesian Sums," he aptly captures the African American experience of anti-Black racism through his articulation of subpersonhood. He argues that "white racism so structured the world as to have negative ramifications for every sphere of Black life."[83] Drawing from the German *Untermensch*, Mills defines a racial subperson as "an entity, which, because of phenotype, seems... human in some respects but not in others."[84] In response to this racial marginalization, Mills observes that Black philosophers have engaged in the politically dogged "insistence of one's Black humanity in a racist world."[85] A consequence of this political engagement is the understanding "from a Black perspective" that the "now-triumphant mainstream liberalism" has "provided inadequate conceptualizations of the polity."[86] With such a searing indictment of liberalism and enlightening articulation of Black philosophy's contribution to political theory, it is surprising that Mills did not connect those dots in the "Moral Duty" article. To better understand this omission, it is helpful to examine his more prescient account of liberalism and anti-Black racism in *The Racial Contract*, published the year prior.[87]

Mills deploys the theoretical "Racial Contract" as a descriptive tool to "*explain* the actual genesis of the society and state, the way society is structured, the way the government functions, and people's moral psychology."[88] The Racial Contract, for example, consists of moral and legal doctrines that are foundational to the sustainment of white dominance. These doctrines included three "subsidiary" contracts, namely the expropriation contract, the slavery contract, and the colonial contract. These contracts ensured the formal codification of nonwhite subordination. Mills asserts that from this vantage point, we can observe that European moral and political theory within the context of the Racial Contract understood that "only Europeans were human."[89] I remain aligned with Mills's account of Europeans' humanist myopia, but I take issue with his consideration of gender.

Mills claims that gender, or sexual difference, is not historically locatable, unlike the Racial Contract. Therefore, one would have to conclude that the Racial Contract is not gendered.[90] By reducing his analysis to a narrow, single axis of oppression, Mills misses key opportunities to strengthen his argument by utilizing an intersectional approach to disclosing the racialization of liberal modernity. For instance, when taking up the slavery contract, Mills is correct in his assertion that for Black people, "the degradation of *racial* slavery" entailed that "*slavery acquired a color.*"[91] However, we know that nonpersonhood was not meted out in the same way across enslaved Black people. Chattel slavery was a gendered American institution. Numerous feminist scholars have provided thorough analyses of the gendering of the American slave system. Of note is Angela Davis's seminal article "Reflections on the Black Woman's Role in the Community of Slaves."[92] In defense of his deficient approach, Mills notes that his focus on the singular axis of racial oppression is based on the "absence of that chimerical entity, a unifying theory of race, class, and gender oppression."[93] As demonstrated earlier, Black queer feminist theory provides a wealth of resources that express what is only fantastical for Mills. In my view, single Black motherhood is a conceptual tool that embodies the chimerical entity that could have enriched our understanding of the Racial Contract.

Let us consider the marriage contract in relationship to Mills's description of the Racial Contract, which both norms space and delimits personhood and subpersonhood. Mills writes that "The Racial Contract demarcates space, reserving privileged spaces for its first-class citizens."[94] Further, he highlights the "intimacy of the connection between place and subperson."[95] Explaining the economic consequences of this demarcation, Mills writes, "This raced space will also mark the geographic boundary of the state's full obligations."[96] He states that majority-Black communities will be condemned to negative economic outcomes, like poverty and high crime rates. He concludes that the Racial Contract ensures that "the *political space* of the polity is not coextensive with its *geographical space*," such that the rules governing white spaces are not applicable in Black space.[97] As I will discuss in greater detail, this dynamic is demonstrable when considering the institution of marriage. There is no more intimate space than the home place. It is a site of consequential geographical and political dimensions. The marriage contract, as an institution of settler sexual citizenship, demands the formation of nuclear families. But home places headed by single Black mothers fall outside of the political and geographical spaces protected by the Racial Contract. Attending critically to the marriage contract provides a theoretical opening to explore the Racial Contract with a robust accounting of race, gender, and sexuality. To be sure, acquiescence to the inevitability of the marital institution is not unique to Africana philosophy. There is no correlate of marital reform or abolition literature within the canon of Black scholarship that matches the volume of literature in the white canon. I aim to demonstrate that gender-inclusive racial justice movements necessitate critical interrogation of state-regulated marriage.

By necessity, this book is "undisciplined" in its interdisciplinary approach.[98] Christina Sharpe's astute call for undisciplined research methodologies is particularly germane for Black philosophers centering feminism and queerness in our work. We are compelled to engage in novel research and pedagogical methodologies to counter the "epistemic violence that we know to be violence against others and ourselves" in our efforts to capture the fullness of the Black experience.[99] The commitment to remain undisciplined allows us to bypass the production of "legible work in the academy" that does "violence to our own capacities to read, think, and imagine otherwise."[100] In this book, I dispense with the presumed justificatory norms that prompt the exasperating question posed to Black women philosophers, namely "how is this work philosophy?"[101] The exclusionary aspects of this culture of justification within professional philosophy, according to Kristie Dotson, beckon a shift to a culture of praxis that places "value on contribution, multiple canons, and multiple forms of disciplinary validation."[102] Dotson notes that the culture of justification assumes "that philosophy and philosophizing are not a widespread, human activity. It contains the assumption that there is something special about philosophizing that is in the purview of professional philosophy alone."[103] We know this assumption to be false. Patricia Hill Collins, in her canonical *Black Feminist Thought*, makes it clear that theory, and Black feminist thought specifically, is generated by Black women from all walks of life. Thus, I aim to expand the philosophical canon by defying the boundaries of our myopic discipline, drawing upon the wisdom of a multiplicity of scholar-activists both within and outside of the academy.

In particular, I employ a Black queer feminist lens in my exploration of single Black motherhood. In 1994, Evelyn Hammonds observed that "Black feminist theorizing about Black female sexuality, with a few exceptions . . . has been relentlessly focused on heterosexuality. The historical narrative that dominates discussion of Black female sexuality does not address even the possibility of a Black lesbian sexuality, or of a lesbian or queer subject."[104] In the intervening years, Africana studies has enjoyed an abundance of scholarly contributions to Black queer theory. Africana philosophy, however, has yet to address the topic of sexuality in a substantive manner. The absence of meaningful theorization centering queerness undermines the liberatory import of our work. The study of the ontological, epistemological, and social-political dimensions of Black existence continues to be incomplete as long as it does not fully attend to queerness. This theoretical scarcity is a pity. As Joanne Barker reminds us, "gender and sexuality are core constitutive elements of imperialist-colonialist state formations."[105] Barker encourages us to remain attentive to "the gendered, sexist, and homophobic discrimination and violence on which those formations are predicated."[106] I strongly believe that a core principle of Black philosophy's liberation work in the 21st century must be the fervent inclusion of a radically expansive engagement with sexuality, gender identity, and their relationship to family formations.

To that end, this book considers queerness in four dimensions: definitional, ontological, social-political, and liberatory. Queerness informs my gender-expansive definitions of "woman" and "mother." Each term is inclusive of all individuals who live and consistently identify as women and mothers. Unbound from the narrow constraints of biology, the concept of unmarried motherhood encompasses the broad spectrum of those who identify as mothers, including cisgender mothers, transgender mothers, Ballroom House mothers, and beyond. Through the queering of motherhood, I develop an account of Black mothering that is situated beyond traditional accounts of family. This framework allows for the inclusion of single Black mothers, who head both biological and chosen families.

The preponderance of literature on Black women and marriage focuses on heterosexual unions. This queer exclusion not only ignores a significant population of Black women, but it also undermines discerning deliberation on heterosexual women. Black embodiment in the United States has been tethered to queerness in the white imaginary dating back to the era of chattel slavery.[107] According to Jafari Allen, Black people are "always already queer relative to normative ideals of the person."[108] As I will discuss in further detail in Chapter 4, our positionality as nonnormative in an anti-Black world remains odd, strange, or queer. The ontological dimensions of Blackness as queerness ground my explorations of our intimate relations, which stretch beyond one's sexual proclivities. Single Black motherhood as a conceptual tool compels a queer sense in which to encompass the richness of our familial, sexual, and romantic ties.

In his analysis of the 2014 protests held in Ferguson, MO, against state violence, Jeffrey McCune observes that the violence precipitated by the murder of Michael Brown illuminates the "queerness in being and living Black."[109] Attending to the social-political dimensions of Blackness as queerness, McCune states that "the frequency of Black death is itself queer. Strange. Out of place."[110] Our queer personification is expressed within the incessant attempts by the state to annihilate Black bodies. The eliminative experience of state violence is often discussed in the context of the prison-industrial complex, health inequities, and economic disparities. This violence, I will argue, is also encompassed within the marital institution.

Finally, the signification of Blackness as queerness is not solely defined as an expression of negativity or of a death-bound existence. In this book, I uplift the positive dimensions of queerness that are evident in "its relationship to living and creativity."[111] The life-giving aspects of queerness are manifest within the liberatory practices of Black activism, art-making, and practices of restorative resistance. The freedom dreams or radical imaginary born out of Black queer feminism provides a rich seedbed of social-political praxis. The interventions offered by Black queer feminism invite us to meditate upon our intimate familial ties with a fresh perspective.

In this book, I develop an account of *marital shade*, which provides a conceptual structure through which I attend to both the experience of systemic harm and the liberatory praxis of single Black motherhood. *Marital shade* is inspired by legal scholar Ariela Dubler's account of unmarried women living under the shadow of marital law's normative framework.[112] Dubler provides an astute account of unmarried women, who live in *"the shadow of marriage,"* and yet are still subject to regulation "by marriage's normative framework even as they have inhabited terrain outside of its formal boundaries."[113] *Marital shade* attends to the racial specificity of the impact of marriage and nonmarriage in Black communities. The forthcoming chapters disclose the dynamism of *marital shade*, with its valences of meaning, which capture the complex interplay of single Black motherhood as both a site of vilification and a resource for Black liberation.

In Chapter 2, I argue that the marital institution is wielded as a weapon of state oppression against unmarried Black mothers. Specifically, the state uses the marital contract as a ruse through which to claim nonrecognition of unmarried mothers and thereby an excuse to deny material benefits and social support. I define marital shade in this context of state regulation as the *performance of illegibility*. In support of this claim, I consider two significant historical periods pertaining to the marital institution. First, I focus on the pivotal role that the marriage contract plays in sustaining anti-Black racism in the wake of Emancipation in the mid-19th century. Paying particular attention to the "Marriage Rules" enacted by the Freedmen's Bureau, I contend that the state utilized the marital institution not only as a means to codify patriarchy but also to sustain the machinations of US settler colonialism. The disadvantaged position of single Black mothers in the 21st century can be traced back to this particular machination of white supremacy, which contributed to the material, social, and moral deprivation experienced by newly freed Black women. Second, I challenge the positive assessment of the Supreme Court's majority opinion in *Obergefell v. Hodges*, which granted same-sex couples the legal right to marry.[114] Critics of the *Obergefell* decision observe rightly that it serves as a contemporary codification of the rigid heteronormative model of family and sexual citizenship articulated by the Founding Fathers.[115] I make the further claim that *Obergefell* not only reifies the purported deviance of nonnormative families, writ large, but that it also curtails racial justice efforts by reinforcing a myopic vision of romantic and family life that exacerbates the stigmatization of unmarried Black mothers across the continuum of sexual and gender identities.

In Chapter 3, I examine the occurrence of marital shade within racial justice movements trained upon anti-Black racism. I argue that a core principle of 21st-century racial justice movements must be the fervent inclusion of radically expansive notions of sexuality, gender identity, and family formations. Movements for Black lives that address the machinations of anti-Black racism often attribute negative life outcomes to single mothers. Consequently, racial justice advocates frequently advance moral platitudes and policy initiatives in response to anti-Black racism that are linked to the marital institution, either implicitly or explicitly. I define this type of marital shade within Black communities as adherence to the *Black married maternal*. Such shortsighted modes of redress that uphold settler sexual citizenship serve to reify the purported moral failings of families led by Black mothers. I argue that Black people must decouple the pursuit of racial justice from the marital institution and allegiance to the Black married maternal such that unmarried Black mothers are valued as worthy recipients of liberation.

In Chapter 4, I make the case that the familiar narrative of American women's shared objections to the patriarchal facets of the marital institution often obscures significant points of divergence between Black and white women's relationship to the state, political freedom, and marriage. I contend that these salient moments of divergence have impoverished work within contemporary liberal political philosophy on marital reform and abolition. In support of this claim, I offer a close reading of debates between queer theorists on the efficacy of same-sex marriage and debates between marriage reformers and abolitionists. I conclude that on either side of these debates, one finds the gross underestimation of the state's role in race-based harm, and more significantly, white women's active role in upholding white supremacy. This myopic view grounds a third type of marital shade, namely *theoretical blackface*. Theoretical blackface is the recognition of the propensity of white women to claim falsely that the lived experience of white wives is equivalent to the lived experience of enslaved Black women. The postmarriage liberal state envisioned by white abolitionists leaves the race-based problems experienced by unmarried Black women living within marital shade fully intact. To flesh out this claim, I situate contemporary abolition arguments within the broader context of white women's active political role in fomenting anti-Black racism through the marital institution.

In the final chapter, I propose a Black queer feminist case for marriage abolition. In so doing, I consider Black feminist articulations of abolition democracy and decoloniality as a possible mode of redress for single Black mothers. In the context of Black queer feminism, marital shade is defined as the defiant act of *throwing marital shade*. The act of throwing shade upon the marital institution is a categorical rebuke of settler sexual citizenship. I contend that a developed account of Black queer abolition feminism must include the critical interrogation of marriage.

Foremost, this book is a declaration of commitment to Black queer liberation. Liberation that conjures and manifests freedom dreams beyond the realm of possibility of the settler-colonial imagination; a liberation that is collective and coalitional; and a belly-laugh-inducing, shake-your-hips liberation that consumes respectability politics. This book revels in Black love: our most intimate relations with ourselves, our lovers, our children, and our communities. Most especially, this reflects a deep, abiding love and enduring respect for single Black mothers. An ode. A praise song. A love letter. This is for you. This is for us.

2
Canaries in the Mine

In her bestselling memoir *Becoming*, Michelle Obama recounts her experience of June 26, 2015, as the juxtaposition of deep mournfulness and joyful restoration.[1] Her day began with the funeral service for Reverend Clementa Pinckney, one of nine Black people gunned down by an avowed white supremacist during Bible study at Emanuel African Methodist Episcopal Church in Charleston, South Carolina. President Barack Obama, who delivered a moving eulogy for Reverend Pinckney, senior pastor at Mother Emanuel and a state senator, explicitly addressed the ills of anti-Black racism before leading those gathered in a rendition of "Amazing Grace."[2] In her retelling, First Lady Obama acknowledged that the presence of a Black family in the White House had assuredly stoked the flames of racial animus that incites white supremacist violence—a reactionary form of violence that is encouraged by the erroneous belief that the gains of the racial Other necessitate the erosion of resources enjoyed by white people. This dangerous worldview sees for humanity only hierarchy and finite possibility where there might instead be equity across differences and abundance for all.

As evening drew near on June 26th, First Lady Obama noticed that the exterior of the White House was bathed in the light of the rainbow. A colorful symbol of LGBTQ+ pride was on display to commemorate the Supreme Court's affirmative ruling in the *Obergefell v. Hodges* marriage equality case, issued earlier in the day.[3] Obama recounts the great lengths to which she and her youngest daughter Sasha went in order to evade the Secret Service so that they could join in the revelry of those rejoicing outside the White House. The euphoric celebration of the landmark decision "helped buoy us through a sad day in South Carolina."[4] Obama's account of the day links two seemingly disparate events: one evincing the deep-seated, hateful violence of anti-Black racism woven into the fabric of America and the other demonstrating our country's progressive sensibilities, its striving to honor difference and overcome the bigotry embedded in our liberal democracy.

The First Lady's sense of buoyant jubilation is also reflected in Justice Anthony Kennedy's majority opinion, or "love letter," to the marital institution.[5] In his wistful account of marriage's history, Kennedy acknowledges that the lifelong union, which "always has promised nobility and dignity to all persons," has been fraught with varying forms of inequality.[6] Over the course of American history, however, marriage has evolved away from its nefarious past of arranged couplings, coverture, and the illegality of interracial unions.[7] In this contemporary moment of significant political and cultural advances for LGBTQ+ communities, the *Obergefell* case offered the Supreme Court an opportunity to address a remaining marital injustice by granting same-sex couples the legal right to marry.[8] The *Obergefell* decision reflects Kennedy's belief that the ruling is a measured step in the direction of perfecting our imperfect union.[9]

However, Kennedy's sanguine depiction of the marital institution prompted the ringing of alarm bells by family law scholars,[10] who were wary of the negative implications this decision would have upon the life prospects of the nonmarried.[11] Among them, Melissa Murray raised concern that *Obergefell*'s "rationale for marriage equality rests—perhaps ironically—on the fundamental *inequality* of other relationships and kinship forms."[12] She warns that the decision's unequivocal endorsement of marriage over nonmarriage "forecloses the possibility of further developing the jurisprudence of nonmarriage."[13] Clare Huntington is troubled that the Court based its decision upon the Due Process Clause instead of the Equal Protection Clause. By doing so, she argues, the Court limited the decision's scope by locating discrimination within the marital institution and not situating it within a broader context of equal citizenship for LGBTQ people.[14] These are legitimate and troubling concerns for all families of all races existing outside the marital institution.

However, I am particularly concerned that portraying the *Obergefell* decision as an optimistic tale of perpetually perfecting democracy ignores the troubled racial waters beneath the surface. As poet Claudia Rankine observes eloquently *Citizen: An American Lyric*, we cannot put the past behind us, nor should we adhere uncritically to facts that create narratives of inclusion and perpetual progress.[15] A closer look at the historicity of the marital institution reveals that the brutality in Charleston and the hidden material and moral costs of the *Obergefell* decision are two sides of the same coin. They are both manifestations of pervasive anti-Black racism that undermine our most sacred sites of solace: our places of worship and our families.

Black activists and scholars decried the characterization of the Mother Emanuel shooting as a solitary, ahistorical incident of gun violence.[16] They insisted upon accurately naming the bloodshed in Charleston as an act of anti-Black domestic terrorism. And far from being solitary, it was horrifyingly familiar.[17] Black churches historically have served not only as communal sites of spiritual refuge but also as sites for political organizing, where leadership is cultivated; as such, they have not infrequently been targeted by white supremacists.[18]

Nineteenth-century Black feminist scholar Anna Julia Cooper recognized that thriving families were necessary to further both racial progress and national advancement in the wake of Emancipation.[19] She placed her hope for the future of our nation's institutions in their equitable valuation of Black homes, specifically centering on Black motherhood. Cooper's view of the primacy of the home in undergirding the strength of the nation is aligned with sentiments espoused by Justice Kennedy's majority opinion in *Obergefell*. But unlike Kennedy, Cooper recognized that a vital and constitutive aspect of that progress is Black women's flourishing. The true gauge of racial and national progress, according to Cooper, is the aggregated well-being of average African American women and their families.[20] She amplifies the vulnerability of Black mothers and underscores the need to invest in improving their quality of life. Cooper's words are echoed in Kennedy's opinion, but the force of her insistence on racial equity is missing.

The devaluation of Black lives that underlies white supremacist acts of domestic terrorism aimed at Black churches is also evident through the devaluation of Black mothers and their children in the seemingly race-neutral *Obergefell* decision. This is not simply because the marriage equality movement was characterized by many as a political quest for, and by, white, wealthy, gay men.[21] More pointedly, the marital shade cast by the *Obergefell* decision has stark material and moral implications for unmarried Black mothers across the spectrum of sexuality and gender identity. These implications are underscored by family law scholar Robin Lenhardt, who presciently observes that "marriage today reflects black inequality."[22] She argues that the color-blind dignity espoused by Kennedy in *Obergefell* serves to entrench the marital institution's significant regulatory role in maintaining Black disadvantage and segregation.

Lenhardt states that the marital institution's influence upon one's access to state and federal resources, such as affordable housing and public benefits, reinforces racial disadvantage by excluding the unmarried. This disadvantage is demonstrable, for instance, upon consideration of the impact of state and federal statutes that protect against marital status discrimination upon the adjudication of cases involving housing discrimination. Upon close analysis of states with said statutes, Courtney G. Joslin observes that "it would be impermissible to refuse to rent an apartment to a particular woman because she is unmarried or divorced, but it would be lawful to refuse to rent to a couple upon learning that the couple is unmarried even though the landlord would have rented to the couple had they been married."[23] In light of these disadvantages, one may reply that nothing precludes Black people from marrying and thereby gaining access to these resources. In point of fact, doesn't the *Obergefell* decision allow more Black couples the opportunity to wed? In response, Lenhardt notes that structural forms of racial inequality "in areas such as housing, employment, education, and mass incarceration" coalesce to prevent access to the marital institution for a significant number of Black people.[24]

Lenhardt also expresses skepticism that the race-neutral marriage equality decision alone "magically cures the stigma, deprivation, disparate treatment, and harm" experienced by those outside the marital institution.[25] Augmenting Murray's call for parity between marital and nonmarital unions, Lenhardt argues for the development of policies to improve the life conditions of all Black families as a means "to secure black belonging."[26] In her critique of neoliberalism's calculating and obfuscating ideologies of post-racialism and color-blindness, Alys Weinbaum asks "what has today become of the specific form of 'blackness' that rationalized four hundred years of enslavement?"[27] Indeed, the pervasively negative archetype of blackness and impoverished Black motherhood is preserved through the state-regulated marital regime.

Returning to Kennedy's notion of a perpetually perfecting democracy offers a preliminary response to the questions at hand. In the *Obergefell* preamble, Kennedy revisits *Lawrence v. Texas*, in which the Court ruled unconstitutional the Texas "Homosexual Conduct" statute, which barred sexual activity between consenting same-sex adults.[28] Kennedy asserts that the personal freedom and state support accorded to the intimate association of opposite-sex married couples should be enjoyed by same-sex couples as well. Beyond the freedoms of sexual intimacy upheld by the *Lawrence* decision, he contends that this state-sanctioned support should extend to same-sex couples.[29] According to Kennedy, the shift precipitated by *Lawrence* from "outlaw to outcast may be a step forward, but it does not achieve the full promise of liberty."[30] This striking assertion by Kennedy provides a foothold to examine state-sanctioned marital shade.

State-sanctioned marital shade is characterized by a casting out from society. Romantic unions designated as outcasts are denied from enjoying the robust array of federal rights, benefits, and privileges accorded to their married counterparts. The marriage equality decision sustains outcast status not only for romantic couples who do not wish to legally marry but also for biological and chosen families alike, outside of marriage.[31] These couples and families, according to the Supreme Court, are resigned to remain outside the protective bounds of the state. State-sanctioned marital shade serves to relegate unmarried Black mothers to outcast status, lacking the "full promise of liberty." In this chapter, I will draw upon *Obergefell*'s reference to outcasts to examine the historically situated marginalization of unmarried Black mothers within the polity. Specifically, I will argue that the framework of casting out allows the state to enact this marital status–based form of marginalization through institutional performances of illegibility.

The illegibility of single Black mothers is characterized as performative because of the contradictory positionality of Black women in the United States. On the one hand, Black women are clearly recognized by state institutions as a legible, or visible, social category. For instance, persons identified as Black and female are quantified by the US Census Bureau, surveilled by law enforcement, and scrutinized by social welfare agencies. On the other hand, the very same state institutions will characterize the social category of Black women as illegible, or seemingly incomprehensible, when compelled to either acknowledge or rectify their productive role in sustaining Black women's marginalization. Investigations pertaining to the disingenuous performance of illegibility have a long history within Black feminist theory.[32] For my purposes, I will show that state-sanctioned marital shade provides the justificatory means for the denial of material resources to unmarried Black mothers, who are characterized as unassimilable surplus commodities, and as such, are deemed morally unworthy of state resources.

2.1 The Unproductives

> Whereas some doubts have arisen whether children got by any Englishman upon a Negro woman should be slave or free, be it therefore enacted and declared by this present Grand Assembly, that all children born in this country shall be held bond or free only according to the condition of the mother; and that if any Christian shall commit fornication with a Negro man or woman, he or she so offending shall pay double the fines imposed by the former act.— Virginia Law, 1662

The colonial Virginia doctrine invokes the Latin *partus sequitur ventrem*—that which is brought forth follows the belly (womb)—in order to separate the free from the enslaved. By tethering freedom and citizenship to the womb, Jennifer Morgan argues, legislators in our 17th-century slave democracy circumscribed "enslaved women's maternal possibilities," rendering them the "crucial vehicle by which racial meaning was concretized."[33] The "condition of the mother" doctrine constituted the state-sanctioned heritability of blackness as a badge of inferiority. For Morgan, "the physiognomy of subjection was not only heritable but was so indelibly rooted in black women's bodies that it could not be dislodged."[34] Enslaved women understood that the condition of Black motherhood would carry the weight of generational racialized dispossession.

Matrilineal subjection excised the Black maternal bond from the private realm of domesticity and relegated it to the public domain of the marketplace. The codification of *partus sequitur ventrem* transformed childbearing Black women into marketable assets within the American system of racial capitalism. My use of the term "racial capitalism" draws from Cedric Robinson's articulation of the concept in *Black Marxism: The Making of the Black Radical Tradition*.[35] In his seminal text, Robinson challenges the origin stories of racism and capitalism as articulated by Karl Marx and Friedrich Engels. He traces the West's failure to accurately account for the development of racism and the formation of white identity and contends that the creation of whiteness was initiated in Europe prior to European engagement with Africa. Robinson further demonstrates that capitalism was embedded within feudalism and was marked by racialism.[36] As such, racism and capitalism were not a departure from the previous feudal order, as argued by Marx, but rather were constitutive components of feudalism itself. Manifestations of racialism are understood as interwoven within capitalist forms of property and production, and embedded within the "values and traditions of consciousness through which the peoples of these ages came to understand their worlds and their experiences." Robinson writes, "The development, organization, and expansion of capitalist society pursued essentially racial directions, so too did social ideology. As a material force, then, it could be expected that racialism would inevitably permeate the social structures emergent from capitalism. I have used the term 'racial capitalism' to refer to this development."[37] My discussion of matrilineal subjection and state-sanctioned marital shade in this chapter is informed by this development.

The racial inheritance of dispossession and alienation imparted through the reproductive capacities of enslaved women has been explored at length in the context of labor. Critical scholarship abounds concerning the central role enslaved women played in producing fungible commodities essential to sustaining the United States slave economy.[38] Still, more scholarship examines the role of reproduction and labor contracts in preserving Black subjugation after Emancipation.[39]

The stamp of the commodity, which haunts the maternal line across generations, has had a far-reaching impact beyond the labor contract.[40] The deployment of the marital contract to maintain subjection through the reproductive capacities of formerly enslaved women also merits significant consideration. The influence of *partus sequitur ventrem* can be traced historically through the state's treatment of unmarried Black mothers. To fully grasp the marital shade embedded within the *Obergefell* ruling, we must situate it within the racialized milieu of capitalism, contracts, and commodification, which has so profoundly shaped the lived experiences of Black women and our progeny. The constitution of marital shade served to reconstitute the mark of slavery as the mark of purported illegibility.

The revaluation of the reproductive capacities of Black mothers became apparent with the commencement of the Civil War in 1861, as they were considered of no use in the market economy of war. Historian Tera Hunter observes that Black women were determined by Union officials to be expendable in comparison to Black men. The Union prized able-bodied Black male labor and was hostile to caring for the women and children who began to flood contraband camps as the war effort wore on.[41] In reply to a Union officer stymied by the material needs of Black women entering the camps, President Abraham Lincoln replied, "They better set to digging their subsistence out of the ground."[42] The Great Emancipator did not care for the Black mothers whom he considered to be a drain on the finite resources of the Union war effort.

Marriage, however, bolstered Black women's valuation as it served as a useful military tool of the US government in its protracted battle with the southern Confederacy. In dire need of additional troops to serve in the Union Army, Congress used marriage to manipulate the labor of Black men for the purpose of strengthening the North's war effort. This particular form of manipulation served to reify gender inequity by making the marital institution Black women's sole pathway to freedom.

The Militia Act of 1862, which was fervently contested by Congress, incentivized military service by granting freedom to Black men who enlisted in the Union Army.[43] The Militia Act also freed enlisted men's mothers, wives, and children—but only "if their owners were disloyal" to the nation. Meaning that if a slave owner did not bear arms against the United States, then the women and children would remain enslaved even as the enlisted man was freed.

Three years later, President Lincoln signed the Enlistment Act into law in March 1865. This bill granted emancipation to the families of enlisted Black soldiers without regard to the loyalty, or disloyalty, of their slave owners. This law was enacted to further encourage Black men to join the Union army, as many were rightfully concerned about the possibility of violent retribution against their families, left in the hands of slave owners upset by their military service. Unmarried Black women across the South protested against this stipulation in a resolute refusal to accept marriage as a precondition to their freedom.

In the intervening months between the March 1865 Enlistment Act and the ratification of the Thirteenth Amendment in December of that same year, Black women's freedom was tethered to the bonds of marriage. In response to the enlistment measure, historian Amy Dru Stanley observes that it "manifests what abolition was meant to overturn" and what abolition was meant to bring into fruition.[44]

In my view, abolition overturned chattel slavery as the conduit of social death for African Americans, while simultaneously constituting new forms of social death through Black women's inextricable tie to the marital institution. Married Black women transitioned into a new form of domestic bondage, while unmarried Black mothers experienced the castigation of burgeoning state-sanctioned marital shade. Emancipated Black women are often described as experiencing civil death owing to wives being relegated to second-class citizenship in the 19th century. In contrast, newly freed, unmarried Black mothers maintained states of both social and civil death in slavery's afterlife once state nonrecognition is reformulated through the marriage contract as a performance of illegibility.[45] The marriage contract in the era of abolition served as a mechanism for condemning all Black women to a condition of second-class citizenship (civil death) and diminished the humanity of unmarried mothers (social death). An examination of Black women's engagement with the Bureau of Refugees, Freedmen, and Abandoned Lands illustrates this claim.

The Freedmen's Bureau was established by Congress in March 1865 to support Southern reconstruction after the Civil War and to facilitate the transition of the formerly enslaved into freedom as American citizens. While the effectiveness of the Bureau's efforts has been long debated, no one can deny the agency's indelible imprint upon familial and gender relations within Black communities.[46] The legacy of this federal agency's engineering of our family structures remains salient today, even if not in concrete terms but in our collective imagination. I will discuss the internalization of the familial and marital norms encouraged within Black communities by the Freedmen's Bureau in Chapter 3. For now, I will focus on the manner in which Bureau agents wielded the marital institution as a weapon of racially gendered oppression that targeted unmarried Black mothers through withholding material resources, criminalization, and moral disapprobation.

The strength of US market economies, transitioning away from the economy of chattel slavery, necessitated a reconsideration of the market value of Black mothers. The material worth of an unmarried, emancipated mother paled in comparison to her previous market value as a childbearing enslaved woman. No longer branded as human commodities giving birth to future generations of human commodities, how would the state incorporate these women? The enslaved mother as a profitable commodity became a negative surplus to be eliminated in freedom's wake. The machinations of racial capitalism required the refiguration of unmarried Black mothers' subjection through the privatization of material care.[47]

The Freedmen's Bureau "regarded the contract as the governing model for all social relations" and, according to historian Mary Farmer-Kaiser, bureau agents worked diligently "to enforce the relationship between freedom and contract."[48] For Bureau agents, the marriage contract was a symbolic indication of a freedman's manhood and the bestowal of citizenship. The marital contract was also understood as a constitutive component of a freedman's acceptance of his duties of free labor as a citizen.[49] Through forceful coercion into the marital institution, the Bureau was able to meet one of its primary objectives, namely to facilitate the transition of the formerly enslaved into the free labor market, where they would be responsible for providing for their own material needs. Bureau agents placed this financial responsibility squarely upon the shoulders of Black men within the marital union. It was decided that wives and children were the political and economic responsibility of their husbands and fathers.[50] The marital institution was levied by Bureau agents as a mechanism to abdicate federal and state responsibility for providing material resources to formerly enslaved women.

The privatization of material care (its delegation to the marital union) prompted state officials to regard unmarried Black mothers as financial burdens; this represented a sharp divergence from their previous status as profitable human commodities within slave economies. Black mothers in the Reconstruction era, who held exclusive financial responsibility for their children, were referred to as "the unproductives" by Bureau officials. These mothers were met with extreme difficulty in their attempts to navigate labor markets. Performances of legibility and assimilation as properly domesticated wives and mothers were required of Black women to receive Bureau assistance.[51] The Freedmen's Bureau reduced material aid given to freedwomen, or the "unproductives," in order to facilitate the forced domestic regulation of Black families.[52] The government paid these women on an unequal scale compared to their male counterparts under the contradictory logic that men were heads of household. Thus, Black women did not require comparable wages because they were assumed to be dependents of their husbands. The state, reliant upon Black women's labor, belies the traditional gender roles and responsibilities associated with white married couples. The contradictory gender roles and expectations for Black women in the marketplace stood in stark opposition to the prevailing expectation that women's labor would be confined to the private sphere or domestic economy.[53]

National fear of the specter of emancipated, but indigent, slaves disrupting the profitability of transitioning US economies predated the creation of the Freedmen's Bureau during Reconstruction. This unwarranted anxiety was promulgated by the American Freedman's Inquiry Commission, created by the US Secretary of War in 1863 to investigate the condition of ex-slaves freed by the Emancipation Proclamation. The American Freedman's Commission determined that marriage should be a requirement for newly emancipated Black people. Black men were told to assume the role of head of household with their wives and children as subordinates. It was thought that marriage would bring sexual chasteness and domestic order, and help to establish market and civil societies.[54]

In her analysis of democracy and the American penal system, philosopher Joy James writes, "Emancipation is *given* by the dominant, it being a legal, contractual, and social agreement. Freedom is *taken* and created."[55] President Lincoln's Emancipation Proclamation and the subsequent adoption of the Thirteenth Amendment did not free the enslaved.[56] The forcibly imposed regulatory control of the newly freed's domestic relations by the American Freedman's Commission and the Freedman's Bureau is demonstrative of the inadequacies of emancipatory legislative acts to engender human freedom. For James, freedom is an ontological status that can only be made manifest by the individual or collective group. Freedom itself is constitutive of liberation from racial, gender, sexual, and class oppression. The legal recognition of the formerly enslaved's marriage unions exemplifies the contractual rights afforded by emancipation, but these circumscribed rights are not evidence of the actualization and enjoyment of freedom.

The denial of freedom's actualization is evidenced in the manner in which newly emancipated people were consigned to the marital union. Many southern states, including Maryland and Virginia, passed legislation that legally married formerly enslaved couples that were cohabitating, notwithstanding the individual couple's desire to be legally wed to one another.[57] In point of fact, not all of these couples wished to marry the person with whom they were living. Many of these individuals had hoped to return to former loves, who had been separated from them through the barbarism of slavery. The authoritarian application of marriage by fiat explicitly denied the freedom and autonomy of the newly freed to make their own decisions regarding their familial and romantic lives. These acts also cultivated the state's nonrecognition of unmarried mothers by allowing them to be legislated out of existence. Marriage by fiat effectuated the disappearance of unmarried Black mothers and advanced the state's performance of their illegibility.

According to James, the United States originated as a slave democracy that has evolved into the penal democracy of today. Tracing the development of US chattel slavery into the modern-day prison-industrial complex, James maintains that "the Thirteenth Amendment ensnares as it emancipates."[58] Enslaved Black people were transfigured from their existence as the personal property of individual slave owners to existing as prisoners that are property of the state. The transition from enslavement to mass incarceration was not the only troubling facet of the Thirteenth Amendment. The metamorphosis precipitated by emancipation from "slave" to "wife/husband" also bears the mark of injustice. The historical excavation undertaken by modern-day prison abolitionists provides interesting points of convergence through which to critically interrogate how the state used the marital contract as a modality of anti-Black racism to criminalize Black people. I will address the salience of prison abolition and marriage abolition within gender-inclusive racial justice movements in more detail in Chapter 5. For our purposes here, I will examine how the marital contract was used to ensnare the formerly enslaved within the carceral state in emancipation's wake.

The mark of criminality imposed upon the Black body was reinforced by the Freedmen's Bureau's employment of the marital institution as a means to engage Black people within the criminal justice system.[59] In the summer of 1865, Bureau agents received guidance in their attempts to civilize newly freed Black people through the dissemination of the "Marriage Rules," issued by Assistant Commissioner Saxton in South Carolina. The "Marriage Rules" codified northern ideals of domestic life, specifically, male social, political, and economic dominance within a nuclear family structure. To use the parlance of the day, the marriage contract was regarded as a "regularizing" tool, meant to civilize the previously uncivilized slave population.[60]

Failure to conform to the Bureau's marital edict came with a significant punitive price. Black people were threatened with prosecution and punishment, either through incarceration or fines, for not entering into marital unions. Shortly after the Civil War ended, legislators in southern states passed laws that made "cohabitation without legal marriage a misdemeanor punishable by a fine."[61] As Southern state legislatures began to resume their sovereign status during the Reconstruction era, they assumed power from the Freedman's Bureau to regulate Black people's engagement with the marital institution, though Bureau officials would continue arresting those accused of adultery, or those resisting the "regularizing" efforts of the state.

Historian Nancy Cott remarked that these punitive measures were extremely effective in manipulating the domestic lives of the previously enslaved. She shares that one woman married her husband a second time to avoid the possibility of arrest.

The legal recognition of marital unions between the newly freed established the inception of state-sanctioned marital shade. The umbrage cast by marital shade not only imperiled emancipated adults, but its harm extended to their progeny as well. In particular, the children of unmarried Black mothers were adversely impacted by the development of Southern laws and statutes governing state recognition of familial rights. Statutes in Texas and Missouri required newly freed couples to formally marry by way of legal ceremony in order to legitimate their children.[62] In Georgia, every child born during slavery was considered to be the legitimate child of her mother. However, these children would only be considered the legitimate children of their fathers if their parents were cohabiting when they were born.[63] A significant number of southern states only legitimated the children born to parents who were living together during slavery.[64] These cohabitation laws had nefarious implications for Black children when applied to legitimacy and inheritance cases. The rulings in these cases exposed the precarity of Black children's liberty and economic well-being while portraying Black mothers as lascivious and Black fathers as feckless lotharios.

For instance, consider the Texas Supreme Court's ruling in *Livingston v. Williams* 1890, which determined the inheritance rights of children born to different mothers but sharing the same father.[65] At issue in this case was a dispute over property owned by Moses Livingston at the time of his death. Prior to emancipation, Moses joined Fannie in a slave marriage; both were the property of Philip G. Smith. Moses and Fannie cohabited as a married couple for close to fifteen years (1850–1865) and birthed an indeterminate number of children in those years. Within this time period, Moses also lived with another enslaved woman on the Smith plantation, Malinda. The relationship between Moses and Malinda was not sanctioned by their owner. An indeterminate number of children were produced by Moses and Malinda. Moses and Fannie lived together until the fall of 1865 and then cohabitated intermittently until Fannie's passing in 1872.

Malinda and Moses then cohabitated until Malinda's passing in 1876. Upon Moses's death, a lower court ruled that the living arrangements of Moses, Fannie, and Malinda left Moses and Malinda's remaining living child, George Livingston, without entitlement to inherit any property from the Moses estate. The Texas Supreme Court upheld the lower court's ruling, stating that George was not Moses's legitimate heir. According to the ruling, the Texas Supreme Court determined that the Texas legitimation statute was not applicable to slave children whose parents lived together without the express intention of entering into a marital union as husband and wife.

In her analysis of the *Livingston* case, Teri A. McMurtry-Chubb observes that the ruling turned on the Court's interpretation of slave consent and marriage. A slave master's approval was required for slave marital consent to have legal standing. Since Moses and Malinda did not have Smith's permission to marry, their relationship would not merit legal recognition and their children would not be considered legitimate (and thus, would not be legal heirs to their father's property). For McMurtry-Chubb, this legal interpretation turns a blind eye to the constrained autonomy that the enslaved had over their bodies and relationships within the chattel slavery system. Remaining willfully ignorant of the mutability of the enslaved's familial patterns, she asserts, the courts served to create a "legal fiction [that] did not take into account the separation of slave families at death or by sale, and ultimately left children from the non-legal union unprotected and illegitimate with respect to accessing the financial resources of the patriarch living or dead."[66] These fictive legal measures are another instantiation of the state's performance of illegibility. The legal fiction of slave marital consent allowed states to refuse acknowledgment of the reality of kinship formations within the horrors of slavery, which created progeny borne of rape, families torn asunder by sale, and marital unions outside the bounds of a master's approval.

The purportedly illegible children of unmarried Black mothers were left without the protective cover of paternal legitimacy that afforded economic and legal safeguards. The fictive legal interpretations of slave marriage left nonlegitimated children prey to the emerging penal democracy. Children of unmarried Black mothers were subject to apprenticeship laws in former slave states: these were measures that authorized the courts to conscript minor children to apprenticeships if it was determined that their parents were unfit to provide for them financially or virtuously.[67] The vulnerability of these children was exploited through their kinship ties to unmarried Black women, who were left indigent from their enslavement and woefully underpaid in postslavery economies, and whose progeny were denied paternal legitimization.

The aggressive and punitive efforts of the state to reconstruct, or "regularize," domestic relations among the newly freed dramatically transformed the familial structures that existed prior to emancipation. The configurations of slave marriages were far too expansive to fit within the narrow confines of the superimposed "normative, patriarchal, nuclear" ideal.[68] The institution of chattel slavery was a site of nontraditional instantiations of gender roles and familial structures. The terror and violence endemic to enslavement provided fertile ground for the development of alternative ways of performing gender. Surviving chattel slavery created the necessity for slaves to fashion their own gender values and ideals. Within the slave system, the matrifocal unit was the most prevalent family form.[69]

I contend that the prevalence of the matrifocal dyad in African American kinship formations was perceived by the state as an existential threat to the polity. According to Cott, marriage, equated with patriarchy, and labor, defined by capitalism, were the foundational blocks of white American citizenship.[70] Revolutionary-era Americans, heavily influenced by Baron de Montesquieu's *Spirit of the Laws*, likened the formation of the US government to the Christian model of monogamous marriage.[71] The manners and fidelity that one ostensibly finds within the marital home were considered vital to cultivating the nation's strength. The conflagration of bad manners would generate degraded, corrupt citizens. Marriage was viewed as the foundation of national morality, which was the bedrock of a successful nation. White, heterosexual, and masculinist power and citizenship were codified through the marital contract that sustained the republic.

Black female-headed households threatened the conceptualization of US nationhood by undermining the chimera of authority afforded to white male citizenship. Single Black motherhood is traitorous and enigmatic to American citizenship. During her sojourn to Ghana to retrace the Atlantic slave trade route, Saidiya Hartman affirmed that

"I, too, live in the time of slavery, by which I mean I am living the future created by it. It is the ongoing crisis of citizenship."[72] This crisis of citizenship remains evident in the lives of unmarried Black mothers enduring the continued influence of slavery's afterlife.[73]

2.2 Obergefell and Performances of Illegibility

The performances of illegibility exhibited in the *Obergefell* decision are contemporary manifestations of racial capitalism's foothold within the neoliberal state. Justice Kennedy's argument for legalizing same-sex marriage rests upon two familiar, yet deleterious, assumptions, namely a belief in the autonomous individual and tacit acceptance of the unworthiness of some individuals to merit material support from the state. These assumptions are embedded within racial capitalist structures in which the promotion of individual autonomy belies systems of oppression that adversely impact racially marginalized groups. While this observation is far from a novel concern, the harmful consequences stemming from racial capitalism require further attention and disavowal. In the following, I will situate the four premises upon which Justice Kennedy grounded the marriage equality ruling within the context of racial capitalism to support my claim that the ruling is harmful to single Black mothers.

> *Premise one: The right to personal choice regarding marriage is inherent in the concept of individual autonomy.*[74]

Justice Kennedy asserts that individual autonomy includes one's fundamental right to choose a partner to join with in a marital union. Implicit in his claim is the belief that sexual orientation does not negate one's individual autonomy, which therefore must be taken to include the personal choice to marry a person of the same sex. However, as was shown in the previous section, the concept of personal choice concerning the marital union was illusory for unmarried Black mothers in the wake of emancipation. An examination of anti-Black racism embedded within contemporary market forces reveals that the illusion of individual autonomy regarding the marital institution remains relevant today.[75]

David Harvey, in *A Brief History of Neoliberalism*, defines the neoliberal state as "a state apparatus whose fundamental mission is to facilitate conditions for profitable capital accumulation."[76] Neoliberalism, as a political project, seeks to promote the conditions necessary for capital accumulation and to reaffirm the power of the wealthy ruling class. In service to this political project is the promoted belief that freedom of the market is necessary to ensure individual freedoms. The *Obergefell* decision rests squarely within this milieu of neoliberalism, specifically within the context of neoliberal "marriage markets."

In *Marriage Markets*, family law scholars June Carbone and Naomi Cahn argue that the significantly changing demographics of the American family should be attributed to economic inequality.[77] They claim that the marital union is a product of market exchange, which is dependent on supply and demand. These "intimate markets" reflect the manner in which class impacts marriage markets, including who will get married, who will find living together respectable, and what family structures are considered acceptable for parenting.[78] In defense of their position concerning the primary role market forces play in reshaping contemporary family life, Carbone and Cahn draw upon two notoriously problematic figures for Black mothers, namely, Daniel Patrick Moynihan and Charles Murray.[79]

According to the 1965 Moynihan Report, the configuration of Black familial patterns reflected a debilitating "tangle of pathology" that compelled "national action."[80] Our familial pathology was evidenced, most notably, within the "matriarchal structure" that had been forced upon our communities. This matriarchal pattern, according to Moynihan, "retards the progress of the group as a whole and imposes a crushing burden on the Negro male."[81] The children in matriarchal households were also endangered, as matriarchal structures promote "aberrant, inadequate, or anti-social behavior" that perpetuates generational poverty.[82]

Reminiscent of the Freedmen's Bureau from a century before, Moynihan concluded that "a national effort towards the problems of Negro Americans must be directed towards the question of family structure."[83] I maintain that, for Moynihan, Black female-headed households were a threat to the masculinist polity. He writes, "Ours is a society which presumes male leadership in private and public affairs. The arrangements of society facilitate and reward it."[84] State policy efforts to eliminate "matriarchal" households were understood as positive measures to afford Black Americans "full and equal sharing in the responsibilities and rewards of citizenship."[85] The unmarried Black mother, the matriarch, was considered to be outside the boundaries of the state's recognition of American citizenship. Far from providing support and protection, the state was directed to eliminate Black female-headed households.

The Moynihan Report's charges of familial pathology continue to generate intense scholarly debate about Black motherhood.[86] While Carbone and Cahn do acknowledge briefly the pathologizing aspects of the Moynihan Report, they primarily herald the report for what they see as its prescience. The authors believe Moynihan was correct to surmise that male employment loss would significantly impact family structures and that chronic unemployment would have an outsized impact on Black families. Carbone and Cahn characterize 1960s Black families and, by implication, single Black mothers, as canaries in the mine, as these families were the first to experience the ramifications of sustained industrial job loss. And what do the canaries tell us? According to Carbone and Cahn, the contemporary American marital landscape is demonstrative of the Moynihan Report's accuracy. They contend that Moynihan identified correctly that (a) the family was evolving along class lines, (b) race was a factor in this change but we can't identify why race matters, (c) changing familial structures negatively impacted Black children, and (d) a significant factor driving this familial change is the lack of employment.[87]

The "elusive question of causation" raised by Moynihan, namely how employment loss alters cultural norms and how gender affects the resulting change, occupies the authors' attention for the duration of *Marriage Markets*.[88] How race is integrated within marriage markets is not of primary concern to Carbone and Cahn, which is a pity. If one takes racial capitalism seriously, as I do, then one cannot excise a discussion of anti-Black racism from an examination of class, or capital, within marriage markets.

Citing Murray with "some reluctance" in light of his racially biased claims in *The Bell Curve*, Carbone and Cahn challenge his enduring proposition that changes in American familial structures are attributable to moral failings and government dependency.[89] They insist that the evolution of the American family is rooted in economic forces and should not be construed as a morality tale. In my estimation, Carbone and Cahn miss the indispensable role played by those of Murray's ilk in maintaining a justificatory moral pretense in support of the machinations of racial capitalism. The intransigency of anti-Black racism embedded within the American moral and political imaginary regarding the family has profound economic implications for Black familial life.

Eschewing the influence of morality upon marriage markets, Carbone and Cahn look toward the symbiotic evolutionary relationship between cultural familial norms and family law. They assert that current marriage markets are influenced by new marital scripts, which have influenced family law in favor of supporting marital unions for the economic elite. The new marital script upends the traditional nuclear family model complete with a husband as breadwinner and a wife as homemaker. This development can be traced to the 1960s when, according to Carbone and Cahn, women became increasingly more educated and financially independent. Women's entry into the workforce gave rise to marital unions based on dual earners who are financially interdependent. Coupled with the expectation of financial interdependence within marriage, the new marital script rests upon the premise that in the event of marital dissolution, each party will remain financially independent. These expectations are supported by courts that grant no-fault divorces, award equal division of assets upon dissolution, and eschew long-term support for less financially secure spouses. Such changes not only influence life after marriage (i.e., divorce), but they also affect one's decision to enter into the marital institution. The authors contend that these new cultural and legal expectations of an individual's financial independence prior to marriage, an institution now defined by financial interdependence, are a structural barrier that prevents entry for the middle and lower socioeconomic classes. Marriage, Carbone and Cahn conclude, has become the playground of the financially elite.

The "new" marital scripts described in *Marriage Markets* are, of course, not at all new. The economic expectations of these purportedly new scripts have always been woven into the fabric of Black marriage. The "problem that has no name" has never been a problem for Black women in any era.[90] Without regard to marital status, Black women's participation in the labor market has been the prevailing expectation—or a necessity for survival—since the inception of US chattel slavery. Evolving cultural norms and family law have not suddenly become disadvantageous to unmarried Black mothers. Unmarried Black mothers distrusted the touted financial advantages of the marital institution decades before their white counterparts developed a healthy skepticism of the state regulation of their romantic unions. These new scripts, which Carbone and Cahn attribute to the refashioning of white familial structures, should not be attributed to unmarried Black mothers' experience with marital shade.

> Premise two: The right to marry is fundamental because it supports a two-person union unlike any other in its importance to the committed individuals.[91]

In the second premise supporting his argument for same-sex marriage, Justice Kennedy reminds us that married couples enjoy the full magnitude of state support. Marriage, according to Kennedy, "remains a building block of our national community."[92] The marital union is essential to the nation, and it is located "at the center of so many facets of the legal and social order."[93] Those who enter the marital institution, which animates civic and private life, are generously rewarded by the state. Kennedy notes that the States have influenced the character of the marriage right through the 1,000+ federal provisions accorded to married couples. The marital contract represents American society's pledge to support the couple by "offering symbolic recognition and material benefits to protect and nourish the union."[94] This sanguine depiction of marital benefits provides a robust narrative for those in support of the legal recognition of same-sex unions. Concomitantly, this articulation of the marital institution lays bare the stark moral and material consequences of state-sanctioned marital shade. One must ask why the state would ignore other kinship formations. More specifically, why are unmarried Black mothers left unprotected and malnourished?

Racial capitalism, according to Jodi Melamed, is defined by the accumulation of capital.[95] This accumulation produces and moves through modalities of severe inequality. She writes, "These antinomies of accumulation require loss, disposability, and the unequal differentiation of human value, and racism enshrines the inequalities that capitalism requires."[96] Melamed asserts that this is accomplished by the displacement of unequal life opportunities onto the fictive notion of varying human capacities between differing racial groups. Racial capitalism maintains racialized inequities within the reigning state-capital orders, while simultaneously espousing liberal terms and tenets of inclusion. For Melamed, neoliberalism's idolization of the individual has advanced this cause by limiting the capacity of antiracist logic to "recognize the economic, legal, political, and epistemic structures that so inconspicuously produce racially unequal outcomes."[97] This lack of recognition has enabled liberal discourses to portray themselves as antiracist "even as they misattribute racialized social and economic dysfunction to the choices and personalities of individuals."[98]

Melamed situates racial capitalism within what she describes as a "state-finance-racial violence nexus."[99] This nexus describes the inextricable tie between racial violence and political and economic governance. The state-finance-racial violence nexus, according to Melamed, "enables ongoing accumulation through dispossession by calling forth the specter of race (as threat) to legitimate state counterviolence in the interest of financial asset owning classes that would otherwise appear to violate social rationality."[100] Melamed cites the extrajudicial killings of Black youth and the letting die of impoverished persons of color as examples of this state violence. I maintain that marital shade is also located within the state-finance-racial violence nexus.

The marital institution, or marital shade, serves to exacerbate inequality through the privatization, or withholding, of federal resources and privileges from the unmarried. Marital shade for single Black mothers is made manifest through the perpetuation of systemic poverty, lower educational attainment for our children, unsafe living conditions, and marked health disparities. Our positionality on the lowest tiers of socioeconomic status is neither by accident nor by our failing. Our lived experiences are an indicator of state-sanctioned racial violence. The threads of racial capitalism woven forcibly into the reproductive capacities of enslaved Black women remain ever present in the lives of single Black mothers today.

In *Marriage Markets*, Carbone and Cahn conclude that an improved economy would allow more couples the financial means to enter into the marital institution. This conclusion is unsatisfying. Seeking a pathway to encourage more marital unions within the neoliberal capitalist system leaves racial capitalism intact. Furthermore, increased economic opportunities will not address the underlying problem of restrictive, anti-Black notions of familial normativity. Without challenging the prevailing view that mothers should be married, unmarried Black mothers will still be designated as social and legal outcasts, even in more economically prosperous times. The maintenance of the state-finance-racial violence nexus requires its villains, its outcasts—those unworthy of societal care or resources. Marital shade acts in service to this endeavor as a regulatory discipline to manage unassimilable Black commodities.

Justice Kennedy's insistence that entering the ostensibly color-blind marital institution is simply a matter of individual choice conceals the structural, racialized market forces that hinder participation by Black mothers. The first two premises in support of the *Obergefell* decision are demonstrative of the machinations of the neoliberal state to impose its economic and social-cultural will upon unmarried Black mothers. Justice Kennedy has subtly demarcated the racial boundaries of those empowered (white economic elites) and those disempowered (structurally impoverished Black families), all under the guise of individual autonomy and government neutrality.

> *Premise three: It safeguards children and families and thus draws meaning from related rights of childrearing, procreation, and education.*[101]

Justice Kennedy makes it clear that the fruits of the marital institution are also enjoyed by the progeny of these unions. Marriage not only provides a material advantage for children, but it also confers the profound benefit of allowing them "to understand the integrity and closeness of their own family and its concord with other families in their community and in their daily lives."[102] In his third premise, Justice Kennedy creates an undeniable moral hierarchy between married and nonmarried families. Integrity is found within families legally forged through a marital contract. Woe unto those families living outside the marital institution. Kennedy does acknowledge that same-sex couples, who were granted adoption privileges prior to the marriage equality decision, formed loving and supportive familial bonds. However, these families were relegated to outcast status. According to Kennedy,

> Without the recognition, stability, and predictability marriage offers, their children suffer the stigma of knowing their families are somehow lesser. They also suffer the significant material costs of being raised by unmarried parents, relegated through no fault of their own to a more difficult and uncertain family life. The marriage laws at issue here thus harm and humiliate the children of same-sex couples.[103]

Kennedy's explicit references to harm and humiliation disclose the Court's unequivocal disapprobation of unmarried parents. In this particular incarnation, marital shade manifests as the feigned illegibility of nonnormative families.

In her critique of the legal justification grounding the *Obergefell* opinion, Clare Huntington is rightfully concerned by the Court's reification of the marital union as the ideal site for childrearing. The marriage equality argument was grounded by an interpretation of the Due Process Clause, which meant that the Court had to both define marriage and provide an account of its "social importance" in American society."[104] Huntington contends that the reliance on the Due Process Clause compelled the Court to reify marriage as the bedrock of family and thereby magnified the marginal status of nonmarital families.[105] She acknowledges that the law plays a significant role in either reinforcing or changing the "social fronts" of familial life, including our normative expectations of proper gender roles, parental responsibilities, and family structure.[106] She believes Kennedy erred in using the Court as a legal mechanism to alter the social front of marriage. Transformations to the social front of marriage as significant as the legal recognition of same-sex unions should have remained, she argues, within the purview of legislative bodies. The legislative process, according to Huntington, is better suited to expand the definition of marriage because more voices are included in the process. Justice Kennedy, according to Huntington, overstepped an important legal boundary by using the Court to change both the law and culture.

Huntington argues that Justice Kennedy should have drawn upon the Equal Protection Clause to support the marriage equality decision. An affirmative argument based on Equal Protection would have allowed the Court to develop a thinner notion of marriage that would have avoided the problematic—thicker—definition of marriage noted above. Furthermore, by not drawing upon Equal Protection, the Court limited the scope of the decision by locating discrimination within the marital institution and not situating it within the broader context of equal citizenship for LGBTQ people. Huntington asserts that an Equal Protection Clause foundation for same-sex marriage would have established that "whatever marriage means culturally, a state cannot deny access to it without distinctions that have a *state* (as opposed to a private, cultural) interest as a basis."[107] Justice Kennedy missed an opportunity to provide a broader, and more substantive, wellspring of legal support for LGBTQ communities and their families.

Huntington rightly identifies the conservatism embedded in Kennedy's ostensibly progressive legal opinion. The most troubling facet of the ruling, however, is not found in the debate over Due Process versus Equal Protection, or the efficacy of a court ruling versus a state ballot measure. The process through which same-sex marriage is accorded legal recognition is immaterial to the lived experience of single Black mothers across the spectrum of gender and sexual diversity. As Jodi Byrd notes, "U.S. neoliberal biopolitics govern bodies, rights, and access through state-sanctioned normativities that expand access only to ensure incorporation as non-transformation."[108] This observation is reflected in the strong resistance to the heteronormative implications—tantamount to queer erasure—raised by LGBTQ+ opponents to marriage equality prior to the *Obergefell* decision. The performative influence of jurisprudence upon societal norms and expectations regarding *proper* families extends to marital law and remains resistant to the nonnormative. The dialectical relationship between our laws and modalities of social legibility reinforces state-sanctioned marital shade, which contributes to unmarried Black mothers' experiences of material deprivation and moral disapprobation. The marital institution is not a site for ensuring, let alone broadening, legal rights and state protections for families headed by racially marginalized women. The marriage equality decision reifies the harm and humiliation that denotes the deviant families outside of the marital institution. I will make the case for the moral advantages of deviance in Chapter 3.

> Premise four: This Court's cases and the Nation's traditions make clear that marriage is a keystone of our social order.[109]

In his final premise, Justice Kennedy is unequivocal in the view that legal precedent and national tradition uphold the marital institution as the foundation of societal order. Kennedy's bold assertion leaves unmarried individuals, as Melissa Murray observes, "in a constitutionally precarious position."[110] This precarity is evidenced by the Court's performance of illegibility when adjudicating cases involving both nonnormative families and sexuality outside the marital union.[111]

The SCOTUS decision in *Lawrence v. Texas* (2003) is widely viewed as a precursor to the *Obergefell* ruling. What is intriguing about Justice Kennedy's majority opinion in this case is that the consensual, casual sexual encounter between the plaintiffs was rendered unintelligible by the Court. Evidence suggests that John Lawrence and Tyron Garner were casual lovers, who met only weeks prior to their arrest.[112] However, the language used in the majority opinion intimated that their romantic relationship was akin to a marital union. The sexual activity between the uncommitted lovers was not simply sex for the sake of sex but rather was evidence of "a personal bond that is more enduring."[113] The unmarried and uncommitted gay lovers central to the *Lawrence* case could not be accorded state recognition and moral valuation outside of the marital context. The state logics undergirding the *Lawrence* and *Obergefell* decisions illustrate how the Court, under the guise of respecting difference, employs the marital institution to reinforce traditional "social order" through the juridical calcification of heterosexual, familial, and socioeconomic normativities.

Foreshadowing the analysis offered in *Marriage Markets*, Nancy Cott asserts that the 20th-century marital institution played a lesser role in the concretization of political citizenship and the establishment of moral virtue than was seen in centuries prior.[114] According to Cott, the utility of modern-day marriage has become more economically focused, for example, the decrease in marriages across socioeconomic classes. This particular historical narrative, which diminishes marriage's considerable role in conferring citizenship and moral status, does not reflect an understanding of the institution's design upon unmarried Black mothers.

The years-long struggle to legalize same-sex marriage nationally was not merely a fight for the civil rights of queer couples. Recognizing marriage as a primary site for citizen production, Amy Brandzel asserts that the marital union is "a key mechanism by which the U.S. nation-state produces a properly heterosexual, gendered, and racialized citizenry."[115] She describes citizenship as inexorably exclusive, privileged, and normative. It is sheer folly to believe that one can enjoy the full rights, benefits, and privileges accorded to US citizens simply by virtue of jus soli or birthright citizenship. One must be deemed worthy of its privileges. Acceptance of same-sex marriage, according to Brandzel, both reifies and reproduces the properties of exclusivity, privilege, and normativity ascribed to citizenship. As a normative discourse, citizenship "presupposes universality and therefore exacerbates and negates difference."[116] The marital union thereby upholds the social order of citizenship by universalizing familial expectations and negating those families that exist in the marital shade.

The Supreme Court's performance of illegibility in the *Obergefell* decision reinforced unmarried Black mothers' outcast status. By virtue of our illegibility, marital shade preserves anti-Black racism through the demarcation of proper and improper citizens. Centuries removed from chattel slavery, the perpetual confluence of unmarried Black mothers' second-class citizenship, moral devaluation, and material deprivation allows the flourishing of racial capitalism in the neoliberal state.

Sociologist Mignon Moore challenges the normative critiques of same-sex marriage as presented in this chapter. She argues that Black queer marriages occur within a racialized context that "is experienced by those in the community as a radical and transformative act."[117] Moore contends that marriage confers a particularly desirable social signification to Black queer couples seeking validation and respect within Black communities that do not support same-sex unions.[118] She is optimistic about the positive potential of *Obergefell* to engender "greater equality" for the LGBTQ+ community.[119] However, I believe that the price of retaining a "radical" marital pedestal is paid by single Black mothers, and it is much too high to justify advocating for the ostensibly transformational act of same-sex marriage. We cannot afford to sacrifice the needs of unmarried mothers and their families in order to promote Black queer marriage. The exigencies of marital shade outlined in this chapter highlight the need to move beyond accepting equality within the neoliberal state. Marriage equality is, indeed, a befitting shorthand for the *Obergefell* decision. Equality does not provide racial equity. Equality does not achieve justice for unmarried Black mothers in slavery's afterlife. As I will argue in Chapter 5, a commitment to gender-inclusive racial justice necessitates advocacy for marriage abolition, which offers a radical transformation of state-sanctioned marital shade.

3
Black Liberation and Deviant Moralities

A clarion call for the abolition of the state-regulated marital regime has resounded within white feminist circles dating back to the 19th century. Moreover, a vocal faction of white queer scholar-activists decried the legal usurpation of same-sex romantic relationships decades before the federal recognition of same-sex marriage.[1] Lesbian scholar Claudia Card captured this collective sentiment by declaring that she would rather "the state *de*regulate heterosexual marriage than see it begin to regulate same-sex marriage."[2] One could reasonably assume that there would be a correlate abolitionist discourse within a population steeped within the cultural iconography of the single Black mother. One, however, would be wrong in this assumption. Despite the ubiquity of unmarried Black motherhood within the Black academic, artistic, and activist imaginary, marriage reform and abolition are almost completely absent from the conversation. Few, if any, scholar-activists within these circles question the integrity of the very institution that so often harms single mothers.[3]

While many Black feminist scholars have disputed the devaluation of nonnuclear familial configurations, their theoretical interventions often treat state-regulated marriage as an immutable institution. Consequently, the specter of the marital regime lurks subtly underneath the promotion of diverse familial configurations. Why does this immutability occur within one racialized canon and not the other? One notable difference between Black and white feminists' analyses is that for Black communities, marriage is not simply a matter of gender-based harm. In contrast to our ostensibly low marriage rates and purported progressive attitude toward raising children out of wedlock, the marital institution plays a significant role in our collective conception of racialized Blackness. Further, it influences our responses to anti-Black racism, such that marriage has been interwoven historically within Black liberatory praxis.

The tacit affirmation of the marital institution within Black communities exemplifies another form of marital shade leveled against unmarried Black mothers. Marital shade in this context is made manifest through the outsized significance assigned to what I call the *Black married maternal*. The Black married maternal is marked by the communal understanding that the pinnacle of Black motherhood is achieved within the confines of the marital institution. To the detriment of unmarried Black mothers, specifically, and Black people, in general, the Black married maternal is interwoven into the theory and practice of racial justice movements. Accordingly, the Black married maternal is an impediment to Black revolutionary work.

***

As presented in Chapter 2, the mark of racialized Blackness was reproduced through the debased reproductive capacities of enslaved Black women. The potency of *partus sequitur ventrem* continues to endure quietly as a maternal wraith in our contemporary grapplings with anti-Black racism. Attending to this presence compels measured deliberation upon the manner in which reproduction, or Black maternity, affects the problem of the color line.[4] C. Riley Snorton suggests that we supplant W. E. B. DuBois's infamous entreaty "What does it feel like to be a problem?" with the question "What does it mean to have a black mother?"[5] This substitution illuminates how the representation of Black mothers "reproduces the borders between a black self ... and racial blackness."[6] Snorton asks us to consider how self-identity—the rich interplay between individual interiority and its mediation in a world of anti-Blackness—is also a mediation with the Black maternal. More pointedly, I offer that this mediated relationship extends beyond the universal Black mother to the Black married maternal.

This shift in vantage point beckons us to revisit phenomenological accounts of Black existence with our focus trained upon the ways the Black married maternal figures into our ontic-epistemic theorization. In *Visible Identities*, Linda Alcoff develops a compelling case for the epistemic salience and ontological realness of raced and gendered identities that is helpful in the elucidation of the historicity of the Black married maternal. Of particular note is her account of the embodied interpretive horizon, which discloses how raced and gendered identities "operate as epistemological perspectives or horizons from which certain aspects or layers are made visible."[7] Attending to the embodied interpretive horizon illuminates how our Black maternal inheritance shapes both the contours of our relationality with ourselves and others as well as the manner in which our historicized understanding of marriage and motherhood influences our perception of liberation.

Hans-Georg Gadamer's philosophical hermeneutics is foundational to Alcoff's conception of the embodied interpretive horizon. Consciousness of the hermeneutical situation, for Gadamer, is constitutive of an awareness of consciousness that is affected by history. Indeed, "the very idea of a situation means that we are not standing outside it" and, as such, we are unable to attain objective knowledge of it.[8] The situation itself is then characterized by a perspectival horizon. Gadamer defines the horizon as "the range of vision that includes everything that can be seen from that vantage point."[9] The experience of the present horizon is perpetually in the process of formation as we continuously encounter the past. A sustained engagement with the past is therefore necessary to the generation of the horizon of the present.

The horizon, however, should not be interpreted as solely individualistic or an experience of monadic isolation. An individual's interpretive process is "produced through a foreknowledge or historical a priori that is cultural, collective, historical, and politically situated."[10] Alcoff explains that the relationship between one's identity and the other is understood through "the necessity of history to the articulation of an individual's life."[11] Identities are significations of historical relationships, which affirms that "aspects of our horizon are inevitably group-related or shared among members of a social identity."[12]

Alcoff turns to Maurice Merleau-Ponty's phenomenological account of embodiment to strengthen our "understanding of embodiment in relation to our concept of the self and of subjectivity."[13] Merleau-Ponty's phenomenological focus on embodiment illuminates how embodiment "structures and organizes the relational and epistemic possibilities."[14]

The interpretive horizon is not solely cerebral or constituted by immaterial thought cognition; rather, it is "manifest as a kind of presence in the body."[15] The situatedness of horizons should be understood as a material, embodied situatedness. One's interpretive horizon is constitutive of "a wealth of tacit knowledge located in the body."[16]

The embodied interpretive horizon showcases the dynamic interplay between temporality, interiority, and sociality that enlivens human existence as racialized and gendered beings. Alcoff's contribution serves "to capture the dialectics of social identities, in which we are both interpolated into existing categories as well as making them our own."[17] As human beings, we have agency in the constitution of our subjective experience while our subjectivity simultaneously remains attached to the world, "never standing free and clear, capable of producing its own foundation."[18] Our freedom lies within the milieu of this dialectic between individual agency and sociality. And freedom's realization is found through our attempts to flourish within a social world filled with meanings, whose significations have already been determined.

Returning to the specific experience of Black existence in the United States, the embodied interpretive horizon provides a method of analysis to explore the impact of marital shade upon our understanding of Black motherhood conjoined with social expectations regarding gender and sexuality. The machinations of marital shade strike at the heart of our grappling with the ever-present weaving of *partus sequitur ventrum* into the fabric of our contemporary confrontations of the past in concert with futural visions of Black freedom.

Toni Morrison captures the aesthetic dimension of this dialectical dance in her essay "The Site of Memory," in which she expresses her discontent with the absence of interiority in the works of slave narratives. She recounts that enslaved writers maintained a veil over their interior selves in an effort to hide the monstrous experiences of their lives. This lack of disclosure reflects an intentional attempt to appease white readers, whom they sought to enlist in the fight to end chattel slavery. Enslaved authors knew this audience would not tolerate an honest accounting of the violence wrought by whiteness. Morrison maintains that as a writer who is both Black and a woman, it is incumbent upon her to determine "how to rip that veil drawn over 'proceedings too terrible to relate.'"[19] Eschewing the veil requires her to rely upon, and trust, both her memory and the memories of others. Memory itself not being sufficient on its own, she recounts that "only the act of imagination can help me."[20] For Morrison, the imaginary act is tethered to memory.

Morrison's ontic-epistemic reflections upon the veil, which masks the full articulation of Black subjectivities, expand beyond the literary realm. Her insight brings the embodied interpretive horizon of Black Americans into full relief as it is situated within the phenomenal world, which "constantly folds back on itself, adding to what has come before and what remains still in the background of the present moment; the past is that which has been surpassed, yet remains within."[21] For Morrison, as Kristie Dotson observes, "one's own recollections and the recollections of others form the orientations of our lives, but also the beings that we are."[22] And these recollections are indelibly marked by the transition from the formation of familial and romantic relations outside the bounds of state recognition to the subsequent disciplinary regulation of sexual citizenship post-Emancipation.

Sexual citizenship expresses the settler-colonial logics, or colonial imagination, that informs the formation of the marital institution and its concomitant precepts of sexual desire and family formation. This colonial imagination upended interpersonal relationships within Indigenous nations and vitiated the self-determination of the formerly enslaved. Scholars at the intersection of sexuality and settler colonialism emphasize that the brutal disciplinary regulation of Indigenous communities taught "any non-Natives witnessing or inheriting its effects, the meaning of being subjected to modern sexuality as settler sexuality."[23] Jennifer Nez Denetdale expresses the fullness of this brutality in her account of the activities within the Bosque Redondo prison camp.

As the nation was embroiled in the Civil War, federal officials interned thousands of Navajo people (Diné) at the Bosque Redondo prison camp (1863–1868). The prison camp marked a shift from military violence enacted against Indigenous people to civil acts of violence aimed "to create 'perfected Natives' who would never be treated as equals but who would be relegated to the lower echelons of American society."[24] This civil violence included the coerced acceptance of the primacy of heterosexual patriarchy, monogamy, and rigid gender binaries. The actions undertaken by US officials precipitated the coercive transformation of Navajos "from people enmeshed within a matrilineal system that included polygamy and recognized genders beyond the binaries of feminine and masculine into American citizens."[25] The Diné at Bosque Redondo experienced the profound "erosion and disappearance of their ways of life, including their philosophies and customs around family, marriage, and sexuality."[26] The machinations of colonialism with its demands for sexual citizenship, according to Denetdale, have refashioned "the Diné in the image of the white man, but without the full benefits and entitlements accorded white male citizens."[27] The privileging of heterosexual patriarchy as normative within the Navajo nation reflects the "imposition of Western democratic principles" that have unduly influenced "the making of the modern Navajo nation."[28]

The subversion of sexual desire and familial practices that reshaped the Navajo Nation has a correlate within Black communities that is often expressed through the Black married maternal. This correlate preserves the marital shade experienced by single Black mothers. The proliferation of marital shade discloses the import of those memories and lived experiences that capture our collective imagination and those that do not. The historical vestiges of our indoctrination into sexual citizenship influence which subjectivities are amplified and which remain veiled in our understanding of acceptable Black romantic and familial life. To bring this to light, I will consider the divergent articulations of marriage, sexuality, and motherhood offered by the Black Club movement and blues women in the wake of Emancipation.

One may think it a belabored exercise in the 21st century to examine the disparate dimensions of historical Black feminism in relation to the marital regime. As noted by Brittney Cooper, the predominance of Black marriage politics within the cultural and political discourses of Black intellectual circles has been evident since the 19th century. I contend, however, that it is this very predominance, which sustains the contemporary influence of the Black married maternal, that makes this topic worth revisiting.

Race women in the late 19th century engaged in theory production about race and gender in tandem with their activist pursuits. The work of these race women is typified by the Black women's club movement, which advanced respectability politics and marriage promotion.[29] Faced with harsh material conditions and acute sexual precarity owing to unrestrained white male sexual violence, these scholar-activists effectuated the chaste image of the Black married maternal. Cooper, rightly I think, asks contemporary feminists to be more understanding of the need for respectability politics in light of the "sexual vulnerability that animated these women's calls for 'refinement.'"[30] Notwithstanding where one falls on the continuum of respectability politics critique, one cannot deny the sustained influence that these women wielded on the role and divisiveness of the Black married maternal within the conceptualization of acceptable Black womanhood and movement work.

The ready acceptance of the tenets of US sexual citizenship is demonstrated most notably within middle-class Black communities that fastened upon the pursuit of the marital regime. Historian Anastasia Curwood notes that middle-class Black people "agreed with those middle-class white Americans who also believed that morality in family life was the cornerstone of morality in public life."[31] At the turn of the 20th century, the presentation of female chastity, monogamy, and heteronormativity was regarded as ballast for respectable marriages. More to the point, this community held the conviction that the "marital relationship itself helped lift the race" by providing a public display of morality and by allowing each spouse the foundation needed to engage in race work.[32]

Public records indicate that Black women activists were married or widowed at far higher rates than white women activists. Race women were beholden to the marital regime as a requisite for participation in the fight for Black liberation. Black women were held to a political double standard. If Black middle-class women desired to engage in race work in the public sphere, Curwood states that "they stood the best chance of success if they were married."[33] Unmarried women were at an extreme disadvantage, as "they were assumed to be sexually loose if they appeared in public without a man's protection."[34] The tethering of activism to the marital regime provides insight into the absence of marriage abolition literature within the Black feminist liberatory canon.

The thoroughgoing adoption of the settler-colonial interpretation of sexual citizenship is readily apparent in the spate of marriage articles written by prominent Black women in the mid-20th century. These articles include Ann Petry's "What's Wrong with Negro Men" (1947) and Gwendolyn Brooks's "When Negro Women Leave (1951)." While Petry and Brooks provide searing critiques of the intolerable gender imbalances motivated by patriarchal norms, they do not go as far as questioning the virtue of the marital institution itself. Of these articles, none encapsulates the disturbing consequences of the settler-colonial influence more than Pauli Murray's "Why Negro Girls Stay Single (1947)."

Murray's substantial intellectual contributions, including her theoretical formulation of Jane Crow, are finally receiving their due after years of subdued attention.[35] According to Cooper, Murray's formulation of Jane Crow "sought to name a powerful system of gender disciplining within Black intellectual communities."[36] Her understanding of the punitive measures of gender regulation extended beyond the binary, cisgender constructs of man/woman, as Murray herself struggled intensely with gender dysphoria.[37] Upon rejecting her given name, Anna Pauline Murray, she settled on "Pauli," as it was both reflective of her masculine-identified gender identity and acceptable to public audiences who regarded her as female. Murray fervently researched her "boy-girl" self early in life as she was convinced by the science of the day that she was a pseudo-hermaphrodite. Though endocrinological tests and later surgery indicated that she was not intersex, Murray refused to assume a gay identity, choosing instead to identify as a heterosexual man existing in a woman's body. Her rejection of queer identification also conveys her adherence to 20th-century stereotypes that supported her presumption that a desire to marry a feminine, heterosexual woman was evidence of her own heterosexuality.

Contemporary engagement with her work exposes fissures where intraracial suppression may have curtailed the full articulation of her scholarship concerning gender and race.[38] From her undergraduate years at Hunter College, as a law student at Howard Law School, to her professional career, Murray's travails with her nonnormative gender and sexual identities infringed upon her scholarly endeavors. Throughout her adult life, she wrestled with both the mental health stressors that accompany conformity with community norms and the intimate erasures required for race women to participate in the public domain. For instance, while at Howard Law, Murray disclosed a crush to (its object) a female undergraduate, who responded unfavorably to the overture. The romantic rejection and ensuing gossip led to a three-week leave of absence from school during which time she missed her final examinations. In correspondence with her Aunt Pauline, Murray explains that she is trying to abide by "society's standards;" however, "the effort 'causes me such inner conflict that at times it's almost unbearable... This conflict rises up to knock me down at every apex I reach in my career.'"[39] Murray's existence was circumscribed by the limitations imposed within Black communities that are beholden to settler sexuality.

Given her subjection to the "disciplining forces of racial heteronormativity," the publication of "Why Negro Girls Stay Single" is lamentable, though unsurprising.[40] Biographer Rosalind Rosenberg attributes its composition to 35-year-old Murray being "compelled to explain" her uncomfortably visible unmarried status,[41] a compulsion that does violence to her richly nuanced, yet socially reprobate, manner of being. She invokes familiar tropes in this piece to defend her single status. First, she cites a lack of marriageable men, referring to men who have the same educational and professional standing as career women. Second, she blames "sex mis-education," whereby Black men and women accept patriarchal gender roles within the marital home. These roles, according to Murray, belie the lived experience of Black women, who are in the workforce, and Black men, who are unable to fulfill the settler breadwinner role. The disjunct motivated by sex mis-education causes marital discord and, at times, thwarts marital unions altogether. Murray not only claims that sex mis-education engenders alienation between Black men and women, but she also alleges that it "intensifies homosexuality."[42] Murray's homophobic allusion drives home the violence wrought upon her by the compulsion to disguise her authentic self.

Blues women in this historical era offer a vision of Black existence—of liberation—that embraces queer embodiment and renounces the inheritance of settler sexuality in the guise of the Black married maternal. In *Blues Legacies*, Angela Davis offers an extensive treatment of gender and sexual politics within working-class communities through her exploration of blues women. A striking aspect of the blues, the most popular genre of music post-Emancipation, is the prominent role that women held within the industry—none more so than Gertrude "Ma" Rainey and Bessie Smith, who were two of the most renowned blues artists of their time. In her study of Rainey and Smith, Davis notes that these two artists contradicted mainstream expectations of sexuality, marriage, and motherhood in the 1920s and 1930s.

Blues women are seldom wives and almost never mothers. For instance, the corpus of Rainey and Smith, spanning 252 songs, reveals only a few references to marriage. On the contrary, these artists wrote and performed songs that were overtly sexual, inclusive of queer imagery, and rarely mentioned the marital institution. The omission of the Black married maternal in blues music, according to Davis, is not evidence of a repudiation of mothering by blues women; instead, it signifies a lack of concern about predominant conventions of familial life. The absence of motherhood and marriage in these creative works is of considerable significance.

Davis's analysis of Smith's "Sam Jones Blues" is of particular interest here. In this song, Smith centers marriage only to portray its dissolution. Smith sings:

> I used to be your lofty mate
> But the judge done changed my fate
> Was a time you could have walked right in and called this place
>   your home
> sweet home
> But now it's all mine for all time, I'm free and living' all alone
> [spoken]
> Don't need your clothes, don't need your rent, don't need your
>   ones and twos
> Though I ain't rich, I know my stitch, I earns my struttin' shoes.[43]

Throughout her rendition of "Sam Jones Blues," Smith vacillates between "standard" English and Black working-class English. Davis suggests that this linguistic disjunction highlights the oppositional valuation of the marital institution between adherents of settler sexuality and those who reject it. Smith's lyrics offer an alternative to sexual citizenship, which prioritizes the preservation of marital unions despite deceitful infractions, for instance, infidelity.[44] Smith's protagonist exercises her economic, sexual, and personal freedom by divorcing her philandering husband and living independently.

We find an explicit rejection of the tenets of settler sexuality embraced by 20th-century race women in the work of Rainey. Throughout her career, the marital institution "often was cavalierly repudiated with the kind of attitude usually gendered as male."[45] Encouraged enthusiastically by her audiences, Rainey exhibited a brazen disavowal of Black bourgeois social conventions about sexuality and gender expression. Rainey's songs are replete with lyrics that renounce marital fidelity, the confinement of sexual pleasure within the bounds of marriage, and the expectation of female sexual modesty. For example, in "Big Boy Blues," written by Rainey, she sings:

> There's two things I can't understand
> There's two things I can't understand
> Why these married women crazy 'bout that back door man
> [spoken]
> Lord, toot it, big boy, toot it
> Lord, that's my back door man.[46]

Rainey's recordings and performances reflect an affirmation of her "independence from the orthodox norms of womanhood" exhibited through the bold flaunting of her lesbian identity.[47] Rainey openly displayed her romantic and sexual desire for women through her discursive lyrics and manner of dress. For example, in "Prove It On Me Blues," written by Rainey, she sings:

> I went out last night with a crowd of my friends
> They must've been women, 'cause I don't like no men
> It's true I wear a collar and a tie...
> Wear my clothes just like a fan
> Talk to the gals just like any old man.[48]

Blues women, like Smith and Rainey, were held in reverence by their working-class audiences precisely because of their unabashed deviation from settler sexuality. These creative cultural artisans, according to Davis, "were expected to deviate from the norms defining orthodox female behavior."[49] Their performances generated a shared cultural space for working-class Black women. A space, per Davis, "in which the coercions of bourgeois notions of sexual purity and 'true womanhood' were absent."[50] Put differently, the women of the blues modeled divergent, or queer, manifestations of Black existence that were devoid of the Black married maternal, and their audiences loved them for it.

The queer performance of love and sexuality found in blues feminism are expressions of Black freedom. Blues music "created a discourse that represented freedom in more immediate and accessible terms," as the recently emancipated enjoyed a newfound autonomy in their romantic and sexual lives. Rainey's and Smith's invocations of sexual love "articulated a collective experience of freedom."[51] This inclusive affirmation of romantically, and sexually, diverse modes of being was not centered solely on women. Rainey also references expansive gender and sexual identities among Black men.[52] Davis concludes that a denial of sexual agency is itself a denial of freedom. These dual denials bring into question the culpability of Black middle-class women, who actively imposed their perception of marriage and motherhood upon Black working-class women. The transgression purportedly committed by blues feminism extends beyond the denunciations of moral integrity and, more critically, undermines Black liberatory praxis. If we are to properly understand the act of cleaving sexual agency, queerness, and Black womanhood away from marriage and motherhood as freedom work, then the Black married maternal can be more clearly understood as an enduring impediment to liberatory praxis.

Revisiting the legacies of historical Black feminisms returns us to the prescience of Morrison's aesthetic call to unveil our individual and collective recollections of freedom dreams germane to sexual desire, gender expression, and their mediation within the institutions of marriage and motherhood. This calling beckons an expansive notion of race women, inclusive of aesthetic dimensions of intellectual production that ground racial uplift.[53] Race women, who inspired Black communities through their oration and writings, were indeed persuasive public.[54] However, blues feminists should not be simply regarded as mere entertainers engaging audiences in folly. Artists like Rainey and Smith, I maintain, were also public orators who contributed to the pursuit of racial uplift.

This observation brings to mind Gadamer's reflections on the aesthetic consciousness and the interpretive horizon.[55] He states that our experience of the aesthetic is a "mode of self-understanding" that "always occurs throughout understanding something other than the self."[56] This understanding occasioned by the aesthetic experience "includes the unity and integrity of the other."[57] One can imagine Ma Rainey's rapt audience, engaging in call and response, as she sang about her experiences as an unmarried, same-gender loving, sexually free, masculine-identified woman. The reverence bestowed upon the beloved Rainey by her primarily cisgender, heterosexual audience provides a glimpse of the "unity and integrity" held within that communal performative space.

Art is a form of knowledge, according to Gadamer, and "experiencing an artwork means sharing in that knowledge."[58] Thus, "aesthetics becomes a history of worldview, i.e., a history of truth, as it is manifested in the mirror of art."[59] Blues feminism points to historical worldviews, or historical truths, that underscore the deviations within the Black ontic-epistemic experience that are not aligned with settler sexuality. These deviations remain obscured in our historical imaginings, or collective recollections, which inform Black theoretical and political praxis. The juxtaposition of Rainey's unabashed masculine presentation and proud lesbianism and Murray's fictive heteronormative contortions typifies the subordination of the deviations espoused by blues feminisms to those iterations of Black feminisms closely hewed to sexual citizenship. Murray's Jane Crow epitomizes the strategic erasures of Black queer identities within liberatory praxis and ontic-epistemic scholarship.

This subordination, which animates the marital shade experienced by single Black mothers, still figures heavily in 21st-century conceptions of racial justice. Mainstream movement work often reflects a tacit acceptance of settler sexual citizenship, such that racial progress is measured by degrees of proximity to full assimilation within the US political regime. Assimilationist aspirations call attention to the ever-present political dissonance between Black elites and working-class Blacks. Keeanga-Yamahtta Taylor writes, "The Black political elite has no *fundamental* political differences with the status quo in the United States."[60] Consequently, the responsibility for the ramifications of anti-Black racism, such as poverty, the achievement gap, and mass incarceration, is often placed upon an assumed deficiency within Black culture. In lieu of scrutinizing the "material causes of Black inequality," the occurrence of juvenile crime, for example, is regarded as the result of unsatisfactory parenting and value formation.[61] Persistent negative outcomes in Black communities, according to Taylor, are attributed to inferior familial formations and cultural practices by liberals and conservatives alike due to the "shared limits of their political imagination."[62] The rhetoric of marital shade is often heard among the Black elite as the whispers of the maternal wraith— *What does it mean to have a Black mother?*—abound in these political circles.[63]

Marital shade was evident during the 2014 racial uprising in Ferguson, Missouri. Teri McMurtry-Chubb brings this to the fore in her analysis of gendered parenthood in the wake of Michael Brown Jr.'s murder at the hands of a white police officer.[64] When St. Louis County Prosecutor Robert McCulloch stated that the officer would not be indicted for Brown's death, Michael Brown's stepfather, Louis Head, was videotaped atop a car yelling "Burn this motherfucker down! Burn this bitch down!"[65] Head's emotional utterances reflected "an expression of the building rage in Black communities over the deaths of unarmed Black men and women by state and extrajudicial violence."[66] His remarks, according to McMurtry-Chubb, "were not sanitized for a white audience and not the scripted lines for a highly-coordinated movement."[67] Benjamin Crump, the Brown family attorney, quickly denounced Head's remarks as inappropriate. McMurtry-Chubb attributes this denunciation to Crump's realization that capturing political attention for the murders of Black children has historically been achieved through Black motherhood.

Aligned with his National Association for the Advancement of Colored People (NAACP) forebears, Crump began to transform the maternal image of Brown Jr.'s mother, Lezley McSpadden. Crump recasts McSpadden in patriarchal terms by restoring Brown's biological father's place by her side. According to McMurtry-Chubb, these actions "began the fiction of Mike Brown Sr.'s role as the head of a household where Mike Brown Jr. figured prominently."[68] This fictionalized depiction belied the facts of the relationship between

Brown Sr. and McSpadden. At the age of sixteen, McSpadden gave birth to Brown Jr. She raised her son with support from members of both families, immediate and extended. According to McSpadden, Brown Sr. did not contribute to his son's upbringing financially or emotionally, despite living in his parents' home. She recounts suffering from intimate partner violence at the hands of Brown Sr. for years, ending only after the final dissolution of their relationship. Notwithstanding his history of neglect and abuse, Brown Sr. was installed in his "rightful" place as Brown Jr.'s father, appearing next to McSpadden in televised interviews and at speaking engagements.

The sanitization of unmarried Black motherhood was displayed two years earlier with the tragic killing of seventeen-year-old Jordan Davis. Davis was murdered by a white man at a gas station in Jacksonville, Florida, after a dispute over loud music.[69] In response to this grievous injustice, Jordan's mother, Lucia McBath, engaged in activism. In her exploration of Black maternal activism, Erica S. Lawson explains that McBath asserts an image of mothering that serves to "challenge problematic tropes about Black mothers," specifically "against the discursive representation of the single Black mother who is thought to raise irresponsible children."[70] This is evidenced in McBath's interviews with Ta-Nehisi Coates, in which she shares the importance of portraying herself as an upper-middle-class woman, successfully coparenting with her former husband, and providing her son with the well-resourced home life of a classic American middle-class teenager.[71] In fact, two-parent, financially well-off households are atypical in the United States. Even when bearing the weight of the unthinkable—the murder of one's child—it is important to portray the trappings of the Black married maternal. To ensure that we care for Jordan, to ensure that he is worthy of our activism, his mother must first demonstrate that she is a good steward of Black married maternalism.

* * *

Contemporary queer of color and Africana philosophical scholarship has broadened conceptions of family formation and mothering by challenging attempts to flatten the fullness of Black women's sexual and gender identities and reproductive practices. Yet, even with differing approaches to address anti-Black racism by confronting the historical consciousness that sustains remnants of bourgeois Black womanhood, the specter of the Black married maternal remains.[72] I will turn to Cathy Cohen's "politics of deviance" and Tommie Shelby's "political ethics of the oppressed" to support this claim. Their respective engagement with the ethico-political dimensions of anti-Black racism illuminates the intransigence of settler sexuality's disciplinary regulation. Their insights draw attention to the porous boundaries between the political and the moral, demonstrative of how these mutually reinforcing and intertwined forces reify marital shade in Black communities.

Cohen posits that the experience of unmarried, poor Black mothers is a ground from which a "politics of deviance must begin" and where "Black queer studies must be rooted."[73] The social location of unmarried, poor Black mothers is home to government surveillance, nominal agency, and exclusion from the spoils of full citizenship. Marginalization from the dominant society precipitates the choices of these mothers to exercise their diminished power through behaviors that are contrary to normative expectations. This behavior includes family formations and sexual choices that are perceived to be "morally wanting" in contrast to the "normative moral super structure"[74] Resistance to dominant normative prescriptions by the marginalized serves to "create new or counter normative frameworks" from which we can make moral judgments.[75] It is from a position of "limited agency," according to Cohen, that deviant practices around family structures and sexuality emerge. The "space created by deviant discourse and practice" engenders the possibility of a "new radical politics of deviance."[76]

Cohen heralds a politics of deviance as a welcome alternative to "the unfulfilled promise of access through respectability."[77] She maintains that the transformative qualities of deviant practice point toward a political strategy that could advance the life conditions of the most marginalized members of Black communities. By focusing on deviant practices, Cohen states that "we are witness to the power of those at the bottom," who demonstrate daily a refutation of "the basic normative assumptions of a society intent on protecting structural and social inequalities under the guise of some normal and natural order to life."[78]

Before an academic inquiry into deviance can commence, Cohen asserts that Black scholars must first scrutinize the normative assumptions that underlie Black social and political life. Such scrutiny is necessary to unearth the people and life activities that are considered deviant. She states that Black political scholars, who operate from a respectability politics lens, tend to only engage the marginalized members of our communities "when they conform to traditional understandings of what constitutes legitimate politics."[79] Cohen offers a moment of intervention to allow for a confrontation with the ethico-political gap between socioeconomically disadvantaged Black people and Black scholars in the academy. This gap is expressed by the latter's desire to be subsumed within the American Dream and to demonstrate assimilation, or conformity, through the marital institution.

The persistence of the Black married maternal is a manifestation of what Cohen describes as Indigenous moral panic in Black communities. This moral panic is a reaction to the supposedly deviant, or immoral, behavior of certain members of the Black community. This moral panic, according to Cohen, "serves as a catalyst for actions meant either to eliminate the behaviors or designate them as something foreign and unacceptable to respectable black people."[80] The censure of those whose sexual and familial practices stray outside heteronormative boundaries is the embodiment of "the anxiety of the black middle-class threatened with incurring" the loss of political and economic security in a political environment rife with anti-Black racism.[81]

The invitation to Black scholars to reflect upon their relationality to the Black married maternal is an important one. Cohen is not simply requesting a modification of the foci of one's research agenda, perhaps shifting away from an approach that centers on middle-class values and aspirations. Rather, her call beckons an extensive and collective ontic-epistemic shift. One that requires us to examine our relationship to our historical Black mother—the enduring maternal wraith that is intertwined with our sense of being and belonging. However, by situating single Black motherhood within the moralistic realm of deviance, the transformative reckoning with the Black married maternal is diminished.

Cautioning us against collapsing sexual difference into deviance, L. H. Stallings writes, "Real resistance to negative stereotypes . . . would mean destroying systems of gender and sexuality that make the stereotypes possible."[82] The destruction of settler sexuality would encourage the evolution of "radical Black female sexual subjectivities."[83] At present, the realization of radical Black sexual subjectivities is hindered by the marital institution and by the political and academic Black elite beholden to the ethico-political commitments of sexual citizenship. Cohen's brilliant analysis affirms that the limitation of agency experienced by single Black mothers is not to be found in the purportedly deviant practices of romantic love, sexual desire, and parenting outside the marital regime. But rather the limitation is revealed in those who are disciplined away from their authentic selves (e.g., Pauli Murray) by the overwhelming disciplinary force of the Black married maternal. However, the politics of deviance does not get to the root of marital shade because it remains within the binary loop of the normative and nonnormative. We need to move beyond this form of moral limitation to a more expansive, generative discourse that lies outside the neoliberal embrace of differing gender identities, sexual orientations, and family structures.

This concern is captured in Lewis Gordon's warning against articulations of decoloniality that eschew addressing the "political conditions of political problems" in favor of "a quest for the moral subordination of political life."[84] He states that the "resulting moralism is compatible with neoliberalism, which privileges the moral individual over political subjects" and sustains structural inequalities.[85] Gordon illustrates this compatibilism through the example of racism and our societal penchant for the well-worn emphasis on privilege. In this case, those privileged through white embodiment can espouse feelings of guilt, shame, or other negative moral traits, which leaves those of color in a position of moral superiority. After the acknowledgment of the purported moral hierarchy, "both the privileged and the deprived return to their relative unequal material conditions in a society that remains structurally intact."[86]

Similarly, Black scholars and activists can espouse platitudes of moral approbation for single Black mothers, while simultaneously eschewing an examination of the harms inflicted by the marital institution itself. The acceptance of heretofore deviant behaviors allows marital shade to flourish without transformative action to drive a political movement that improves the lives of unmarried Black mothers. The elite quest for increased political and economic power through acquiescence to sexual citizenship remains unaffected. Thus, I contend that the problem of marital shade is not exclusion from settler sexual citizenship but rather settler sexual citizenship itself. Heeding the lessons provided by blues feminism, I suggest that we reframe the narrative of single Black motherhood as a limited agency resulting from deviance to an understanding of it as a deviation from the manacles of settler citizenship. I will now turn to an examination of Shelby's treatment of unmarried Black mothers in *Dark Ghettos* to further elucidate my nagging apprehension about a discourse on deviance.

Shelby outlines three main objectives in his meticulously researched volume. He provides an argument in support of the claim that ghettos are products of systemic injustice, then identifies the normative limits that should be placed upon state antipoverty interventions, and finally, he develops an account of "a political ethics of the oppressed." Black women's reproductive capacities serve as paradigmatic examples in support of his threefold objective. Significant attention is devoted to the legacy of intrusive state interventions that undermine reproductive choice. He considers whether these reproductive choices or families headed by single mothers are possible explanatory factors both for the fruition of "ghetto conditions" and for their persistent existence.

Shelby provides a liberal-egalitarian argument to expose systemic injustices that adversely impact impoverished single Black mothers. He confines this inquiry to assessing the moral acceptability of three aspects of welfare reform, drawn from the 1996 Personal Responsibility and Work Opportunity Reconciliation Act. He adeptly provides justificatory grounds to reject these welfare reform policies, which include structuring welfare benefits to discourage childbearing outside of marriage, advancing marriage promotion initiatives, and regulating child support enforcement. He writes, "I believe that under seriously unjust conditions, the state lacks the moral standing to make such forceful interventions into the lives of the oppressed." Given that the underlying structure of US society is unjust, Shelby concludes that principles of corrective justice do not allow the state to use welfare benefits as a means to coerce poor Black women into delaying, or foregoing, procreation.

Returning to my argument in Chapter 2 concerning the state's role in fomenting anti-Black racism through the marital regime, I think that Shelby's analysis of two marriage-specific state policies is insufficient to address the varied facets of state harm. He is, of course, correct in refuting state involvement in the manipulation of Black women's family forming and in any attempt to coerce marital unions. However, Shelby still leaves single Black mothers subject to the firm hand of corrective justice by supporting the legal binary of married and unmarried, with its concomitant material and social costs and benefits. As discussed in Chapter 2, we must remember that the illusion of personal choice in the marriage market is just that. Marriage markets foment a material reality of choicelessness for many of the very women Shelby studied. Shelby misunderstands the most serious effect of state injustice on unmarried Black mothers. Without a doubt, 20th-century welfare policies inflicted undue burdens upon Black families, but this narrow focus will not redress current injustices. Setting state harm aside, what is most intriguing for me is the role racialized Blackness plays in Shelby's analysis of single Black mothers.

After providing a negative account of state activities, Shelby offers a positive account of justice, defining the "political ethics of the oppressed." The objective of this undertaking is to determine what the Black urban poor are "morally required and permitted to do in response to the unjust conditions" that they face in their lives.[87] Put differently, he aims to establish "what would constitute a responsible and dignified response" by the urban poor to confront their unjust conditions.[88] Given the gross injustices endured by the urban poor, he claims that they have different obligations to established societal norms. This includes the moral authority to defy established political and economic norms due to their alienation from the wider society. He claims that "actions of the ghetto poor that are interpreted as deviant" should be "understood as moral responses to injustice." By interpreting some behaviors of impoverished Black people as moral responses to injustice, he writes, "we gain insight into the political ethics of the unjustly disadvantaged and can better evaluate when these responses are reasonable and permissible or blameworthy and self-defeating."

Attending specifically to unmarried Black mothers, Shelby acknowledges that they are often found blameworthy for their own material conditions and as a contributing factor to the plight of Black communities. In contrast to this view, Shelby neither promotes the marital institution as the morally preferable site of procreation and parenting nor believes that the nuclear family is superior to other familial configurations. He agrees with Black feminists who argue that the normalization of the nuclear family unfairly stigmatizes Black single mothers. Though he disagrees with the claims that the wrongness of the dual parent model lies within their account of moral disapprobation. For Shelby, the dual parent norm is wrong because it is "unjustified on a liberal-egalitarian conception of the family's role in a just social order."[89] He surmises that the societal disparagement of single Black mothers is not attributable to their marital status. Rather, panic over the increased number of female-headed households arises out of concern over impoverished single women having children that they cannot afford to care for in meaningful ways. Thus, these families will not have an escape from poverty. He writes, "The problem is not the decline of patriarchal family units, which from a liberal-egalitarian point of view is a welcome development."[90]

Shelby's account of the lived experience of single Black mothers is enveloped within an oddly race-neutral account of anti-Black racism as systemic injustice. It is important to tease out who exactly is in a position of judgment in Shelby's articulation of a "political ethics of the oppressed." One would hope that all American citizens were supportive of ameliorating the injustices incurred by anti-Black racism, white supremacy, and racial capitalism. Such hope, however, would miss the reality of the Black liberation movements. The pursuit of our liberation is not an undertaking being pursued by the masses of white Americans, even in this time of racial reckoning.[91] Firmly ensconced within the tenets of US liberalism, according to Yahmatta-Taylor, the views of the Black political elite regarding settler citizenship do not differ appreciably from those of mainstream society. By erasing the specificity of Black liberation activists from his account, Shelby is unable, in his response to anti-Black racism, to properly attend to the Black married maternal and its symbiotic relationship with settler sexuality.

The invocation of an "us vs. them" ethical-political model is reminiscent of the judgment imposed by race women of the club movement. Shelby appears to have eluded this characterization by giving a progressive nod to the purportedly deviant choices of single Black mothers. The subjugation of unmarried Black mothers to the binary moral discourse of normative and nonnormative allows political power, inclusive of ontic-epistemic power, to remain intact as Shelby's progressive "we" remains privileged to evaluate "them."

As described previously, a hallmark of the Black married maternal is the disciplinary regulation of gender and sexuality in accordance with heteronormativity. Insufficient attention to this regulation animates Shatema Threadcraft's critique of Shelby's elision of "important issues regarding gender and power relations surrounding sex and reproduction in his discussion of child support."[92] She considers this oversight to be particularly "upsetting because he expressly condemns such problematic power relations across racial lines."[93] Threadcraft's theoretical framing of "intimate justice," which considers the particularity of gender-based anti-Black racism as experienced by impoverished Black women, is quite a valuable intervention. Both Shelby and Threadcraft, however, focus their astute theorization on cisgender and heterosexual members of the community. Notwithstanding the requisite parenthetical references to queer folks, Shelby's entire analysis of Black motherhood focuses on cisgender, heterosexual relationships. Where are the lesbian mothers? Where is the consideration of Black trans mothers? This unfortunate absence reinforces Marlon Bailey's and Rashad Shabazz's observation that "black gender and sexual minorities are rendered as outside the spatial formation of black communities."[94]

The urban geographies considered by Shelby include queer people, who are unable to "freely choose the neighborhoods or urban spaces in which they live and move."[95] Their survival amidst homophobic and transphobic violence is dependent on the cultivation of creative reservoirs to sustain nurturing communal life. One such resource is the formation of houses within ballroom culture. These houses consist of families of choice or familial bonds that are socially constructed as opposed to biological. Ballroom houses are headed by mothers and fathers. House mothers are typically either transgender women or gay men, and fathers are usually transgender or gay men. House mothers in this kinship network impart love and guidance to their children to foster their growth and well-being.

To be fair, Shelby maintains a broad conception of family and parenting that includes biological, moral, social, and legal parents. He notes that moral parents, those with "moral rights or responsibilities of parenthood with respect to another person," may not be legally recognized, and the law may indeed "construct parenthood in ways that are not morally justified or that are even unjust."[96] This gesture, however, does not convey the fullness of systemic injustice endured by Black queer families. Queer of color and Black feminist scholars have emphasized at length that the perpetual process of norming binary sexual and gender identities is performed in relationship with the norming of hierarchical racial identities. There is a particularity of "Blackness" within Black queerness that cannot be ignored or subsumed under other "forms of oppression." Our experience of homophobia and transphobia internal to Black communities cannot be separated from anti-Blackness or systemic injustice within the nation-state. There is a specificity to the oppression faced by Black queer and trans mothers that is exacerbated by marital shade.

A cisgender-heteronormative theoretical framework is not comprehensive enough to capture our imagination around the Black married maternal. This progressive, yet myopic, framework can indeed recognize the possible legal sleight of hand within the context of US liberalism. But the absence of queer Black mothers in the framework is demonstrative of its inability to recognize the dominating force of the Black married maternal, insofar as it does not make room for this form of fictive kin. Further, without troubling the waters of allegiance to the marital regime itself, queer families will continue to experience alienation through intraracial homophobic/transphobic violence and by the withholding of state resources.

At the bottom, I agree with Shelby's view that there are myriad factors that engender the injustices faced by the poor, of all races. The crux of my concern here is echoed by Christopher Lebron's worry about what he calls the sterility of Shelby's learned account of the Republic's gross injustices against Black Americans.[97] In his reply to Lebron's critique, Shelby notes that he purposefully uses the terms "structural injustice" and "systemic injustice" in lieu of "systemic racism" because the injustices faced by the ghetto poor are not caused by white supremacy alone. I believe Shelby is too quick to dismiss the virulence of anti-Black racism that adversely impacts single Black mothers across sexual, gender, and class lines. The hastiness of the dismissal leads to palliative remedies to address racially motivated injustices that miss the mark.

For instance, Shelby cites Dorothy Roberts's seminal *Killing the Black Body*, in which she exposes the racism that undermines Black women's flourishing as mothers through the state's attempts to (1) use policy measures as a mechanism to oppress Black motherhood and (2) to perpetuate negative stereotypes of our mothering capacities. Shelby praises her work, accepting Roberts's claim that the experience of Black motherhood is impacted by anti-Black racism. He deems her account of anti-Black racism, however, irrelevant to the "question of whether there is a valid justification for welfare policies that deter reproduction among poor single women."[98] Not everyone who endorses such policies, he argues, is motivated by anti-Black racism. For example, some policymakers may believe these policies will redress Black poverty or improve life conditions for impoverished Black women. Shelby concludes that the "basic structure of U.S. society is unjust and that principles of corrective justice do not permit" using welfare benefits to coerce poor Black women into delaying/foregoing procreation.[99]

Our conclusions concerning the morality of poor women procreating are the same. Notwithstanding nefarious intent, the mere act of poor women choosing motherhood is neither morally wrong nor is it an unfair burden on the state.[100] Yet, it is important to consider the "Black" in single Black motherhood. Otherwise, we are left with a form of marital shade that ignores the Black married maternal and its role in the praxis of Black liberation. I believe Shelby underestimates the angst that many Black people feel regarding unmarried Black mothers across the socioeconomic spectrum. Consequently, he undervalues the role of the Black married maternal in social justice movements.

Twenty years ago, Roberts proposed that we properly consider the relationship between racial justice and reproductive rights. In the intervening years, the reproductive justice movement has successfully demonstrated that reproductive justice is far more expansive than securing the legal right to abortion.[101] This broader understanding of reproductive justice—extending beyond a "woman's right to choose"— reflects the racialized gender disparities within our liberal democracy. Moving one step forward, I posit that unmarried Black mothers exist precariously at the fulcrum of the marital regime and reproductive justice. As a precedent, the state penalizes those regarded as "unworthy of procreation."[102] For Roberts, the denial of Black women's procreative rights "functions to preserve a racial hierarchy that essentially disregards Black humanity."[103] She writes, "the government need not be concerned with social practices that create such vague injuries as the devaluation of Black mothers."[104]

The litany of manipulative procreative policies enacted within the liberal state operates as institutionalized forms of state punishment or, put differently, as methods of disciplinary regulation for Black women, qua Black women. These are not race-neutral policies. They are policies aimed at preventing single Black women from bearing children. Roberts provides a chilling example in *Killing the Black Body* to underscore this point. In 1958, Mississippi state representative David H. Glass "introduced a bill mandating sterilization for any unmarried mother who gave birth to another illegitimate child."[105] His explicit aim was to reduce the number of Black women and children receiving government benefits. He raised the familiar trope of the Black welfare queen to justify his stance. Roberts asserts that these efforts serve as punitive measures to "penalize single, rebellious Black mothers."[106] It is the rebellion that invokes the lineage of blues feminism and its blatant rejection of settler citizenship. It is the rebellion that unsettles those invested in being accepted as proper stewards of settler sexuality.

I imagine these stewards include the well-meaning middle-class Black folks that Shelby envisions are crafting race-neutral welfare policies to address Black poverty. What a careful reading of Roberts reveals is that such stewardship is a peculiar reaction to anti-Black racism that is defined by its determination to properly configure Black families in alignment with settler sexuality. This peculiarity is evident in marriage-related juridical precedents. Historical analysis of the jurisprudence of nonmarriage shows that the Supreme Court tentatively supports nonmarital families in the context of "serving and supporting" only when marital families are not an option.[107] A survey of 1977 *Moore v. East Cleveland* demonstrates not only the intransigence of the marital regime in US jurisprudence but also the stronghold of the Black married maternal.[108]

The case involved the plaintiff, Inez Moore, a Black mother and grandmother who lived with her son and his child. She also resided with John Moore Jr., the son of her late daughter. Moore received notification from the City of East Cleveland that her grandson, John Jr., was not a legal resident of her home per the city's housing code. The notice stated that in order to be in compliance with the housing code, she must permanently remove John Jr. from her home. Moore resolutely refused to cast out her grandson, whom she had been raising since his mother's death when he was an infant. In response to her refusal, the City of East Cleveland filed a criminal case against her and sought prosecution. Upon hearing the case, the Supreme Court ruled in favor of Moore and concluded that the "East Cleveland housing ordinance, which limited occupancy of a dwelling unit to members of one single family, violated the Due Process Clause of the Fourteenth Amendment."[109]

In its opinion supporting Moore's due process claim, the Court affirmed that it "has long recognized that freedom of personal choice in matters of marriage and family life is one of the liberties protected by the Due Process Clause of the Fourteenth Amendment."[110] This freedom of choice begets a "private realm of family life which the state cannot enter."[111] Thereby, the Court dismissed the City of East Cleveland's claim that "any constitutional right to live together as a family extends only to the nuclear family."[112] The Court asserted that its decisions "establish that the Constitution protects the sanctity of the family" because the familial institution is so "deeply rooted in this Nation's history and tradition."[113] This history is not limited to "bonds uniting the members of the nuclear family."[114] On the contrary, there is a rich tradition "of uncles, aunts, cousins, and especially grandparents sharing a household along with parents and children."[115] Consequently, the Court concluded that the Constitution does not uphold East Cleveland's attempt to compel its residents "to live in certain narrowly defined family patterns."[116] This Constitutional right is especially important in "times of adversity" when extended family members "come together for mutual sustenance and to maintain or rebuild a secure home life."[117]

On its face, the Court's opinion appears to undercut my claims about the parochialism of settler citizenship and the Black married maternal. Under closer scrutiny, however, we see that this is not the case, as evidenced by the critique leveled by Angela Onwuachi-Willig. She writes that the "assumption of African American deviance in families is so strong that even the U.S. Supreme Court's two most progressive justices at that time—Justices Brennan and Marshall—failed to acknowledge and appreciate the inherent strengths of extended family forms when presented with an opportunity to do so."[118] For instance, in his discussion of the importance of extended families to the well-being of immigrant families, Justice Brennan "did so in a way that implied that such immigrant families quickly and rightfully left behind those purported 'nonideal' family forms once they had climbed out of their economically depressed situations."[119] While it is true that the Court held that discrimination against nonnuclear families was unconstitutional, the moral binary of "ideal" and "nonideal" still reigns within the settler-colonial juridical imagination. Thus, this ruling, in its failure to decisively reject this limiting hierarchy, is ineffective in ameliorating the detrimental impact of marital shade experienced by single Black mothers.

Onwuachi-Willig also asserts that the intraracial implications of this case reveal the schism between the middle-class and working-class Black communities. The Justices' decision, according to Onwuachi-Willing, "failed to acknowledge and explain how the actions of the Black middle class in East Cleveland constituted a form of racism, not just classism, against poor and working-class African Americans."[120] She states that an exploration of the intraracial biases exhibited in *Moore* "could have revealed the pressures that African Americans have faced (both in history and at that time) to conform to the nuclear family structure."[121] In so doing, the Justices "could have revealed the internalization of myths about African American familial deviance by the black middle class in East Cleveland that has resulted in racial discrimination by African Americans against other African Americans."[122] Onwuachi-Willig's surfacing of the vital necessity for such a revelation animates my concern with Shelby's race-neutral analysis of single Black motherhood. We may attribute the shortcomings I have identified as a symptom of Shelby's analytic approach. Since he is working within the tradition and language of analytic philosophy, Paul C. Taylor notes that Shelby did not concern himself with the reduction of moral reflection or the import of social meaning-making within sociopolitical life.[123]

This shortsightedness is not endemic to heteronormative liberalism alone. David L. Eng also defines queer liberalism as "the forgetting of race and the denial of racial difference."[124] For Eng, "the 'completion' of the racial project that marks the advent of colorblindness in the U.S. nation-state" is a "condition of possibility for the historical emergence of queer freedom."[125] My charitable reading of Shelby acknowledges that he is not being purposefully obtuse about racial injustice or openly endorsing color blindness. To the contrary, we observe that he is simply working with the tenets of neoliberalism, which requires a tempering of the specificity of anti-Black racism's impact on Black people across varying iterations of systemic injustice. Thus, Shelby's positive portrayal of queerness and diverse family formations is allowable under liberal-egalitarian principles as long as they remain in contradistinction to a robust racial analysis.

In a sense, one could say that his meticulous parsing of the injustices of state welfare programs prevents him from seeing the forest for the trees. Through his subtle dismissal of the Black feminist accounts in *Dark Ghettos*, Shelby misses their attempts to guide us beyond entanglements with the maternal wraith that impede the flourishing of unmarried Black mothers. These Black women understand that the struggles of single Black mothers are based, in part, on the intraracial social meanings concerning the particularity of this social identity. This is not simply a matter of "ideology," but rather reflects the very fabric of our humanity in relation to ourselves and our communities. The embodied, situated person is, according to Merleau-Ponty, in direct contradistinction to the "modern, liberal picture of the separate, autonomous self."[126] Shelby's "black radical liberal" approach overlooks the grave importance of social meaning-making, which is a constitutive aspect of the phenomenological account of the embodied interpretive horizon. As beings in the world, we engage in a mutually conditioning dance between the interplay of individual interiority and sociality, and our freedom is experienced through our interaction with a world of meanings thrust upon us.

The gaps presented in Cohen's "politics of deviance" and Shelby's "political ethics of the oppressed" reveal the difficulties faced by Black scholars committed to challenging the pernicious existence of single Black mothers. Phenomenology provides significant resources for this academic endeavor, especially Africana phenomenology, which draws upon "the Africana context to see what we tend not to see."[127] Africana phenomenology is a fruitful theoretical approach as it expands "options in a world where the lack thereof leads to meaningless choices and, consequently, human suffering."[128] This expansion, however, necessitates a queering of Africana phenomenology. Disruption of the Black married maternal depends on it. Pursuits in Africana philosophy must confront the consistent denigration of familial, gender, and sexual fluidity within Black communities if we are to contribute meaningfully to Black liberation.

Sara Ahmed points us toward the advantages of a queer phenomenological approach that begins "by redirecting our attention toward different objects, those that are 'less proximate' or even those that deviate."[129] Ahmed expounds upon the possibilities of redirection through reference to the landscape architecture term "desire lines." Desire lines are the "marks left on the ground" by people using unofficial pathways that "deviate from the paths they were supposed to follow."[130] The marks created by deviation hold the generative potential to occasion even more alternative lines. The lesbian landscape, for Ahmed, is a manifestation of such a desire line. It is one that deviates from the socially prescribed straight line.

There is a "significance of 'deviation' in what makes queer lives queer. To make things queer is certainly to disturb the order of things."[131] Our queer orientations exemplify this disturbance through the defiance of straight cultures' expected spatial and temporal dimensions. Spatially, we humans are oriented toward specific objects, paths, or directions. On a temporal plane, we develop sexual orientations over time. The queer subject's deviation from the spatial and temporal norms of straight culture is "made socially present as deviant."[132] To be clear, it is our deviations, our desire lines, that are perceived, or interpreted, as deviant. Queerness is not deviant in itself, only appearing as such within a sociality dominated by an orientation toward settler citizenship.

Deviation is an imaginative act that inspires us to reach beyond what is known and familiar. Queer phenomenology leads away from deviance and points toward expansive, generative modes of being, theorizing, and loving within our homes and communities. This creative potential returns us to Morrison's imperative to give voice to those silenced behind the veil. This ontic-epistemic work must be inclusive of the markings left by queer desire lines. This queer aesthetic process "frequently contains blueprints and schemata of a forward-dawning futurity."[133] Queerness is an as-yet realized ideality, according to José Muñoz, which grounds the possibility of our imaginings of the future.[134] I will address this possibility as the ground for overcoming marital shade in Chapter 5.

4

Corrupted Intimacies

Intimacy lies at the heart of this exploration of single Black motherhood in the United States. Subject to unveiling are the intertwined familial intimacies between generations of Black mothers and children, both biological and chosen. Laid bare before us are the romantic and sexual intimacies whispered between lovers across a vast spectrum of gender and sexual identities. This project of intimate disclosure roots us within the very meaning of intimacy itself. Derived from the Latin intimatus, the past participle of intimare, intimacy is to "make known, announce, impress." And stemming from Latin intimus, it is also defined as "inmost, innermost, deepest." The innermost facets of ourselves, coupled with our deepest human connections, are not left hidden within our individual subjectivities; these inclinations are made known through their impressions upon the social world.

Sexual citizenship encapsulates these dual aspects of intimacy as embodied intersubjectivity and as a site of power. Love and kinship in our contemporary era of liberalism, with its emphasis on individualism, "are anchored in a particular conception of the subject, the body and its extension in the world."[1] Put differently, our familial formations and sexual relationships are not confined solely to the private realm. Our intimate choices are "infused with worldliness," such that these choices are imbued with "specific political, social, and cultural meanings."[2] The state-regulated marital regime, or the legal regulation of love, for example, "reflects the constitutive role of intimate attachments in the formation of nation-states—and vice versa."[3] Familial and sexual intimacies exist in dialectical interplay with the liberal state socially, politically, and economically.

Sexual citizenship is situated within the larger milieu of settler citizenship in the United States. The perversion of anti-Black racism, which is embedded within settler citizenship, serves to vitiate Black intimacies through the legal regulation of love. The extension of marital rights to the formerly enslaved, according to Roderick Ferguson, demonstrates "the ways in which the law as it pertained to postslavery attempted to 'absorb all responsibility' for intimacy" and thereby undermined efforts to form diverse intimate relations.[4] The bestowal of marriage rights thus "created new technologies for attenuating forms of African American intimacy."[5] I attempted to flesh out these deleterious techniques by articulating forms of marital shade advanced by the state through marriage equality and Black scholar-activists wedded to the neoliberal marital regime.

It is reasonable to conclude that the problems raised in the aforementioned chapters could be addressed through marriage abolition or the end of the legal codification of romantic relationships through state-sanctioned marital contracts. I wholeheartedly agree with this sentiment and will offer support for marriage abolition in Chapter 5. I remain wary, however, of the transformative potential of marriage abolition as it is currently articulated and argued for by its proponents. An examination of white women's theoretical contributions aimed at advancing the abolition, or even reform, of the marital regime reveals that the travails of unmarried Black women would remain intact. I purposefully single out white women's sustained critiques of marriage because there is no correlate within either Black feminist literature or Africana philosophy.

White women's arguments against marriage have spanned centuries.[6] From the 18th- and 19th-century objections to coverture and white women's lack of political/legal autonomy to 21st-century arguments steeped in liberal theory, white women have fought against gender- and sexuality-based marginalization embedded within the marital regime. What is not prominent within these arguments related to the marital institution is a substantive examination of racial marginalization, specifically anti-Black racism. While contemporary scholars most certainly reference the racialized hardships faced by Black women, they do not scrutinize the negative impact of their own whiteness upon their theoretical endeavors. This circumvention beckons an exploration of platonic intimacies between women-identified scholars. More pointedly, I posit that there is a corruption of platonic intimacies that compromises marital abolition discourses offered by white-embodied scholars within the liberal political tradition.[7] Recognizing the ephemeral or "phantom-like nature of liberalism itself," my interest here is not to denounce liberal discourses.[8] Rather, I aim to illustrate how unchallenged whiteness bound within these intimate discourses maintains racial inequities.

The refutation of the marital regime is often situated within condemnations of patriarchy, heterosexism, and capitalism. These matters are often coded implicitly as male and invoke the specter of cisgender, heterosexual, white male privilege as foundational to sexual citizenship. Less problematized is the racial privilege enjoyed by white women. As many have pointed out in recent years, white supremacy is not confined to cisgender, heterosexual men. White women, whether cisgender, transgender, heterosexual, or queer, are active agents in the propagation of anti-Black racism. As moral agents, they are culpable for the establishment and maintenance of white supremacy. Far from mere victims, white women are beneficiaries of the economic, political, and social privileges accorded to whiteness. This race-based power and privilege is evident within white women's calls for marital abolition. The absence of a robust racial reckoning in their arguments for abolition contributes to a tertiary form of marital shade, namely theoretical Blackface.

The invocation of theoretical Blackface is a nod to Black minstrelsy, a popular form of theatrical performance developed in early 19th-century America, in which primarily white men performed caricatures of Black people.[9] In its heyday as a preeminent national art form in the 1840s, E. Lott asserts that the minstrel show "began to ease the friction among various segments of the working class, and between workers and class superiors, by seizing on Jim Crow as a common enemy."[10] The minstrel show "buried class tensions and permitted class alliances along rigidifying racial lines."[11] The grotesque performance of white transmogrification through Black caricature was a catalyst for the uplift of less powerful, working-class white people into the ranks of the more powerful upper class through the codification of whiteness as a unified racial caste. The pervasiveness of Blackface performances, its words and deeds, remains significant within the contemporary white imaginary. This gendered iteration of minstrelsy does not call for solidarity across racial lines in pursuit of the liberation of all women. In lieu of unification, theoretical Blackface personifies the desire to gain entry into the ranks of white-embodied power, alongside white men.

Marital shade, as expressed through theoretical Blackface, evinces a bilateral defilement of Black intimacies. On the one hand, the sanctity of Black women's intimate lives has been upended by anti-Black racism effectuated by white women. On the other hand, the fruition of genuine platonic intimacies between Black and white women is stymied by the latter's evasion of culpability through fanciful imaginings of embodied racial equivalence. In the following, I will provide a brief genealogy of white women's racialized weaponization of the marital regime spanning across the past two centuries. This historical account provides the seedbed from which I will explore the presence of theoretical Blackface in contemporary white feminist literature on the marital regime. Specifically, I will show how marital shade permeates the marriage debates between lesbian feminists Claudia Card and Cheshire Calhoun.

The entanglement of the marital regime, the enslavement of African-descended people, and the white women's rights movement can be traced back to the earliest days of the republic. Antislavery abolitionists and southern slaveholders alike employed references to marriage to both condemn and defend the master-slave relationship. Abolitionists argued that it was cruel to prevent enslaved Black people access to legal marriage because it denied them the opportunity to live in accordance with Christian values, including sexual chastity and monogamous romantic relationships.[12] They also decried the contradictory behavior of purportedly Christian slaveholders, who flouted their marriage covenants through the rampant sexual assault of enslaved Black people.[13] Meanwhile, proponents of the peculiar institution believed that "slavery, like marriage, was a relationship of unequals benefiting both parties."[14] They claimed that enslavement benefited Black people in the same way that women were suited for domestic servitude as wives, as God and nature intended.

White women activists in the mid-19th century seized upon the "convergence of proslavery and antislavery rhetorics on marriage . . . to compare the wife and the slave" and likened their subordinate roles in marital unions to abject subjugation.[15] They appropriated the plight of Black women to advance their own crusade to champion legislative and social changes to benefit white womanhood.[16] This gross misconstrual of kindred sisterhood obscures the utter disregard for Black love and bodily autonomy held by white men and women, respectively. While the plantation mistress did experience victimization due to patriarchy, Ann duCille states that "she was also in many instances the victimizer, either as the silent/silenced codependent enabler or as the abuser, physically, emotionally, and in some cases sexually assaulting, tormenting, and terrorizing the enslaved."[17]

This predatory behavior extended beyond physical and emotional abuse as plantation mistresses contributed actively to the American slave economy. Preceding the marriage markets of the modern era, these women played a significant role in sustaining racial capitalism, as, what Stephanie E. Jones-Rogers calls, the mistresses of the market. Hewing closely to its original meaning, Jones-Rogers defines "mistress" as a woman who governs, who holds capital, or who is able to deploy rule or power. "By definition and in fact," she posits that "the mistress was the master's equivalent" as Southern slave owners in their own right.[18] The substantial economic investment in chattel slavery made by these women "were fundamental to the nation's economic growth and to American capitalism."[19] The conception of slavery and capitalism as solely male domains is rendered untenable, according to Jones-Rogers, when one considers that "the enslaved people women owned before they married or acquired afterward helped make the nineteenth-century scale of southern cotton cultivation possible."[20]

Slave-owning wives were not exempt from the challenges posed by coverture regarding women legally owning property. Plantation mistresses took great care to retain ownership and control "over the enslaved people given to them by loved ones or bought or acquired upon, during, and after marriage."[21] The complex legal maneuvers undertaken by slave-owning white women is a testament to their vested commitment to the institution of slavery—a commitment that supports Jones-Rogers's claim that for these women, slavery was synonymous with their own freedom. This freedom was continuously created "by actively engaging and investing in the economy of slavery."[22] The subjugation of Black people allowed these women, these wives, a modicum of respite from a diminished existence circumscribed within the domestic sphere. Plantation mistresses participated in 19th-century marketplaces and were afforded economic security, for themselves and for their families.

Emancipation did not diminish the vital role played by white women to preserve racial dominance through the degradation of Black familial and romantic intimacies. The end of chattel slavery merely signaled a refashioning of the enforcement of racial hierarchy. The system of entrenched racial segregation maintained through white supremacist politics in the first half of the 20th century, according to Elizabeth McRae, was very often constructed and maintained by white women. Through their mobilization and political training efforts, "these women guaranteed that racial segregation seeped into the nooks and crannies of public life and private matters."[23] The mobilizing force of white supremacist women, per McRae, was not contained in the south, and neither was it limited to a particular political party or socioeconomic, marital, or educational status. More pointedly, she asserts that white women "were the mass in massive resistance."[24]

White women employed in state agencies during the 1920s were able to leverage their positionality to conjoin white supremacist politics and intimate domestic relations, including sex, marriage, and parenthood. Their political power allowed for the bureaucratization of white supremacy within social welfare infrastructures and granted them state-sanctioned legitimacy to control the most intimate aspects of Black life. These female employees, according to McRae, "translated their gender-specific authority as white mothers into public authority as workers for the state."[25] In support of her claim, McRae cites Virginia's Racial Integrity Act (RIA), enacted in March 1924, to illustrate the control that local clerks were granted to determine racial classification and maintain white purity through the issuance, or denial, of marriage licenses.[26] Through their work, these white, college-educated women "designated racial lines, labeled families, and drew boundaries around Black and white in their communities."[27] By racializing womanhood, McRae concludes, "white women embodied a political system that elevated whiteness and imbued women with political power based on their exclusion of African Americans."[28]

It is from the historical situatedness of white woman as slave master and later arbiter of white supremacist politics that I explore the manifestation of theoretical Blackface in white feminist scholarship. I am far from the first to engage in such analysis, as Toni Morrison provides us with a compelling entry point for inquiry of this sort. Her examination of white literature reveals that "a real or fabricated Africanist presence was crucial" to white authors' understanding of themselves as American.[29] Morrison's literary curiosity fastens upon the epistemological and ontological consequences of "playing in the dark" for non-Black writers, or as she puts it, "the impact of racism on those who perpetuate it."[30] She seeks to understand "what racial ideology does to the mind, imagination, and behavior of masters."[31] The import of her literary query is correspondingly significant within academic scholarship. The Africanist presence in literature made explicit by Morrison has an often implicit, yet constitutive, correlate within white scholars' collective identity as American women. How does this Africanist presence, or playing in the dark, influence their collective understanding of white wifedom and subsequent theorization of the marital regime?

4.1 Queer White Women and Marital Shade

Carol Pateman's classic work *The Sexual Contract* is often heralded as a laudable feminist treatment of contract theory's patriarchal roots. It is at its most instructive, however, as an exemplar of theoretical Blackface that vitiates the import of white women's marital scholarship to the betterment of Black women's lives. To be clear, Pateman's origin story is not race-blind. She posits that the men "who (are said to) make the original contract are *white* men," and this contract includes "the slave contract that legitimizes the rule of white over Black."[32] The rule of whiteness that Pateman acknowledges is inclusive of white women, as the violence wrought by chattel slavery and anti-Black racism has not been solely executed by white men. By invoking the analogy between the white wife and the Black slave, Pateman is able to code anti-Black racism as male through the convergence of the marital and slave contracts. Appeal to the marital regime thus allows for the gendering of white racism and grants white women absolution from their culpability in the perpetuation of racial harm.[33]

The marriage contract, according to Pateman, "reflects the patriarchal ordering of nature embodied in the original contract."[34] She posits that the contradiction revealed in institutional slavery, namely the simultaneous denial and affirmation of the enslaved's humanity, is also evident in patriarchy. The marital contract considers women as both property and persons, as the "contract demands that their womanhood be both denied and affirmed."[35] Pateman assumes that an ostensible equivalence of contradiction should be regarded as an equivalence of lived experience between white wives and enslaved Black women.

Noting that 18th-century white women abolitionists frequently compared their condition as wives to that of their slaves, Pateman attempts to provide evidentiary support for this amalgamation. She states that (a) adult male slaves were called boys and wives were called girls; (b) "until late into the 19th century the legal and civil position of a wife resembled that of a slave," declaring that white wives were civilly dead; (c) slaves were forced to take their owner's name and wives took their husband's name, including "the great American suffragist" Elizabeth Cady Stanton; and, finally, (d) as an exemplar of this horror, "the most graphic illustration of the continuity between slavery and marriage" was wife selling in England.[36] She reports that between 1073 and the 20th century, 387 women were sold.[37]

The absurdity of these comparisons should be readily apparent to the astute reader with even a cursory understanding of the travails of chattel slavery. Pateman herself cites, in her words, Orlando Patterson's "striking formulation" that the slave is "a socially dead person."[38] This acknowledgment alone should have rendered the comparison of the civilly dead white wife to the socially and civilly dead slave obsolete. But her commitment to the white wife/Black slave analogy is quite extraordinary. One wonders what exactly is at stake for Pateman to equate the sale of approximately 400 white women over the course of 800 years to the 12.5 million Africans entrapped within the transatlantic slave trade and the 3.5–4.4 million enslaved Africans in the United States.[39]

With the transmogrification complete, Pateman is freed from the burdensome task of admitting to and atoning for white women's active participation in slave economies and the perpetuation of anti-Black racism post-Emancipation. The fictitious solidarity forged by the white wife/Black slave analogy allows Pateman to uncritically center white women in her marital regime discourse, even when acknowledging the systemic sexual violence endured by enslaved Black women. She writes, "the figure of the slave-owner's wife was a peculiarly dramatic symbol of patriarchal right for other (white) wives of the period."[40] This figure was dramatic, according to Pateman, because their husbands' repeated acts of rape were emotionally injurious to their white wives. The sustained sexual assault of Black women is treated strictly through the lens of aggrieved white wives. The fruition of genuine intimacies between Black and white women is impeded by such fanciful flights from the realities of sexually violent acts committed by white women married to slave owners and from the significance of married mistresses of the market, who were themselves slave owners.

Pateman concludes that the white wife/Black slave analogy does not hold in contemporary times, given that white women now enjoy full citizenship. While white wives are no longer civilly dead, she cannot fully part from the analogy and writes, "perhaps a wife is like a civil slave."[41] The propensity of this peculiar analogy within white literature does not have a correlate in the Black feminist canon. When afforded the opportunity to publish in the 19th century, Black feminists did not describe their existence as analogous to their white married counterparts. Quite to the contrary, these intellectuals decried the anti-Black racism of white women.[42] Further, critiques of patriarchy within the marital institution are not absent from the Black feminist intellectual tradition. Ann Petry laments the regressive attitude held by some Black men toward Black women, which "comes straight out of the Dark Ages."[43] Gwendolyn Brooks explains that some women leave marriages troubled by infidelity or financial impropriety to "maintain dignity and self-respect."[44] It is telling that actual descendants of slavery and those living in its aftermath do not compare ourselves to our enslaved foremothers. Are there any sustained examples of Black feminists ever comparing wifedom to the enslavement of our foremothers?

* * *

The cannibalization of Black women's intimate lives extends beyond heterospecific considerations of the marital regime. The marriage equality debate waged between Claudia Card and Cheshire Calhoun demonstrates how marital shade proliferates within the ontic-epistemic imaginary of LGBTQ+ white scholars as well. Both Card and Calhoun erase the facticity of unmarried, queer Black mothers through their use of theoretical Blackface.[45] As with Pateman and their white foremothers, these lesbian feminists cast themselves in the guise of Black womanhood and circumvent a meaningful reckoning with the relationship between race and American marriage. This avoidance forestalls a weakening of their powerful positionality as white-embodied women within the hierarchy of sexual citizenship. I will begin with a close reading of Card's seminal article, "Against Marriage and Motherhood" to support my claim.

Card considers the institutions of marriage and motherhood to be "so deeply flawed" that they are unworthy of "emulation and reproduction" by lesbian and gay romantic partners and parents.[46] She locates her skepticism of these two institutions, marriage and motherhood, within the feminist moral theory and lesbian and gay activism. The germination of racial cleavage between wives, mothers, and queer women is present in her opening critique of care ethics. Card rejects the arguments posed by white, feminist care ethicists, who mine the experience of motherhood as a source of ethical values.[47] She is more receptive to the concept of mothering as theorized by Black feminists Patricia Hill Collins, bell hooks, and Audre Lorde. She considers Collins's work to be more capacious because her models of motherhood expand beyond the nuclear family to include "othermothers" alongside "bloodmothers." These models, in concert with those of bell hooks, represent "instances of 'revolutionary parenting.'"[48] Card endorses these parenting models because they focus on the needs of children in a broader communal environment than the traditional nuclear model.

She states that revolutionary parenting is unsupported by the marital regime, which prioritizes and protects the nuclear family. Thus, the state-aligned familial configurations championed by same-sex marriage activists and white, feminist care ethicists alike are antithetical to the revolutionary parenting model espoused by Black feminists. To counter this view, Card focuses her critical attention on the marital regime because "it is legal marriage that sets the contexts in which and the background against which motherhood has been legitimated."[49] As she shifts from motherhood to the marriage equality debate within the LGBTQ+ community, we lose sight of the concrete specificity of Blackness altogether. While featured prominently in the conversation about motherhood in general, Black, queer women, as wives and mothers, are conspicuously absent. In fairness, white theorists and activists dominated the marriage equality discourse in the march toward *Obergefell v. Hodges* (2015). As noted in Chapter 2, Black queer theorists and activists pursued a divergent set of priorities to address the needs of LGBTQ+ people.[50] In light of this racial disjunct, one could submit that Card's shift away from racial inclusion is reasonable, given that the marriage equality movement can be legitimately coded as white. But I think there is something else going on here for Card as demonstrated by her argument against marriage equality. I contend that the loss of racialized Blackness in her argument against marriage can be attributed to theoretical Blackface.

Like a moth to a flame, when Card begins to scrutinize the marital regime, she likens it to slavery. At the outset, Card clarifies that her opposition to the pursuit of same-sex marriage does not mean that the state is right in its refusal to legally recognize same-sex unions. She draws on an analogy of slave-owning women in a "mythical society" to support the claim that we can say it is wrong for the state to deny marriage rights to same-sex couples while claiming simultaneously that we are not obligated to fight for that denied right. In the proposed analogy, we are asked to imagine a society where women were denied the ability to own slaves due to sexism. It stands to reason that we can declare that it is wrong to deem women unfit to be slaveowners while also acknowledging that it would be wrong for women to fight for the right to own slaves. This analogy serves to sow the seeds of the gendered coding of white supremacy, which is one aspect of theoretical Blackface. As Card begins her foray into playing in the dark, we see that white women in her moral imaginary are freed from culpability pertaining to enslavement. Slavery, in this mythical place, is the domain of men. Not only are white women depicted as innocents, but they are portrayed as the victims of sexism or the denial of their full humanity. This is indeed quite the mythology, given the significant role white, slave-owning women held as mistresses of the market. This casual, imagined flight into moral innocence, one that so starkly belies reality, undermines the trust necessary to engender shared interracial intimacies between Black and white women.

Card also invokes the white wife/Black slave analogy in her defense of her support for the inclusion of queer people in the military but exclusion from the marital institution. The argument that the wrongness of legal exclusion does not necessarily imply that we should argue for inclusion does not apply in the case of military service. According to Card, "the case of marriage seems to me more like the case of slavery than like that of the military."[51] She claims that "marriage (like slavery) is much worse" than military service because "its impact on our lives is usually greater."[52] First, marriage, unlike military service, is a lifelong commitment. Second, marriage is coercive for women. Finally, marriage has the potential to become violent, or a "dangerous trap."[53] In response to those who argue that not all marriages are violent, she writes that this "seems to me analogous to pointing out, as many slave-owners did, that many slave-owners were truly emotionally bonded with their slaves, that they did not whip them, and that even the slaves were proud and honored to be the slaves of such masters."[54] This formulation of the white wife/Black slave analogy rests upon a deracialized comparison of militarism and marriage. The assertion that marriage impacts "our lives" to a greater degree than the military beckons the question: whose lives? While it is beyond the scope of this chapter to explore in detail, there is a wealth of literature that chronicles the disastrous material and psychosocial impact of the US military upon Black and brown people both in the United States and globally.[55]

Card points to the crux of her position as she writes, "I would rather see the state *de*regulate heterosexual marriage than see it begin to regulate same-sex marriage."[56] She is fundamentally opposed to state involvement in romantic relationships. She rejects granting the state the power to define intimate relationships. But she does not problematize the racism inherent in the state itself, as evidenced in her elucidation of four problems with the marital institution. First, she says, material benefits are granted to married couples that are denied to unmarried, queer couples (e.g., employer-sponsored health benefits). Second, the legal complexities of divorce are more cumbersome for married couples than break-ups between the members of queer couples, such that some heterosexual spouses are compelled to remain in unhealthy marriages to retain material benefits. Third, marriage necessitates monogamy, which would continue to nullify legal protections for polyamorous relationships enjoyed by many lesbian couples. Finally, marriage can exacerbate violence in relationships because it can be difficult for an abused spouse to separate from her abuser, given the strength of marital law (e.g., that governing property rights).

The specifics of Card's subsequent examination of these four problems are of less interest here than what her commentary reveals about her conceptualization of sexual citizenship as defined by the state. It is evident from her critique that sexual citizenship is heteronormative and patriarchal, but it is not white. Card surmises that the first three problems identified could likely be addressed through changes in marital law. With such legal amendments in hand, same-sex couples could receive the "State's blessings" through same-sex marriage. The blessing of marital status would allow a lesbian wife to enjoy both increased material benefits and an "improvement in one's social reputation as a reliable citizen."[57] As argued in previous chapters, Black people are prey to the machinations of racial capitalism, which undermines the attainment and subsequent enjoyment of the material benefits referenced by Card. One needs stable employment to garner shared health benefits and equitable access to ownership to enjoy property rights. The obstacles to marriage endured by Black people of all sexual orientations and gender identities far exceed the problems identified by Card. And we must not forget that these anti-Black obstacles often originate from and are sustained by the state.

The whiteliness of Card's sexual citizenship is further demonstrated in her notion of reliable citizens. "Whiteliness" in this context refers to both the social locations and the epistemological position of whiteness. "Seeing whitely," according to Paul C. Taylor, "tends to involve a commitment to the centrality of white people and their perspectives."[58] I believe we can conclude without undue controversy that the conferral of marital rights to Black heterosexual couples in the 19th century has yet to deem Black individuals as reliable American citizens in the eyes of the Republic, despite the best efforts of the staunchest advocates of respectability politics. Card's implicit trust in the racialized state is also evidenced through her example of a possible perk to be gleaned from same-sex marriage. She amusingly observes that once married, lesbian and gay spouses would be precluded from being compelled to testify against each other. The playful invocation of the criminal justice system lies in stark contrast to gross injustices faced by Black people ensnared within it. Dismantling the atrocities committed by the criminal justice system is a central pillar of racial justice movements for Black people of all walks of life, whether married or unmarried, queer, or straight. It is quite striking that an offhand remark in Card's argument for marriage abolition is in tension with the most sustained contemporary argument for abolition in the Black community, namely prison abolition.

Card returns to the institution of motherhood after arguing against the merits of the marital regime for same-sex couples. Having subsumed mothering within the marital institution and employing theoretical Blackface through the gendering of white supremacy and the white wife/Black slave analogy, Card is able to assume herself as an interracial "us" and can move forward without truly including an "us." She dons the cloak of bell hook's revolutionary parenting and discusses mothering exclusively in the context of white families. Black women are engaged as a melanated accoutrement, but we are not included substantively within her argument of either marriage or mothering. This racial exclusion is demonstrated in her concluding treatment of single mothers, deviancy, and the state.

Card posits that motherhood has historically been a central component of patriarchy. The branded mark of deviance stamped upon single mothers is attributed to the absence of "prestige or social and legal support available to patriarchal mothers."[59] Card and I stand in agreement regarding the branding of single Black mothers as deviant. However, as was argued in the previous chapter, the source of this deviancy extends far beyond parenting outside of the normative bounds of patriarchy. One must attend to the elements of anti-Blackness at work to offer credible theoretical analyses of deviance, motherhood, and Black women. Just as failing to attend sufficiently to the triumvirate of marriage, motherhood, and deviancy negatively influences the impact of Black social justice movements upon the lives of single Black mothers, it also mars the viability of Card's queer, white analysis.

Card rightly argues that children's needs extend beyond "stable intimate bonds with adults."[60] Children require a positive and stable environment to thrive, including quality education, access to healthcare, and so on. In lieu of providing these necessities, she writes that "what the State tends to enforce in motherhood is the child's access to its mother."[61] Can we legitimately say that what the state enforces in Black communities is the "child's access to its mother?" From the sale and murder of enslaved children in the 19th century, to overly involved state welfare agencies that routinely removed children from their mothers in the 20th century, to the precarity of Black maternal health outlined by the Reproductive Justice movement in the 21st century, this claim is ludicrous when applied to Black mothers and their children. If Card is unable to accurately identify the multivalent sources of injustice endured by single Black mothers, how can she be trusted to provide suggestions for their remedy?

On the other side of the same-sex marriage debate, Cheshire Calhoun posits that lesbians and gays should enjoy the totality of rights, benefits, and privileges afforded by state-defined sexual citizenship. She opens her positive case for marriage equality in *Feminism, The Family, and the Politics of the Closet* with an unfortunate, yet familiar, attempt to isolate race from sexual orientation. Calhoun takes pains to demonstrate that "lesbian and gay subordination differs substantially in form from gender and racial oppression."[62] Why does Calhoun consider it necessary to excise race from an argument supporting state recognition of same-sex romantic unions? I believe this excision, whether conscious or not, is necessary for the preservation of sexual citizenship, which requires forsaking an honest interrogation of whiteness and romantic/sexual intimacies. The pursuit of the state's protection of one's romantic union negates a crucial critique of anti-Blackness and racial capitalism—both foundational to sexual citizenship in the United States. As such, Calhoun must remove the import of racialized Blackness for queer Black women from her argument. This weakens her analysis of the marital regime's benefits and obscures its harm for single Black mothers. In what follows, I will demonstrate how Calhoun's marriage equality argument exemplifies the fracturing of interracial, platonic intimacies between Black and white women striving to eliminate injustices embedded within the state institutions of marriage, sexuality, and the family.

Calhoun prioritizes the development of an "abstract concept of lesbian and gay subordination" that is unencumbered by considerations of intersecting forms of oppression.[63] This abstraction is necessary, according to Calhoun, because "one cannot even begin to give a complex analysis of the interpenetration of race, sex, and class unless one has attempted to delineate the basic structures of, say, racial oppression in abstraction from other forms of oppression."[64] In support of this methodological approach, she constructs a pointed distinction between Black feminist and lesbian feminist critiques of mainstream feminism. While Black feminists emphasized "their *difference* from white, middle class feminists," she claims that lesbian feminists emphasized "the potential *commonalities* or continuum between lesbians' and heterosexual feminists' experience."[65] Further, she posits that Black feminist critiques underscore "the racial and class *biases* encoded in dominant feminist theorizing" while lesbian feminists underscore "the *incompleteness* of dominant feminist theorizing's resistance to gender oppression."[66]

Calhoun's insistence upon cleaving race from gender from sexuality does violence to the very being of queer Black women by fancifully dismissing the racial and class biases encoded within lesbian feminist theorizing. Indeed, some lesbians are also white, middle-class women. Her attempted flight into abstraction is, more precisely, a flight into tacit whiteness that serves to create a false feminist dichotomy that negates the existence of Black lesbian feminists. Black feminist scholars across the spectrum of gender identity and sexual orientation have argued extensively, and convincingly, against the merits of theories pertaining to our lived experience that separate race from gender.[67] No one has made this argument better, perhaps, than Anna Julia Cooper in her classic 19th-century text *A Voice from the South*.

Cooper takes the Black woman to occupy a unique, and advantageous, moral position because she "is confronted by both a woman question and a race problem," while remaining "an unknown or an unacknowledged factor in both."[68] Cognizant of the distinctive nature of the prejudice experienced by Black women, she challenges the exclusive discourses of Black men and white women.[69] When addressing the woman question, Cooper states that white women are not additionally hampered by the racism experienced by Black women. To illustrate her point, Cooper recounts an experiment conducted by a group of American women to determine the safety of women traveling throughout the nation unaccompanied by male escorts. She observes that this travel experiment will afford these women limited insight into American sexism, as it will not uncover the particularity of racialized sexism experienced by Black women. While traveling alone, Cooper famously recounts that at a train stop, "I see two dingy little rooms with 'FOR LADIES' swinging over one and 'FOR COLORED PEOPLE' over the other; while wondering under which head I come."[70] Cooper's pithy observation offers a material example that underscores the simultaneity of Black women's confrontations with both gendered iterations of anti-Black racism and racialized iterations of heterosexism.

My purpose here is not to recount the points of weakness apparent in Calhoun's methodological approach to developing an analysis of race, gender, and class in the United States. Rather, I am interested in her subsequent attempt to forge a semblance of solidarity between Black and white women in the wake of tearing us asunder. She establishes a shared intraracial intimacy through the invocation of theoretical Blackface in the form of an iconic trope of Southern slavery, namely mammy.

Black feminist scholar Patricia Hill Collins asserts that "intersecting oppressions of race, class, gender, and sexuality could not continue without powerful ideological justifications for their existence."[71] She contends that the oppression of Black women in the United States has been legitimized by our portrayal as "stereotypical mammies, matriarchs, welfare recipients, and hot mommas."[72] These stereotypical images, according to Collins, "take on special meaning" for Black womanhood as they illuminate the authoritative power of dominant groups to "manipulate ideas about Black womanhood."[73] She states that this manipulative control is necessary because outsiders "threaten the moral and social order" of the dominant society.[74]

Despite Collins's grounding of the interlocking architecture of Black women's oppression and her insistence concerning the specificity of these controlling images to the lived experience of Black women, Calhoun maintains that Collins's analysis is applicable to white women too. She writes, "without denying these are racist images, we can say a lot about what makes these images gendered images, and how they function in a general pattern of Black and white women's oppression."[75] Of the four controlling images Collins explores in *Black Feminist Thought*, Calhoun singles out the Black maternal trope of mammy to take as her own. The image of mammy, according to Calhoun, "trades on broad cultural associations between women and domesticity, between women and self-sacrificing virtues, and between motherhood and asexuality."[76] In this iteration of theoretical Blackface, we move from the analogy of white wife/Black slave to white woman/Black mammy. This act of minstrelsy serves as a foundational step in Calhoun's positive argument for the inclusion of gays and lesbians within the state-sponsored marital regime. Before addressing her argument for same-sex marriage, it is important to clarify the patent falsehood of a white woman/Black mammy analogy.

A generous reading of Calhoun's assertion that the mammy image has "broad cultural associations" would grant that she is simply pointing out that certain stereotypical aspects of this image are applicable to all women, regardless of their racial embodiment. However, the enduring legacies of chattel slavery and anti-Black racism do not allow for such a simplistic reading of the mammy image. In the context of the United States, one cannot apply general cultural assumptions about women writ large and their relationship to domesticity in a race-neutral manner.[77] The historical record speaks to the racial particularity of the mammy.[78] For example, in the early 1900s, the United Daughters of the Confederacy lobbied for the erection of a monument in the nation's capital to honor the mammies of the South. On December 8, 1922, Senator John Sharp Williams, a Democrat from Mississippi, introduced the first mammy monument proposal bill (S. 4119) to Congress. Weeks later, Representative Charles Manly Stedman from North Carolina introduced an identical bill to the House in January 1923.[79] The bill passed in the Senate but failed in the House due to vehement resistance from Black women activists, including Mary Church Terrell.[80] The proposed mammy monument, according to Raquel Kennon, "reflects a state-sponsored nostalgic desire for the immutable symbolic subjugation of the Black woman's body."[81] While the state-sponsored bill does reflect the desire of white male Congressmen for Black subjugation, we cannot ignore white women's shared culpability as the bill was introduced at their behest. White women campaigned for mammy to be "publicly fixed in stone as a romanticized enslaved woman of Southern Plantation lore."[82] To ascribe a gendered coding to the racial domination of Black women through the enduring mammy image would be inaccurate. Both white women and men are equally responsible for the propagation of this tool of subjugation.

The iconography of mammy was forged in the white imaginary in the Antebellum South as the "juxtaposition of Black and white womanhood."[83] According to historian Micki McElya, the term "mammy" was applicable to both Black and white women before the 1830s "as a maternal endearment or an indication of enslavement."[84] With the rise of abolitionist opposition to chattel slavery, the term's race-neutral connotation began to shift. McElya writes, "the figure of the faithful slave" as mammy "came to bear much of the burden of slavery's defense."[85] Southern slaveowners propagandized the mammy figure as loving and grateful to offset abolitionist claims of chattel slavery's violent foundation. Consequently, the moniker "mammy" became associated primarily with enslaved Black women after the 1830s and was no longer ascribed to white women.

Mammy symbolizes fidelity to the white home: she is a maternal figure who cares for each member of "her" family. As McElya puts it, "the scene of Black loyalty was almost always the white home."[86] Calhoun's suggestion that the mammy figure is an appropriate image to examine race-neutral implications regarding "women and domesticity" is misguided. The domestic sphere is not one of shared experiences between Black and white women. The proverbial homeplace with its gendered occupants is a racialized space. The site of the white domicile is also a site of Black subjugation. Mammy labors for white women and thus frees them from the tedium of domestic responsibilities. It was the mistresses of the market who purchased Black women to perform domestic work, including the raising of their children. Mammy has worked in the homes of mistresses of the market, mothers of mass resistance, and she probably remains in the homes of some white women professors today. Further, mammy is relegated to unmarried Black motherhood in two respects. First, she is the unmarried, surrogate mother of white children. Second, mammy is characterized as unmarried in the sense that she is separated from her actual Black family.

While the depiction of mammy as a loving, faithful servant functions to enhance slaveowners' paternalistic image, the casting of mammy as asexual serves another duplicitous aim. The de-sexualized, grandmotherly mammy figure was crafted as the "antithesis of desirable white femininity" to conceal white men's sexual violence against enslaved Black women.[87] The mammy image was employed as a rebuttal to abolitionist depictions of the sexual, physical, and emotional violence rife within chattel slavery. Calhoun's uncritical reference to mammy's applicability to a generalized notion of "motherhood and asexuality" obscures the sexual violence experienced by enslaved Black women. Far from evoking interracial solidarity or shared intimacies between Black and white women, the asexual mammy image functions to privilege the purported virtues of white womanhood while simultaneously denigrating Black women.

The mammy figure emerged as a national icon by the 1850s, in large part owing to the popularity of Harriet Beecher Stowe's *Uncle Tom's Cabin*. The faithful mammy in this abolitionist novel, Aunt Chloe, "bears an uncanny resemblance to the trademark Aunt Jemima, a figure that can in turn be traced to the minstrel stage of the nineteenth century, which generated endless adaptations of *Uncle Tom's Cabin* for Blackface performance."[88] The endurance of the faithful mammy can be attributed to white Americans' desire "to live in a world in which African Americans are not angry over past and present injustices, a world in which white people were and are not complicit, in which the injustices themselves ... seem not to exist at all."[89] The iconography of the faithful slave "is deeply rooted in the American racial imagination."[90] So enduring is this narrative that while champions of the Washington, DC, mammy monument may not have seen the erection of their statue, white Americans have long enjoyed the comforting mammy image on grocery store shelves across the nation as bottles of Aunt Jemima and Mrs. Butterworth syrups.[91] It was not until the nation was rocked by a seismic racial reckoning in the wake of George Floyd's murder in 2020 that corporations deigned to rebrand the long-protested mammy images of Aunt Jemima and Mrs. Butterworth.[92]

Mammy's entrenchment within the white racial imagination helps to explain Calhoun's comfort with replicating this form of Blackface performativity. Her foray into playing in the dark allows her to write from a position of authority when discussing people of color, as she has essentially "become" us. In so doing, actual Black queer women and unmarried Black mothers are misrepresented through the white woman/Black mammy amalgamation. By invoking theoretical Blackface, Calhoun can focus on state-defined sexual citizenship and the inclusion of lesbians and gays within the marital regime without the necessity of attending to their race-specific impact upon single Black mothers.

Calhoun is deeply troubled by the displacement of lesbians and gays from civil society. She claims that the displacement of lesbians and gay men is theoretically distinct from the subordination of Black people and women in the United States. Unlike anti-Black racism, Calhoun states, subordination of lesbians and gays "does not materialize in a disadvantaged *place*" that thwarts social group access to "basic social goods like income, wealth, education, employment, and authoritative social positions."[93] Lesbians and gay men do not inhabit a disadvantaged place because their oppression "consists in the systematic *dis*placement of gay men and lesbians to the outside of civil society."[94] They are expelled from the public sphere owing to the forced adoption of heterosexual comportment as a requisite of access. They are also displaced from the private sphere through restrictions on marriage and family (e.g., through gay adoption bans). Further, lesbians and gay men are "displaced from civil society's future" by civil policies "whose aim is to prevent future generations of lesbian and gay people."[95]

This triad of displacement from the public sphere, private sphere, and the future suggests for Calhoun that lesbians and gay men "do not appear to be located in any particular social structural places."[96] The understanding of queer existence as marked by nonlocation has two implications for Calhoun. First, she claims that a specific socioeconomic position cannot be attributed to lesbians and gay men. Second, she posits that the proverbial closet affords gay men and lesbians opportunities to avoid heteronormative discriminatory practices. Within the closet, Calhoun surmises that the social position held by lesbians and gay men "does not appear to be a pervasively and systematically subordinating one."[97]

The displacement of nonlocatable lesbians and gay men renders theoretical models of race and gender oppression incompatible with homophobia. In support of this position, Calhoun judges the "place and numbers" approach—common to Marxist, socialist, and liberal feminist theories that locate women's subordinated positionality within civil society—as inapplicable to same-sex attracted individuals. Such quantifiable locations do not exist for nonlocatable lesbians and gay men in her estimation. She asserts that one cannot visually sort people into categories of sexual orientation because sexuality "is not connected to any visible bodily marker."[98] Given that one can intentionally conceal one's sexual orientation, Calhoun states, "persons who *are* lesbian or gay often evade being socially treated *as* lesbians or gay persons."[99]

An evasion of a different sort is at work in Calhoun's disaggregated analysis of human existence. This Frankenstein approach of disaggregation does not provide insight into queer nonlocation but rather creates nonhumans. As Audre Lorde famously writes, "there is no such thing as a single-issue struggle because we do not live single-issue lives."[100] She implores us to "face with clarity and insight the lessons to be learned from the oversimplification of any struggle for self-awareness and liberation" lest "we will not rally the force we need to face the multidimensional threats to our survival."[101] Calhoun's oversimplification of the simultaneity of raced, classed, and gendered queer embodiment is supported by the use of theoretical Blackface at the outset of her argument. Through the arrogation of Blackness for herself, she can evade confrontation with the undercurrent of white privilege and its attending socioeconomic advantages that inform her analysis.

Contemporary Black scholars have discussed the queering of Black identity at length. Black-embodied people of all sexual orientations are marked for oppression, even without overt queer disclosure. Put differently, as a Black woman, my encounters with the world are most certainly connected to a visible bodily marker that invites heterosexist anti-Blackness. As Cathy Cohen observes, heteronormativity rooted in "white supremacist ideologies" has been deployed by the "state and its regulation of sexuality, in particular through the institution of heterosexual marriage, to designate which individuals were truly 'fit' for the full rights and privileges of citizenship."[102] The historical denial of marital rights to enslaved Africans, coupled with the contemporary barriers to entry into the institution for heterosexual Black people, are emblematic of the queering of Black personhood in the United States.

Further, the dismissal of an integrated analysis of race, gender, socioeconomic status, and sexual orientation based on the assertion that we cannot locate lesbians through a "place and numbers" analysis is a negligent dismissal of the stark material disparities faced by queer, Black mothers. The overwhelming majority (79.5%) of children living with a same-sex couple are in households headed by women.[103] Female-led households are almost twice as likely to receive food stamps (21%) in comparison to opposite-sex households (12%) and same-sex male households (9%).[104] These economic disparities are more pronounced when race is taken into account. According to the 2019 Williams Institute study, "LGBT Poverty in the United States," Black LGBT adults fare worse than non-LGBT adults "in almost all areas of economic and social vulnerability, such as employment, income, food insecurity, and healthcare access."[105] Specifically, the study found that 30.8% of Black LGBT people live in poverty, while 15.4% of white LGBT people live in poverty.[106] The disparity in poverty rates triples when looking specifically at Black, cis-lesbian women (31.3%) and white, cis-lesbian women (10.7%).

We cannot begin to address the purported merits of the state-regulated marital regime for queer Black mothers if we eschew the material and sociopolitical realities of Black embodiment. Calhoun's moral argument in support of same-sex marriage is compromised by her invocation of the white woman/Black mammy analogy, which allows for the evasion of such realities. In the absence of direct confrontation with the considerable implications of white supremacist ideologies in the preservation of sexual citizenship, Calhoun's marriage equality argument fails Black mothers. Calhoun attributes opposition to same-sex marriage to the pervasive characterization of lesbians and gays as morally deficient. Gays and lesbians are denigrated for their apparent "gender deviance, lack of sexual self-control, and unfitness for family life."[107] The right to marry would, according to Calhoun, "affirm gays' and lesbians' fitness to participate in this foundational institution."[108] State recognition of same-sex marriage would "put in to cultural circulation legal arguments that directly challenge the ideology sustaining gays' and lesbians' social inequality."[109]

Calhoun's examples of moral denigration levied against queer people are consonant with the barbs of moral turpitude lodged against Black people historically, namely our sexual animality, gender deviance, and failings as parents. Our characterization as immoral beings unworthy of the state protection afforded to proper sexual citizens has endured despite being granted the legal right to marry in the 19th century. In other words, our entry into the state's marital regime has not tempered negative assessments of our fitness for nuclear familial life. One could attribute Calhoun's speculation that legalizing same-sex marriage would translate into queer social equality to naiveté. An instance of naiveté evidenced by the current social-political climate, which is overtly hostile to LGBTQ+ civil liberties that only recently appeared to be settled law. Not only has social equality not been achieved, but there is credible speculation that the staunchly conservative Supreme Court may overturn the *Obergefell v. Hodges* marriage equality ruling. However, I do not believe that Calhoun's stance is grounded in naiveté; rather, I posit that it reflects her confidence in white sovereignty—a confidence that fuels her dismay with white, queer exclusion from the racialized domain of state-regulated marriage. Rather than questioning the harms inflicted upon racially marginalized people by the marital regime, Calhoun seeks the state protection promised to white Americans.

Calhoun contends that lesbians' experience of powerlessness within the domestic sphere emanates from "their denial of access *to* a legitimated and socially instituted sphere of family, marriage, and parenting."[110] She states that queer "displacement from a protected private sphere" arises from "the historical construction of lesbians and gays as outlaws to the natural family."[111] Presaging Justice Anthony Kennedy's outlaw rhetoric in the *Obergefell* majority opinion, she writes:

> [I]f gay men and lesbians are to become fully equal citizens, their private lives must be equally protected. Our culture connects full citizenship with being married and having a family... When lesbians

and gays are constructed as outlaws to the family and are told that they cannot marry, they are being told that they are not capable of doing the work of citizens. Thus, lesbian and gays will not be fully equal until the law recognizes same-sex marriages and equally protects lesbian and gay family life.[112]

Calhoun's domestic vision was realized with the 2015 marriage equality decision. And this realization maintains her casting of single Black mothers as outlaws, who remain outside the bounds of the state's "legitimated and socially instituted sphere" of family, marriage, and parenting.

* * *

The pervasive invocation of theoretical Blackface in white feminist marriage literature exemplifies Paget Henry's observation that "race/ethnic orders have deep roots in the national imaginary of a people."[113] These racial orders are embedded within the "institutional structures established for their long-term preservation," such that the national imaginary reflects "the creative imaginations of citizens where self-construction and national construction become inseparable."[114] The "continuous reproduction of narratives of individual and collective origin," according to Henry, "affirm and legitimate the order and growth of the nation."[115] These imagined origin stories, in turn, support state institutions that safeguard the perpetuation of the racial hierarchies "observed by members of the society."[116] Marital shade, under the guise of the white wife/Black slave analogy, serves as one such origin story specific to the corrupted platonic intimacy between Black and white women.

Armed with a fallacious origin story of racial transmogrification, white progressive theorists can readily evade the multifarious ways that whiteness influences sexual citizenship in an anti-Black, settler-colonial state. This evasion is borne out in contemporary marriage abolition debates, which do not offer substantive treatments of white supremacy, anti-Blackness, and their deleterious impact on unmarried Black mothers. The arguments offered by Elizabeth Brake and Clare Chambers are emblematic of this phenomenon. Both philosophers tout single Black mothers as paradigmatic examples of the benefits of marriage abolition/reform in an ideal state. However, these theorists extol these potential benefits without attending to the coterminous institutions that would continue to support racial hierarchies in a postmarriage state.

Brake offers a compelling argument against what she coins amatonormativity, which she defines as "the assumption that a central, exclusive, amorous relationship is normal for humans, in that it is a universally shared goal" that "*should* be aimed at in preference to other relationship types."[117] She posits that amatonormativity incites wrongful discrimination, is legally unjust, and is morally wrong. To counter, Brake advocates for the creation of a unique legal category, deemed minimal marriage, which "allows individuals to select from the rights and responsibilities exchanged within marriage and exchange them with whomever they want, rather than exchanging a predefined bundle of rights and responsibilities with only one amatory partner."[118] She states that the liberal state is required to have a legislative framework for personal relationships.

Arguing from the position of ideal theory, Brake states that "various rights would be overseen by the appropriate governmental agencies and integrated into their policies."[119] For example, she notes that immigration eligibility based on a care relationship would warrant "greater bureaucratic oversight" to discourage fraud. She notes that such oversight "would differ little from investigations in immigration cases now."[120] A proposal for marriage reform that invites increased governmental scrutiny for Black and brown Americans of a sort that differs little from contemporary state investigations is a frightening prospect indeed. In the fantastical realm of ideal theory, laws and policies are applied equitably without regard to race, gender, or sexual orientation. Those invested in social change recognize that racial justice, as Charles Mills rightly observes, is "pre-eminently a matter of non-ideal theory."[121] By appealing to ideal theory, Brake is exempt from "dealing with the legacy of white supremacy in our society."[122] In this particular instance, we can reflect upon the havoc wrought by the mothers of mass resistance, who used the full weight of their bureaucratic power to interfere in the intimate lives of Black people. Further, there is significant literature detailing racial disparities evident in the application of immigration policies.[123] In the world in which we actually exist, anti-Black racism would undoubtedly interfere with the execution of minimal marriage for Black-embodied people.

In *Against Marriage*, Clare Chambers argues that liberalism demands the abolition of state-recognized marriage. In her ideal marriage-free state, "a. personal relationships are regulated, b. the vulnerable are protected, and c. justice is furthered, all without the state recognition of marriage or any similar alternative."[124] While her argument for marriage abolition lies within the realm of ideal theory, she insists that it does not ignore the "realities of power."[125] Given the absence of cited Black scholars in a text that repeatedly references Black women in support of its claims, I believe it is fair to say that the realities of differential racial power are most certainly ignored. Save the citation of an unnamed Black source, Chambers cites white scholar Katherine Franke for all references pertaining to Black people. It is both offensive and intellectually irresponsible for Chambers to present Franke as the sole authority on Black life in a text devoted to romantic and sexual intimacies in the liberal state. This work is an exemplar of playing in the dark, with the full consumption of Black womanhood on display.

An efficacious case for marriage abolition in support of single Black mothers requires the abandonment of imagined origin stories that allow racial hierarchies to thrive. As an alternative to this form of marital shade, our political-ethical deliberations concerning the romantic and sexual lives of unmarried Black mothers are better served by a grounding within José Medina's notion of resistant imaginations. Our imaginative capacity and its subsequent limitations, according to Medina, "go to the very core of our moral sense and political agency delineating the contours of our moral and political sensibilities."[126] The resistant imaginative act must be "pluralized, polyphonic, and experimentalist."[127] By contrast, marital shade as theoretical Blackface disallows consideration of the pluralistic, polyphonic interplay of Black feminist voices from consideration. The excision of the lived realities of Black single mothers prevents the theoretical-political exchanges necessary to create the field of possibility for liberation.

5

An Abolitionist Invitation

Black motherhood was long ago forged as a commodity in the American social-political imaginary, through the proliferation of *partus ventrem sequitur*.[1] The legacy of the forced appropriation of Black women's reproductive capacities for the use of others has branded their progeny as the bearers of anti-Black racism through the present day. Modern Black liberation movements that share the aspiration to realize the end of slavery's afterlife in favor of liberated life after slavery cannot escape a reckoning with the complex dimensions and varied iterations of Black motherhood. The insistence upon Black motherhood's centrality to liberatory theory and praxis reflects a recognition of the concept's significance within movement work.

The policing of normative performance of Black motherhood is a source of pervasive interracial anxiety. Reverence for the proper "Black Family" is thoroughly integrated within discourses of Black liberation. Conversely, the very seeds of Black liberation, namely freedom and love, dwell within the heart of Black motherhood. As Robin D. G. Kelley reminds us, freedom and love are the motivational ties that have bound radical abolitionist movements historically and "may be the most revolutionary ideas available to us."[2] Radical Black motherhood is rooted in the demand for the fruition of unimpeded freedom and in love not only for oneself but for one's children, one's lovers, and one's beloved community.

Frantz Fanon succinctly illuminates the vitality of freedom and love within the revolutionary praxis of the colonized. As human beings, our very existence *is* our freedom, or possibilities, and we exist as transcendence, or a projection into the future. Transcendent human existence can be oriented in one of two directions: aggression or love. Authentic love, for Fanon, manifests itself in "wishing for others what one postulates for oneself, when that postulation unites the permanent values of human reality."[3] The achievement of authentic love would signal the realization of the ultimate stage of ethical orientation.

The salvific wish for humanity, encapsulated by authentic love, prompts derisive laughter from the colonized "when Western values are mentioned in front of him," because those under colonial subjugation understand the contradiction between the West's appeals to dignity and civility and their oppressive rule.[4] The recognition of this contradiction discloses the privileged epistemic and ethical insights of the racially marginalized with respect to the nature of racial oppression that Fanon grounds within the *Erlebnis* of the colonized. Fanon does not deny that the subjective experience of anti-Black racism can be understood by others; rather, he emphasizes that white acknowledgment of the existence of racism and its negative effects is not in itself a monumental achievement.[5] The real challenge of overcoming racial oppression is not simply admitting its existence but rather lies in effectuating a viable political agenda to end it. Fanon posits that white people are incapable of rising to this challenge, owing to their limited understanding of both their own humanity and the *Erlebnis* of the racially marginalized. Adherence to an ethos of anti-Black racism and the myth of white superiority compels white people to "work hard to reach a human level."[6] As a result, the possibility of eradicating racial oppression and achieving a reclamation of humanity defined by authentic love is dependent upon the revolutionary actions of the oppressed.

In this final chapter, I will focus upon the derisive, Fanonian laughter of single Black mothers that resounds in the face of the US marital regime, a state institution that, as I have argued, corrupts the fruition of freedom and love. Dispensing with the destructive forms of marital shade leveled against unmarried Black mothers outlined in previous chapters, I will explore a generative form of marital shade that is expressed as *throwing marital shade*. Originating within the spirited 20th-century ballrooms created by Black and brown queer people, throwing shade is a common phrase within Black communities that denotes a subtle, yet incisive, rejection of someone or something.[7] Throwing marital shade encapsulates the conceptual and experiential modalities of single Black motherhood that simultaneously embody the subversive repudiation of the marital regime and reflect freedom and love as the hallmarks of a liberated life after slavery. Single Black motherhood offers a fertile seedbed for the development of Black, queer, feminist theorization and liberatory praxis that are antithetical to settler sexual citizenship. Throwing marital shade represents the cessation of the reproduction of capitalist, neoliberal, heteronormative modalities of being that have been embraced across diverse political and racial lines. In what follows, I will employ the conceptual lens of throwing marital shade to disclose its productive contributions to feminist abolition movements.

Throwing marital shade is steeped within the Black radical tradition aligned with W. E. B. DuBois's analysis of the marked failings of Reconstruction. According to DuBois, a genuine abolition of slavery requires abolition democracy, or, put differently, the creation of new democratic institutions that fully embrace Black people.[8] In lieu of abolition, enslaved people were granted emancipation, while denied access to institutions that would foster well-being. The perpetuation of material and structural inequities after slavery's end precipitated the development of the prison-industrial complex (PIC). As Angela Davis famously observes, the prison of slavery evolved into the slavery of prison.[9] More pointedly, Davis describes the PIC as demonstrative of the "failed moral imagination of imperial democracies" and the failure to establish abolition democracy.[10]

Although abolition feminists offer a radical revisioning of human relationality that extends far beyond a critique of the carceral state, the predominant abolitionist narrative is trained upon the PIC. This focus is not surprising, given the significant oppression of Black people within the modern carceral state.[11] While there remains disagreement concerning the qualitative and quantitative harms wrought by the carceral state within Black communities, there is little doubt that there is a dire problem in need of some form of redress. What remains less clear in activist spaces is an acknowledgment of the insidiousness of the marital regime, as evidenced by the nearly nonexistent discussion of its reform or abolition. Without doubt, I concede that there is widespread acceptance, or perhaps more accurately, *tolerance* of single mothers. However, this tolerance neither indicts the marital institution itself nor effaces the familial hierarchy that privileges a heteronormative, nuclear configuration.

The failure of those committed to Black liberation to adequately interrogate the marital regime has significant material consequences for single Black mothers. Movement work, according to Beth Ritchie, "subscribes to a very narrow understanding of who is entitled to protection, to services, to resources, and to grants. The more you fit in, the more married you are—and I am talking about queer marriage, too"—the more the movement will advocate on your behalf.[12] Though I wholeheartedly support marriage abolition on behalf of single Black mothers, who are marginalized within movement work, I will not offer an argument for marriage abolition here. Such an argument would be a premature enterprise within an environment that has yet to seriously consider its very possibility. Rather, I will extend an invitation for us to meditate on its promise. This promise is effectuated within throwing marital shade, which is characterized by its commitment to the "indivisibility of abolition and feminism" and the understanding that racial justice and gender justice are indivisible.[13]

The positive expression of marital shade is also necessarily queer, owing to abolition feminism's disavowal of the domination of heterosexual, cisgender feminist discourses. Queer of color theoretical discourses and activism have markedly advanced our understanding of the human condition in relationship to the conceptualization of freedom and love.[14] The continued viability and credibility of movements for Black lives necessitate a robust integration of queer of color ontic-epistemic insights. Black, queer feminists have also illustrated the damage wrought when sexual and gender-based hierarchies within subjugated populations are left to fester. In this current historical moment, heterosexism and transphobia remain rampant within Black communities. This is evidenced in purported safe havens, including Black neighborhoods, places of worship, HBCUs, and sites of respite, such as music festivals and comedy clubs.[15] The malevolence of anti-Black racism does not allow for the implicit, or subtle, inclusion of queerness within movements for Black lives that are truly committed to universal Black liberation. Scholarship and activism dedicated to Black freedom must be bold and explicit in its inclusion of all Black people across the spectrum of gender identity and sexual orientation.

Further, throwing marital shade is situated firmly within the lineage of radical Black feminist intellectuals, who recognized that Black freedom itself is queer. For these scholars, including Cathy Cohen and Audre Lorde, Black feminist motherhood "imagined the death of the dominant capitalist relation, a halt to the reproduction of the state."[16] Radical Black mothering portends this death, according to Alexis Paula Gumbs, because "she who refuses to reproduce the status quo threatens to produce a radically different world."[17] The very act of refusal is queer. The insistence on futurity in an environment of overt hostility, coupled with the affirming declaration of oneself as both Black and mother, is an expression of queerness. In this way, the queerness of single Black motherhood is not derived from a particular sexual orientation or gender identity. Rather, our queerness is born from an abiding defiance that breaks the manacles of settler sexual citizenship. In what follows, I will explore this defiance further by exploring three facets of throwing marital shade.

5.1 Outcast Mothers

In previous chapters, I demonstrated how unmarried Black mothers are perceived as outcasts, who are unworthy of either state protection or esteem within Black communities. From the state's perspective, outcast status provides justificatory grounds to diminish legal safeguards, deny material benefits, and inflict pity and/or scorn upon families headed by unmarried Black women. This sentiment is expressed by Justice Anthony Kennedy in the *Obergefell v. Hodges* preamble, where he describes unmarried same-sex families as outcasts.[18] Justice Kennedy claims that the children of unmarried parents "suffer the stigma of knowing their families are somehow lesser" and they are "relegated through no fault of their own to a more difficult and uncertain family life."[19] The currency of outcast status within the liberal state is not arbitrary. Rather, as Grace Hong writes, "it registers a longer history of political modernity that relies on a category of structuring exclusion."[20] This history is evidenced through the disparaging tropes propagated by the highest office in the land: consider President Lyndon Johnson's Moynihan Report, President Ronald Reagan's welfare queen, and President Barack Obama's lascivious twerking women.[21]

The exclusionary political structuring of outcasts was displayed fully during the height of the COVID-19 pandemic. In the congressional debate over President Joseph Biden's $1.9 trillion COVID-19 relief plan in 2021, Wisconsin's Republican Representative Glenn Grothman argued against the proposed plan because he contended that the expansion of the earned income tax credit for unmarried employees would penalize married individuals. In support of this claim, he states, "I bring it up, because I know the strength that Black Lives Matter had in this last election. I know it's a group that doesn't like the old-fashioned family."[22] In the midst of a global pandemic that occasioned national economic turmoil and extraordinary loss of life, Grothman conjures the specter of the unmarried Black mother as the linchpin in his case against a federal economic relief plan. His remarks concretize the manner in which the marital regime, and the concomitant outcast status of single Black mothers, serves as a building block in a liberal republic that protects the interests of white elites.

In a pointed response to Grothman, US Virgin Islands delegate Stacey Plaskett demanded, "How dare you say that Black Lives Matter, Black people, do not understand old-fashioned families? Despite . . . some of the things that you have put forward that I've heard out of your mouth in the Oversight Committee, in your own district, we have been able to keep our families alive for over 400 years, and the assault on our families to not have Black lives or not even have Black families."[23] The forceful vitality of her rebuttal encourages a possible rejection of state-supported marital shade. Plaskett clearly repudiates Grothman's attempt to ignore the severity of state violence leveled against Black families. What remains untroubled by her statement, however, are the actual merits of the "old-fashioned family." There is an implicit understanding that our families have thrived *despite* relentless assaults that have undermined our ability to form heteronormative, nuclear households. In this heated Congressional exchange, we are witness to the power of outcast status to illuminate the occurrence of marital shade by the state upon Black communities.

The generative potentiality of outcast status to surface deep-seated inequities within settler sexual citizenship is also exemplified within the social activism of Miss Major Griffin-Gracy. Miss Major is a legendary transgender elder, mother, father, and activist, who was present at the inception of the Stonewall Rebellion and survived incarceration at Clinton Correctional Facility in Dannemora. She was appointed as the first Executive Director of the Trans, Gender-Variant, and Intersex Justice Project (TGIJP) in 2010. The mission of TGIJP is to eradicate the human rights abuses suffered by transgender, gender-variant, and intersex people ensnared within the pernicious web of the PIC. In the following interview excerpt, Miss Major succinctly expresses the relevance of outcast status to Black liberation movements:[24]

JAYDEN DONAHUE: I consider TGIJP to be a radical organization. Can you talk a little bit about where your priorities differ from mainstream gay politics?

MISS MAJOR: I eventually do want to get married, to the right person, pet, tree. At this point, I don't care, but I don't want to assimilate myself into a group of people who think that my very existence is abominable. Why do I want to do what they want to do? Why do I have to have a ring on my finger? Why do I have to pass? Why can't I just be recognized and acknowledged for who I am. Well, he's pretty, the man's gorgeous.

JD: Some of the things that you are talking about seem to be indirectly related to the prison industrial complex and maybe address some of the root causes of imprisonment for transgendered women of color.

MM: The thing is, it's hard to see that there is a connection, but there is a definite connection between that kind of stuff and the prison industrial complex. One of the things that happens for a girl getting involved in the PIC is we already, from the moment we decide to be a transgendered person, are living outside the law. The moment this dick-swinging motherfucker wants to put a dress on and head on down the street to go to the store or something like that, they have broken the law.

One cannot escape Miss Major's palpable exasperation with the proverbial *they*, who demand assimilation to settler sexual citizenship. When asked about marriage equality, she invites us to, in the words of Kaila Adia Story, "throw shade on normativity" and "sashay away from a politics of respectability."[25] Miss Major's comical nod to marrying the "right person, pet or tree" affirms a desire for romantic and sexual love while simultaneously resisting the dangers inherent in the marital regime. The dangers surfaced by Miss Major not only implicate the state, which imprisons those it deems abominable, but also indicts the assimilationist bent of mainstream queer movements. This indictment is evidenced in the wake of the US Supreme Court's 2022 decision in *Dobbs v. Jackson Women's Health Organization*, which overturned the longstanding Constitutional right to abortion.[26]

In the months preceding the *Dobbs* decision, leading queer advocacy organizations were engaged in a coordinated, coalitional effort to lobby Congress into passing the Equality Act. This bill would expand the Civil Rights Act of 1964 to ban discrimination based on sex, sexual orientation, and gender identity in public life, including employment, education, housing, and federal funding. These extensive protections would provide clear material benefits to queer people and women, regardless of marital status. However, these lobbying efforts came to an immediate standstill after the *Dobbs* decision due to Justice Clarence Thomas's concurring opinion. While conveying his support for overturning abortion rights, Justice Thomas remarked that "we should reconsider all of this Court's substantive due process precedents, including Griswold, Lawrence, and Obergefell."[27] This explicit threat to same-sex sexual relationships and same-sex marriage had a chilling effect on the pursuit of the Equality Act, as mainstream queer organizations turned their lobbying focus to the Respect for Marriage Act, which codifies same-sex marriage.[28]

The singular focus on same-sex marital unions present within the Respect for Marriage Act symbolizes the fierce political will to preserve the status quo of settler sexual citizenship. The mere mention of revisiting *Obergefell* in a concurring opinion prompted advocacy organizations and Congressional leaders to abandon enacting broad sweeping protections for the queer masses in favor of prioritizing the limited protections offered by the state marital regime. The chilling effect occasioned by the Respect for Marriage Act brings the diminished valuation of single Black mothers into sharp relief. In contrast, marital shade disrupts the entrenched, uncritical belief that the marital institution must be safeguarded. Throwing marital shade rejects the assumption that respect for the exclusive privileges afforded to married couples is more significant than respect for ensuring a queer single mother's access to education, housing, and medical care unfettered by discrimination. Throwing shade invites us to think more creatively, and expansively, about the valuation of intimate relationships.

The entreaty to question the alleged inevitability of the marital regime exemplifies the commitment of queer of color abolitionist movements to offer "a critique of citizenship, of the nation-state, of normalization and heteronormativity."[29] This commitment, according to Amy Brandzel, must eventually extend beyond critique, as "a queer citizenry would refuse to participate in the prioritizing of one group or form of intimacy over another."[30] Brandzel contends that, ultimately, queer abolitionism "would refuse citizenship altogether."[31] Decoupled from the conventions of settler sexual citizenship, outcast families embody concrete manifestations of radical and resistant imaginaries.

Existing beyond the normative bounds of public policy and legal precedent, single Black mothers conjure intimate freedom dreams that oppose the regulatory forces of settler sexual citizenship in a manner resonant with David L. Eng's "racialization of intimacy."[32] The racialization of intimacy, according to Eng, "marks the collective ways by which race becomes occluded within the private domain of private family and kinship" and "it brings critical focus on the processes by which race is exploited to consolidate idealized notions of family and kinship in the global North."[33] The illuminative qualities of throwing marital shade disrupt the persistence of racial occlusion within familial life. Outcast families refute the postulation that the material harm and moral humiliation endured by households led by unmarried Black mothers are attributable to their unmarried status, as Justice Anthony Kennedy suggests in his *Obergefell* opinion. Alternatively, outcast families reveal the duplicity of ostensible divisions between the public and private spheres in relation to familial and romantic intimacies, which serve to undermine Black well-being.[34] The mutable boundaries between the public and private spheres of Black intimate life "not only engineer vulnerability" but also "frequently mask the evidentiary traces of racialized, ableist, and heterogendered violence."[35]

Throwing marital shade identifies the manner in which the marital regime creates vulnerability by either bestowing public reward or state punishment for the intimate choices made by Black mothers in the private sphere. As described in Chapter 2, this manufactured vulnerability is most obviously evident in the 1,000+ federal rights, benefits, and privileges accorded to married couples that are withheld from the unmarried. Marriage positively influences the economic, mental, and physical well-being of couples through a vast array of federal and corporate incentives.[36] As is well known, married couples, who file joint tax returns, may be eligible for higher tax deductions and credits than those who file individual returns. An additional tax benefit extends to the unlimited marital deduction provision within the US Federal Estate and Gift Tax Law, which allows individuals to transfer assets to their spouse without financial liability.[37] Further, if a married couple is subject to capital gain from the sale of a jointly owned home, they can qualify for a tax exclusion that is double the amount of unmarried sellers.[38] Access to insurance benefits and lowered insurance premiums are also enjoyed by married couples. The bestowal of these rewards unto married couples is especially unfair when one considers the significant racial and economic barriers to entering the marital institution faced by Black women.[39]

The marital regime's unnecessary and unwarranted destabilization of unmarried Black familial life is also evident in the contemporary public determination of acceptable household configurations. Improper households are policed through zoning ordinances that disproportionately impact Black families. These public ordinances, which legally prevent unmarried people from sharing a home, still abound almost 50 years since the Supreme Court's 1977 *Moore v. City of East Cleveland* ruling.[40]

Outcast intimacies, however, are not solely negative. The utility of throwing marital shade extends beyond a refutation of oppressive institutions and is inclusive of generative attributes. The racialization of intimacy, according to Eng, "indexes other ways of knowing and being in the world."[41] These racialized intimacies are "an affective life-world within but ultimately beyond the dictates of a liberal humanist tradition."[42] In a similar vein, throwing marital shade allows us to witness a plurality of romantic, sexual, and familial intimacies that transcend the state-regulated marital regime. Single Black motherhood should not be defined as a status to be pitied or maligned; instead, families led by unmarried Black mothers reveal a wellspring of intimate possibilities that more fully capture the diversity of human relationships.

5.2 Unsettled Origin Stories

The proliferation of detrimental origin stories is a unifying theme across the various iterations of marital shade explored heretofore. First, the origin story of the United States is often told using the metaphor of marriage. The nation's "Founding Fathers" employed marital rhetoric to realize a vision of settler citizenship predicated upon domination across gender, race, sexuality, and socioeconomic status.[43] Further, in response to gender injustice, white women have fabricated a shared history of maligned sisterhood with enslaved Black women in an effort to secure social and political parity with white men. And finally, Black activists, who are committed to securing a seat at the American table, recount an origin story of anti-Black racism, which is based, in part, on the lamentable preponderance of families headed by unmarried mothers.

In each of these disparate accounts of origination, single Black motherhood serves as a negative foil or cautionary tale to be avoided. These conventional tales cannot be dismissed as inconsequential historical fodder, as they continue to influence the ethical-political and ontic-epistemic imaginaries that inform the contours of public and private life far beyond the marital institution. As such, collective efforts to overcome the ills of settler citizenship must engage in a confrontation with the marital institution and its role in the perpetuation of harmful imaginaries impeding liberation. Single Black motherhood, or throwing marital shade, provides a compelling negation of the mythos of American marriage.

Hortense Spillers presents us with an entry point to such a consideration through her reconsideration of shadow families during the era of US slavery. Shadow families were formed through the sexual exploitation of enslaved women by their white masters. The ubiquity of this form of violence, for Spillers, defies naming or language.[44] The enduring legacy of trauma and disapprobation endured by families created through such abject violence has been studied, and debated, at length. Spillers shifts the focus of the analytical lens, asking, "to what extent did the presence of these children and their mothers, or the families that lived in the interstices of the institution of marriage, or in the shadows of the 'official' family, transform what went on in the Big House?"[45] In this question, Spillers foregrounds unmarried Black mothers to disrupt fictitious narratives that reverently uphold white intimacy as the paragon of romantic and sexual relations. She calls upon us to dispel our inheritance of an inadequate "sentimental education" or what I call intimate origin stories.[46]

The intertwined concepts of "marriage" and "family," according to Spillers, are two practices that have influenced "the idea of a racialized perception of reality."[47] The prevalence of shadow families, or the genesis of single Black motherhood in the United States, destabilizes this racialized perception as we attend to their impact upon "the entire social calculus of intimate relations across all the demographics that participated in the world of slavery."[48] I addressed one aspect of this destabilization process previously, as I posited that coalitional efforts between Black and white women to confront gender-based marital harm is undermined by the erosion of interracial platonic intimacies owing to the latter's unacknowledged culpability in systemic racial violence. Here Spillers calls upon us to grapple with the blight of romantic and sexual intimacies between white men and women that were created coterminously with the brutal sexual abuse of enslaved women. The existence of shadow families calls into question whether one could even define the relationship between white masters and white wives as a marital relation. What form of ethical marital intimacy can a couple share when the man is engaged in regular acts of extramarital rape while his wife feigns? Spillers wonders "what happens to our concepts of love and intimacy under those circumstances?"[49] Indeed, these considerations upend the idealized narrative of settler sexual citizenship, as it compels acknowledgment of corrupted intimacies at the core of the settler marital relation. The vitality and integrity of our contemporary intimate relationships are reliant upon an unflinching account of the intimate origin stories bound up in the triad of settler-native-slave.[50]

5.3 Throwing Shade at Euromodernity

Alienation is a hallmark of coloniality, according to Lewis Gordon.[51] It arises through Euromodernity's attempt to transform racially marginalized groups into maligned categories (e.g., the enslaved or colonized). For Gordon, alienation is experienced as the suffering of "a unique form of melancholia," in which racially marginalized people are "indigenous to a world that rejects them by making them into problems."[52] Melancholic suffering is nourished through the "specific colonial matrix of power, being, and knowledge that became a central, if not a constitutive, dimension of Western modernity."[53] The state marital regime rests squarely within this colonial matrix and supports racialized alienation through the fabrication of the disparaged category of the single Black mother.

The three iterations of marital shade examined previously clarify how settler colonialism is sustained, in part, through the perpetuation of sexual citizenship. The prioritization of cisgender, heteropatriarchal, monadic familial units continuously reproduces properly ordered citizens that maintain and perpetuate the nation-state. As a matter of its very survival, settler colonialism must cast single Black motherhood as a problem, because the existence of single Black mothers is antithetical to the seemingly natural order of sexual citizenship. The concept of single Black motherhood counters patriarchy with the alternative of matrilineality. The flourishing of households led by a diverse array of unmarried mothers eschews biological, nuclear family units in favor of intergenerational, communal, and nonbiological familial ties. Unmarried Black mothers forsake the limitations imposed by Euromodernity's visions of family, gender, and sexuality. In sum, throwing marital shade encourages decoloniality as it "undoes, disobeys, and delinks" from the alienating settler colonial matrix of power.[54]

Situating single Black motherhood within an abolitionist and decolonial context amplifies Cathy Cohen's prescient appeal for Black queer studies to center the experience of economically disadvantaged single Black mothers.[55] As I argued in Chapter 3, the liberatory force of her insight is not to be found in the development of a "politics of deviance" ostensibly expressed by single Black mothers. Rather,

Cohen's entreaty is most impactful when situated within decolonial marriage abolitionist praxis.[56] Decoloniality, as defined by Walter Mignolo and Catherine Walsh, is a "form of struggle and survival," which is emblematic of unmarried Black mothers' lived experiences.[57] Further, decoloniality is "an epistemic and existence-based response and practice—most especially by colonized and racialized subjects—*against* the colonial matrix of power in all of its dimensions."[58] Decolonial marriage abolitionist praxis is marked by a collective and resolute refusal of settler sexual citizenship that seeks to dominate the racially marginalized.

The potency of throwing shade is evident in Miss Major's emphatic refusal "to assimilate myself into a group of people who think that my very existence is abominable."[59] Our trans elder and mother is offering a defiant response to a settler sexual citizenship that would rather imprison her than embrace the fullness of her vibrant modalities of existence. What fruitful lines of theoretical inquiry and liberatory praxis can be gained if we were to regard the lived experience of Miss Major as an instantiation of the decolonial turn articulated by Nelson Maldonado-Torres as "a vision, a horizon of action, and an orientation that differ from the vision, horizon, and orientation of modernity."[60] Miss Major's defiance evinces the "emergence of an attitude that proposes and reveals Western modernity as a problem to be overcome rather than as a project to complete."[61] In this way, throwing marital shade aligns with the Indigenous refusal of the "gifts of liberalism, democracy, and freedom on the settler nation's terms," in order to affirm "the authority and power of women and queer people."[62] By rebuking these gifts, throwing marital shade envisages a contrasting notion of intimate home places in which to ground our experiences of desire, love, and family unmarred by systems of domination.

The contravening vision of intimate home places resists a secondary aspect of alienation engendered by Euromodernity, namely homelessness. The struggle "with being homeless at home," according to Gordon, is a constitutive aspect of being indigenous to a world that defines our existence as fundamentally problematic.[63] However, the very recognition of Euromodernity's propensity for alienating the proverbial racialized other illuminates the pathway to its transcendence. The disclosure of the particularity of Euromodernity, for

Gordon, affirms the presence of alternative modernities, including Afromodernity. Given the "globality of the Euromodern age," homelessness is not defined geographically but is rather temporal.[64] The present and futural existence of the Afromodern age grounds the threads of decoloniality woven within the underpinnings of Black, queer feminist, and Africana philosophical theory and praxis.[65]

Throwing marital shade is an incarnation of Black futurity, Black modernity, and Black aliveness. Its providence exists in stark contrast to Euromodernity's hegemonic drive to foreclose upon Black life in a quest to maintain an afterlife of slavery. Unmarried Black mothers, on the other hand, "are always harbingers of that promising alternative sociality necessary for a new vision of community."[66] A vision of inclusivity, according to Lyndon Gill, "points toward a new home for our hearts and consciousness."[67] Intimate home places, both material and immaterial, contain guideposts for worlds of possibility and relationality to self and others that remain uncoupled from settler sexual citizenship.

This meditation on alternative home places is not situated within an ideal world—a world far removed from the tensions evident between abolitionist and decolonial ambitions. We must acknowledge explicitly that coalitional efforts between Black and Indigenous liberation movements are complicated by ofttimes disparate contestations of land, sovereignty, and models of redress. Mindful care must be undertaken in our mutual resistance practices.[68] On the one hand, the pursuit of freedom on behalf of Black people, whose indigeneity on this land was forged through chattel slavery, must also consider establishing relationships "with the Indigenous peoples of that land whose survival is so under siege."[69] Conversely, as Jodi Byrd writes, Indigenous scholars must "consider the possibilities of solidarity and resistance where our lands became the grounds for others' oppressions."[70]

An openness to reciprocity within movement work enhances the creativity and expansiveness of Black, queer, feminist freedom dreams. In my critique of Black-led movements for racial justice, for instance, I oppose the primacy of the Black married maternal because of its entrenchment within Euromodernity's schema of family and home. I contend that the prioritization of the Black married maternal in response to colonial alienation and its concomitant material costs is an understandable, yet flawed, approach to Black liberation. Champions of this approach would benefit from attending to Indigenous communities' relationality to land, which "constitutes a different ontological position than liberal property regimes."[71] Land is not experienced as occupation or possession; rather, "it is a place that says who they are, that they are, through which they exist."[72] By shifting our conceptualization of land, we are open to ontic-epistemic possibilities beyond the Black married maternal that capitulates to the capitalist confinement of land as property, in which properly ordered sexual citizens are viewed as marriageable commodities expected to purchase houses for our monadic, heteronormative family units.[73] Throwing marital shade, and its coterminous rebuke of state-regulated marriage, contributes to the fruition of critical, coalitional space to reconceptualize land, home, and collective sovereignty.

An openness to alternative ontic-epistemic possibilities should not be construed as a parasitic appropriation of Indigenous ways of being and thinking. Rather, it reflects an alignment with lineages of US Black feminism that attends to Indigenous displacement in relationship to "horizontal histories of slavery ... that force indigenous peoples to take root elsewhere and in someone else's land."[74] This relationship is exemplified in Kristie Dotson's claim that Black feminist identity politics is "'on the way' to settler decolonization in a US context."[75] The move toward decolonization is evident within the Black feminist demand that "we attend to our 'originating' stories on this land."[76] Foregrounding our origin stories as a method of resistance against Euromodernity's insistence on historical unknowing serves to undermine the endurance of settler futurity.

While it is beyond the scope of this project to engage the ongoing debate concerning the merits of identity politics, what is pertinent here is Dotson's centering of Black feminism within Afromodernity's negation of the seeming inevitability of settler colonialism. Black (queer) feminist origin stories on this land inspire a "thinking with" that deepens critical engagement with decolonial marriage abolitionist praxis that disrupts settler futurity.[77] In previous chapters, I leveled critiques against those who sought to ameliorate the harmful impact of marital shade by "seeking redress and healing through the settler state."[78] I made plain that single Black mothers would not be liberated through same-sex marriage equality, adherence to the Black married maternal, or through renegotiating the terms under which the state regulates our sexual and romantic relationships. Throwing marital shade is a repudiation of the settler state that obliges us to consider "what healing and redress would look like on otherwise or decolonial and abolitionist terms."[79]

As an investment in decolonial marriage abolitionism, throwing marital shade compels an orientation away from conventional academic engagements with theory and praxis. The fecund disruption of settler futurity effectuated by throwing marital shade evokes a commitment to alternative ways of being-thinking-doing. Traditionally, theory and praxis are ofttimes interpreted as siloed endeavors to be pursued in contrasting linear orders. In the first order, one advances an ideal theoretical proposition that will be subsequently put into practice in the "real world." Secondarily, one documents occurrences of indiscriminate practical activity that requires the analytical force of theoretical grounding.[80] Both sequential orderings belie the simultaneous co-creation of theory and praxis, aptly described by Mignolo and Walsh as "theory is doing and doing is thinking."[81] Contrary to positioning theory and praxis at opposing poles, they advance "the idea of theory-and-as-praxis and praxis-and-as-theory."[82]

Single Black motherhood embodies the symbiotic, generative flow among the being-thinking-doing of family in relationship to self and community. The transgressive nature of households led by unmarried Black women exceeds what is considered comprehensible, or acceptable, in the context of settler sexual citizenship. Thus, when one takes flight into the fanciful ideal world of settler colonialism, one cannot account accurately for the positive existence of, for example, a non-biological family helmed by a Black trans mother, like Miss Major. Theory-making from this perspective, which influences public policy and societal attitudes, will default consistently to a nuclear marital configuration. Conversely, the generation of an affirming theoretical model that captures the richness of single Black motherhood in the "real" world is thwarted by the conceptual limitations imposed by settler sexual citizenship. At either pole, unmarried Black mothers are understood as problems to be solved or aberrations to be eradicated. The turn toward the co-creation of theory and praxis is a necessary enterprise to fully embrace and support families that exist in excess of settler sexual possibilities.

By virtue of its resistance to both academic and societal conventions, throwing marital shade is a particularly useful practice for the evolution of Africana philosophy and Black studies—two disciplines that have made significant contributions to our understanding of human existence when it is situated within structures of domination. The queer orientation of throwing shade holds these disciplines accountable for not capturing the full richness of the human condition because the treatment of varied sexualities and gender identities remains wanting.[83] The dominance of cisgender, heteronormative, masculinist sensibilities, especially in Africana philosophy, has proven to be a limitation in the pursuit of subverting systemic, anti-Black racism. But this shortcoming is not insurmountable. Throwing marital shade can help prevent these sensibilities from growing stronger roots.

For Black scholars laboring toward liberation, Leanne Simpson reminds us that "we cannot just think, write or imagine our way to a decolonized future."[84] Try as I might, I cannot write my way to the end of the state marital regime. This decolonial, abolitionist endeavor necessitates engagement with theory-making that "is generated and regenerated continually through embodied practice and within each family, community and generation of people."[85] This crystallizes our generation's work, which, I contend, entails an intraracial reckoning with the queer others in our midst—whether the "queer" unmarried mother parenting outside the boundaries of the respectable Black married maternal or the Black lesbian mother raising her children in defiance of the norming principles of settler sexuality. The alienation occasioned by Euromodernity that foments a sense of homelessness cannot be countered by an uncritical, utopian depiction of Afromodernity. The tendency toward systemic domination and violence is deeply rooted within the fabric of humanity across the color line. If we are to establish nurturing, intimate home places, then we must attend to the sites of domination within Black communities that are as detrimental to Black futurities as settler colonial logics.

We would be well served to place the marital institution under the full weight of our intellectual scrutiny. Take for instance, Katherine

McKittrick's exploration of the dynamic between "geographies of domination (such as transatlantic slavery and racial-sexual displacement) and black women's geographies (such as their knowledges, negotiations, and experiences)."[86] These geographical sites compel philosophical investigation, according to McKittrick, "because existing cartographic rules unjustly organize human hierarchies in place and reify uneven geographies in familiar, seemingly natural ways," and further, "these rules are alterable."[87] I believe this philosophical project will be strengthened by the inclusion of the state-regulated marital regime, alongside considerations of the transatlantic slave trade and urban gentrification, for example.[88] Single Black mothers traverse the geographical sites identified by McKittrick in both "their physical materiality and imaginative configurations."[89] We are witness to these mothers' methods of survival outside the protection of the settler state and traditional sites of Black sanctuary. We are also witness to the resilient and imaginative geographies of unmarried Black mothers, as they create home places of their own desire and design.

McKittrick cautions against succumbing to the seductive and comforting notion that "space 'just is', and that space and place are merely containers for human complexities and social relations."[90] Rather, we must take responsibility for the social production of space as "we produce its meanings."[91] Black communities produce the home place. While settler sexual citizenship was imposed upon us in the wake of emancipation, we are accountable for the continued and dogged adherence to a hierarchical ranking of suitable family configurations. Intraracial geographies of domination are manifested through the negation of the matrifocal dyad as a site of value. The deification of "The Black Family" represents the continuous reproduction of the heteronormative home place that mimics the very settler colonial values that many scholar-activists purportedly disavow.

McKittrick posits that affirming "the alternative geographic formulations" established within subaltern communities constitutes a pathway toward dismantling hierarchies of domination and oppression.[92] Throwing marital shade is an example of an alternative geographic formulation. It is defined by the dynamic charting of new and different cartographies of home-making and familial formations. The pathway to this revisioning is forged, according to McKittrick, through "various kinds of madness," "pathological geographies," and "impossible black places."[93] I contend that Black freedom lies within the "madness" of trans mothering, the "pathology" of the Black matriarch, and the "impossibility" of thriving families headed by women. The very psychosocial disturbance caused by these purported deviants is, in actuality, a clarifying light shone upon the very forms of domination that must be overcome. Thus, single Black motherhood should be considered foundational to the advancement of liberatory theory-praxis.

Single Black mothers inhabit a liminal space between the pernicious settler state and an unfolding existence beyond slavery's afterlife; their negotiations with space and place provide a path to Black liberation. In *Aliveness, or a Poetics of Being*, Kevin Quashie gestures toward life after slavery when he invites us to imagine Black aliveness in place of its antithesis, Black death. Responding to the enduring vocabulary of death that attempts to confine the very meaning of blackness itself, Quashie writes, "Antiblackness is part of blackness but not all of how or what blackness is."[94] While anti-Blackness may be total in the world, "it is not total in the black world."[95] Quashie's exploration of Black world-making is enlivened by Black feminism. For Quashie, "Black feminist thinking might be specific in naming black women, but its ambition has always been the breadth of being alive, the principle that the lived experience of one who is black and female is comprehensive enough to manifest totality."[96] It is within the spirit of verdant aliveness present in Black feminism that I situate the generative capacities of single Black motherhood.

The productive qualities of single Black motherhood are a manifestation of bountiful aliveness. This life-affirming abundance continuously exceeds, or overflows, pervasive delimitations of Black humanity. Throwing marital shade is an expression of the providence that is single Black motherhood. Providential Black world-making is sacred and secular, material and immaterial, and personal and communal. The providence of single Black motherhood inspires the sentiments of the divine in its care for humanity and in its foresight forged through the inheritance of intergenerational wisdom. Defying unimaginative interpretations of social-political orders and spatial-temporal possibilities, the providence of single Black motherhood, as a facet of Black world-making, is a wellspring for Black liberation.

In conclusion, I return to the question "what does it mean to have a Black mother," a query based on C. Riley Snorton's reformulation of W. E. B. DuBois's "what does it feel like to be a problem?"[97] Previously, I demonstrated how Snorton's question influenced the reification of the Black married maternal within movements for Black liberation. Here, I situate the Black mother as conceived by Audre Lorde in her seminal essay "Poetry is not a Luxury" within Gordon's phenomenological accounts of Afromodernity and Euromodernity. Read within this context, I contend that Lorde's renderings of the ontic-epistemic liberatory potentiality of the Black maternal evinces the providence of single Black motherhood. This well-known essay serves as an exemplar for contemporary explorations of throwing marital shade. While Lorde does not address the marital institution explicitly, I read this composition as a work of decolonial marriage abolition praxis crafted in contradistinction to settler sexual citizenship.

For Gordon, the detrimental impact of Euromodernity's grounding within racial hierarchy extends beyond fostering a sense of homelessness for the racially marginalized. The negative repercussions of systemic racism lead to suffering for all those living under its reign, including white-embodied people. One notable aspect of this suffering is the existential notion of anguish, which Gordon considers in legal terms. He defines this particular manifestation of anguish as "the confrontation with the self via the choices one makes."[98] One's options are conditioned by the legal parameters set forth by legislative institutions that determine which activities are permissible and which actions are prohibited. The choices that one makes within our social world, according to Gordon, "could be summarized as one's relation to the proverbial others."[99] Our relationality to others is an inescapable facet of our choices because the law is a form of power enacted by legal institutions, which are a manifestation of intersubjectivity. Given that intersubjective relationality is a constitutive element within legal doctrine, we see that our choices are "exemplifications of power, even where fairly limited."[100] Further, these choices are not simply cerebral cogitations; they are also embodied. Gordon argues that "our actions are the choices made manifest through our body . . . the 'reach' of our choices at that level is concrete: the capacities of consciousness in the flesh."[101]

Gordon offers racial segregation as an example of this juridical instantiation of existential anguish. In a society predicated upon racial domination, or white supremacy, those who are racially marginalized by virtue of Black embodiment encounter limited options from which to make fulfilling life choices. In contrast, legal institutions in a racially stratified society provide its racially dominant members with a wealth of options from which to make meaningful choices. Within this phenomenological framework, Gordon posits that ending racism would entail the creation of laws that maximize the options available to the racially marginalized for choice-making aimed at joyful living, while simultaneously reducing the availability of options that foster racist choices that diminish the quality of Black existence. A racialized manifestation of anguish is also apparent in the legal regulation of our intimate relationships, specifically the marital institution. Marriage epitomizes the dynamism of embodied intersubjectivity enmeshed with the human activity of legal world-making.

Anguish is exhibited in the white feminist use of theoretical blackface in their quest to eliminate gender-based marital harm. Marital shade as theoretical blackface exposes a loss of these women's meaningful connection both to themselves and to others, owing to the preference for colonial unknowing in lieu of a forthright engagement with the domination inherent in whiteness. Ultimately, the evasion of a confrontation with oneself and one's choices, which lies at the heart of existential anguish, results in a lost sense of one's own humanity. James Baldwin, when describing "the Negro's past, of rope, fire, torture," states that "this endless struggle to achieve and reveal and confirm a human identity, human authority, yet contains, for all its horror, something very beautiful."[102] Baldwin is careful to note that he is neither romanticizing Black suffering nor violence. Rather, he is uplifting the truism that "people who cannot suffer can never grow up, can never discover who they are."[103] The prevalence of theoretical blackface in marriage reform literature, as well as an affinity for ideal theory, is representative of the desire to escape from the very anguish or suffering that Baldwin deems necessary for human growth and development. The pursuit of evasion is indicative of a lack of maturation or wisdom, which is invariably reflected within our legal institutions.

Anguish also plagues Black social justice activists, who remain attached to assimilation within settler sexual citizenship through the heralding of the Black married maternal. Anguish abides in the confrontation with the entreaty "what does it mean to have a Black mother?" As will be discussed below, Lorde's maternal poet provides a point of intervention that disrupts anguish and encourages an evolution toward authentic human connection. Lorde instructs us to "never close our eyes to the terror, to the chaos which is Black which is creative which is female which is dark which is rejected."[104] She posits that the affective act of mothering provides the definitional power by which one can face terror or "move through being afraid to whatever lies beyond."[105] Lorde's instruction lies at the heart of marital shade that incites existential terror in the face of the subaltern, the Black other, in our midst. What is more terrifying than a mother who is also a "gorgeous man?"[106] What fears lurk in the wake of the historical legacies of *partus ventrum sequitur*?

Lorde opens "Poetry is not a Luxury" with a phenomenological description of Black existence as a radiant light. Akin to Linda Alcoff's embodied interpretive horizon, Lorde posits that the quality of light by which we view our existence influences our experience of it. This luminescence informs the contours of our freedom dreams or our strivings to make the unknown known and the impossible possible. Lorde identifies this human activity as "poetry as illumination."[107] The poetic is thus far from a luxury because it is the conduit that reveals the pathways to liberation that are necessary to our survival.

The illuminative qualities of the poetic outline both the geographies of domination faced by Black mothers and the architectural schemata for liberated home places. Lorde's articulation of the human condition does not consign us to "what is" without recourse to evolution beyond the suffering engendered by domination. Poetry provides "the skeleton architecture of our lives" because it "lays the foundation for a future of change."[108] The gesture toward architecture is reminiscent of Sara Ahmed's queer phenomenological interpretation of desire lines.[109] In landscape architecture, desire lines denote alternate pathways carved by pedestrians in defiance of the planned routes in the built environment. For Ahmed, the queer desire line beckons confrontation with heteronormative ontic-epistemic norms. The queer desire line, or Lorde's skeleton architecture, provides direction toward the as-yet-unrealized, but achievable, existence as freedom.

Lorde's poetic Black mother is situated within the decolonial milieu of Afromodernity—one that is both queer and feminist. Kara Keeling succinctly describes the decolonial facets of poetry in *Queer Times, Black Futurities*.[110] According to Keeling, "whatever escapes recognition, whatever escapes meaning and valuation, exists as an impossible possibility within our shared reality."[111] The temporal contours of Black liberation "raises the possibility of the impossible within colonial reality."[112] The ontic-epistemic disruption posed by "poetry from the future" "threatens to unsettle, if not destroy, the common senses on which that reality relies for its coherence."[113] The disruptive poetic potentiality affirmed by Keeling is evident in Lorde's rejection of the prioritization of "living in the european mode only as a problem to be solved."[114] She readily dismisses a singular reliance on ideas as the road to freedom.

In contrast, Lorde asserts that when we are aligned with "our own ancient, noneuropean consciousness of living as a situation to be experienced," we can hold fast to feelings and "respect those hidden sources of our power from where true knowledge and, therefore, lasting action comes."[115] She eschews the flight into rationality as a defense mechanism to avoid one's feelings, especially the experience of suffering. In lieu of fleeing, Lorde implores us all to "learn the lessons of the Black mother in each of us."[116] The lessons imparted by the poetic Black mother express Lorde's nuanced understanding of the symbiotic relationship between theory and praxis. Her articulation of the edifying aspects of the Black maternal is rooted within her methodology of "poetic praxis." Lorde's methodological approach is not simply "'theorizing' the possibilities of poetry"; rather, poetic praxis demonstrates one "living it, experiencing it."[117] The rejection of the world of ideas, disassociated from lived experience, is a reflection of her "notion of embodied intelligence."[118] It is from this vantage of radiant luminescence that Lorde writes, "The white fathers told us: I think, therefore I am. The Black mother within each of us—the poet—whispers in our dreams: I feel, therefore I can be free. Poetry coins the language to express and charter this revolutionary demand, the implementation of that freedom."[119]

Lorde's remarks do not perpetuate the false binary that pits the emotional Black mother against the rational white father. Rather, she is pointing out the limitations of European epistemes. Through her assertion that there "are no new ideas," Lorde exposes the finite nature of European consciousness or Euromodernity.[120] She seeks to awaken us from the delusion that "the head will save us" or that "the brain alone will set us free."[121] Freedom cannot be attained through the generation of more ideas but will be realized in "new ways of making them felt."[122] Lorde likens "leaving rationality to the white man" to leaving him with a "road that begins nowhere and ends nowhere."[123] The nowhere road is rendered as groundless and meaningless. In this way, Lorde displaces, or un-homes, whiteness. Afromodernity brings forth another sense of homelessness, not owing to alienation but from Euromodernity itself. The poetic Black mother sets us en route to the formation of new homeplaces.

Poetic praxis is not a passive intellectual enterprise. It requires active engagement with the power that lies within our vulnerability and intimate relationships with ourselves and with others. Lorde beckons us to "learn to bear the intimacy of scrutiny and to flourish within it."[124] As we become acculturated to enduring the weight of intimate scrutiny, the grip of the "fears which rule our lives and form our silences" lessens their hold upon us. The cultivation of our intimate capacities brings forth the spaciousness needed to hold the experience of suffering, as opposed to its evasion as demonstrated in the anguish of marital shade.

If the revolutionary demand of the poetic Black mother compels an unflinching embrace of intimacy and profound intersubjective affinity, then what are we to make of settler sexual citizenship? What poetic freedom dreams of love and family do we hear being whispered by the Black mother who speaks to us all? I consider Lorde's invitation to lean into suffering and to expand our capacities to love ourselves and others to be antithetical to the state marital regime.[125] As Roderick Ferguson asserts, Lorde understands that intimate scrutiny, or attending to one's self, involves personal and collective intentions that are "appointed not for the continuation of liberal social formations but for their abolition."[126] Lorde asserts that genuine human connection resists "living structures defined by profit, by linear power, by institutional dehumanization," in which "our feelings were not meant to survive."[127] Settler sexual citizenship, inclusive of the marital regime, is the epitome of a living structure that thrives on power and profit at the cost of the dehumanization of unmarried Black mothers and their families. It habituates us toward intersubjective relationality that foments political, ethical, and socioeconomic strife through hierarchical rankings from properly ordered familial formations, sexualities, and gender identities deserving of support to the deviant families worthy of scorn. In contrast, Lorde offers us a guidepost toward the liberation of all Black families through the creative poeticism of the Black mother, who abides in us all.

Notes

Chapter 1

1. Paul Hemez and Chanell Washington, "Percentage and Number of Children Living with Two Parents Has Dropped Since 1968," United States Census Bureau, April 12, 2021, https://www.census.gov/library/stories/2021/04/number-of-children-living-only-with-their-mothers-has-doubled-in-past-50-years.html.
2. Pew Research Center, "Rising Share of U.S. Adults Are Living Without a Spouse or Partner," October 5, 2021, https://www.pewresearch.org/social-trends/2021/10/05/rising-share-of-u-s-adults-are-living-without-a-spouse-or-partner/.
3. Chanell Washington and Laquitta Walker, "Marriage Prevalence for Black Adults Varies by State," United States Census Bureau, July 19, 2022.
4. Ibid.
5. Angela Davis, "Reflections on the Black Woman's Role in the Community of Slaves," *The Massachusetts Review*, Vol. 13, No. 1/2 (Winter–Spring, 1972): p. 84.
6. Davis, "Reflections on the Black Woman's Role," p. 81. For further reading on Black women and controlling images, see Patricia Hill Collins, *Black Feminist Thought: Knowledge, Consciousness, and the Politics of Empowerment* (New York: Routledge, 2002).
7. Mignon R. Moore, *Invisible Families: Gay Identities, Relationships, and Motherhood among Black Women* (Berkeley: University of California Press, 2011); Shirley A. Hill, *Black Intimacies: A Gender Perspective on Families and Relationships* (Walnut Creek: Altamira Press, 2005); Gwendolyn Mink, *The Wages of Motherhood: Inequality in the Welfare State, 1917–1942* (Ithaca: Cornell University Press, 1995); Jennifer C. Nash, *Birthing Black Mothers* (Durham: Duke University Press, 2021).
8. See Patricia Hill Collins, "It's All in the Family: Intersections of Gender, Race, and Nation," *Hypatia*, Vol. 13, No. 3 (Summer 1998); Candice M. Jenkins, *Private Lives, Proper Relations: Regulating Black Intimacy* (Minneapolis: University of Minnesota Press, 2007); Lisa B. Thompson, *Beyond the Black Lady: Sexuality and the New African American Middle Class* (Urbana: University of Illinois Press, 2009); E. Franklin Frazier, *The Negro Family in the United States* (Chicago: University of Chicago Press, 1967); Ralph Richard Banks, *Is Marriage for White People?: How the African American Marriage Decline Affects Everyone* (New York: Dutton, 2011).
9. Evelyn Brooks Higginbotham, *Righteous Discontent: The Women's Movement in the Black Baptist Church 1880–1920* (Cambridge: Harvard University Press, 1993); E. Francis White, *Dark Continent of Our Bodies: Black Feminism and the Politics of Respectability* (Philadelphia: Temple University Press, 2001).
10. Paul C. Taylor, "William Edward Burghardt Du Bois," in *The Wiley-Blackwell Companion to Major Social Theorists*, ed. George Ritzer and Jeffrey Stepnisky (Hoboken: Blackwell, 2011), p. 427.
11. W. E. B. Dubois, *The Philadelphia Negro: A Social Study* (Philadelphia: University of Pennsylvania Press [1899], 1996); W. E. B. Dubois, *The Negro American Family*, The Atlanta University Publications, No. 13 (1908).
12. Dubois, *The Philadelphia Negro: A Social Study*, p. 68.

13. Ibid., p. 72.
14. See https://www.mediamatters.org/tucker-carlson/fox-news-guest-blames-Black-single-mothers-killing-tyre-nichols; https://www.essence.com/lifestyle/Black-single-mothers/.
15. https://www.theguardian.com/uk-news/2019/dec/11/modern-slave-19-convicted-of-of-jaden-moodie-14; https://www.thetimes.co.uk/article/half-of-Black-children-do-not-live-with-their-father-and-we-wonder-why-they-re-dying-pj0n3th6g; Rod Liddle, January 13, 2019. Sociologist Miranda Armstrong criticized Liddle's assertion that the violence wrought upon Black youth is the fault of unmarried Black mothers in her op/ed: https://mediadiversified.org/2019/01/22/when-will-we-stop-blaming-Black-single-mother-households-for-violent-crime/comment-page-1/.
16. The US Department of Justice lists the following dissertation on its website as training material: Armine Campbell, "Black Single Female Headed Households and Their Children's Involvement in Gangs," California State University, Long Beach ProQuest Dissertations Publishing, 1992. Campbell concludes that there is a link "between family structure and delinquent or gang behavior. Single-female-headed households seem most at risk of their children becoming gang affiliated," p. 33. She lists considerable stress and lack of church involvement as possible contributing factors.
17. Farah Jasmine Griffin, "Black Feminists and Du Bois: Respectability, Protection, and Beyond," *The Annals of the American Academy of Political and Social Science*, Vol. 568 (March 2000): p. 31.
18. Ibid., p. 31. His progressive views on birth control are also evident in W. E. B. Du Bois, "Black Folk and Birth Control," *Birth Control Review*, Vol. 16, No. 6 (1932): pp. 166–167.
19. W. E. B. DuBois, "The Damnation of Women," in *W.E.B. Du Bois: A Reader*, ed. David Levering Lewis (New York: Henry Holt, [1920], 1995), p. 311.
20. Taylor, "William Edward Burghardt Du Bois," p. 430.
21. W. E. B. DuBois, *Black Reconstruction: An Essay Toward a History of the Part Which Black Folk Played in the Attempt to Reconstruct Democracy in America, 1860–1880* (New York: Harcourt, Brace and Company, 1935), p. 447.
22. Anastasia C. Curwood, *Stormy Weather: Middle-Class African American Marriages between the Two World Wars* (Chapel Hill: University of North Carolina Press, 2010), p. 15.
23. Tera W. Hunter, *Bound in Wedlock: Slave and Free Black Marriage in the Nineteenth Century* (Cambridge: The Belknap Press of Harvard University Press, 2017), p. 293.
24. Shirley A. Hill, "Marriage among African American Women: A Gender Perspective," *Journal of Comparative Family Studies*, Vol. 37, No. 3 (Summer 2006): p. 429.
25. Frances Smith Foster, *Til Death or Distance Do Us Part: Love and Marriage in African America* (New York: Oxford University Press, 2010), p. 64.
26. Hill, "Marriage among African American Women," p. 429.
27. Riché J. Daniel Barnes, *Raising the Race: Black Career Women Redefine Marriage, Motherhood, and Community* (New Brunswick: Rutgers University Press, 2016), p. 5.
28. It is beyond the scope of this project to engage in either the scholarship addressing genealogies or the evolving debates of these terms. For further reading, see D. Bell and J. Binnie, *The Sexual Citizen: Queer Politics and Beyond* (Cambridge: Polity Press, 2000); D. Bell and J. Binnie, "Authenticating Queer Space: Citizenship, Urbanism and Governance," *Urban Studies*, Vol. 41, No. 9 (2004): pp. 1807–1820; L. Berlant, *The Queen of America Goes to Washington City: Essays on Sex and Citizenship* (Durham: Duke University Press, 1997); M. Canaday, *The Straight*

State: Sexuality and Citizenship in Twentieth-Century America (Princeton: Princeton University Press, 2011); A. Cruz-Malavé and M. F. Manalansan IV, eds., *Queer Globalizations: Citizenship and the Afterlife of Colonialism* (New York: New York University Press, 2002); L. Duggan, "The New Homonormativity: The Sexual Politics of Neoliberalism," in *Materializing Democracy: Toward a Revitalized Cultural Politics*, ed. R. Castronova and D. D. Nelson (Durham: Duke University Press, 2002); Bryan S. Turner, "Citizenship, Reproduction and the State: International Marriage and Human Rights," *Citizenship Studies*, Vol. 12, No. 1 (2008): pp. 45–54; J. Weeks, "The Sexual Citizen," *Theory, Culture & Society*, Vol. 15, No. 3–4 (1998): pp. 35–52; Diane Richardson, "Rethinking Sexual Citizenship," *Sociology*, Vol. 51, No. 2 (2017): pp. 208–224.

29. Scott Lauria Morgensen, "Settler Homonationalism: Theorizing Settler Colonialism Within Queer Modernities," *GLQ: A Journal of Lesbian and Gay Studies*, Vol. 16, No. 1–2 (2010): pp. 105–131.
30. Justin Leroy, "Black History in Occupied Territory: On the Entanglements of Slavery and Settler Colonialism," *Theory & Event*, Vol. 19, No. 4 (2016): p. 5.
31. Nancy F. Cott, *Public Vows: A History of Marriage and the Nation* (Cambridge: Harvard University Press, 2002), p. 2.
32. Ibid., p. 3.
33. Ibid.
34. Jodi A. Byrd, "Weather with You: Settler Colonialism, Antiblackness, and the Grounded Relationalities of Resistance," *Critical Ethnic Studies*, Vol. 5, No. 1–2 (Spring 2019): p. 207.
35. Maile Arvin, Eve Tuck, and Angie Morrill, "Decolonizing Feminism: Challenging Connections between Settler Colonialism and Heteropatriarchy," *Feminist Formations*, Vol. 25, No. 1 (2013): p. 14.
36. Leroy, "Black History in Occupied Territory," p. 10.
37. Zainab Amadahy and Bonita Lawrence, "Indigenous Peoples and Black People in Canada: Settlers or Allies?" in *Breaching the Colonial Contract: Anti-Colonialism*, ed. A. Kempf (Ontario: Springer Science + Business Media, 2009), p. 107.
38. Ibid., p. 119.
39. See Tiffany Lethabo King, Jenell Navarro, and Andrea Smith, "Beyond Incommensurability toward an Otherwise Stance on Black and Indigenous Relationality," in *Otherwise Worlds: Against Settler Colonialism and Anti-Blackness*, ed. Tiffany Lethabo King, Jenell Navarro, and Andrea Smith (Durham: Duke University Press, 2020).
40. Cheryl Harris, "Of Blackness and Indigeneity: Comments on Jodi A. Byrd's 'Weather with You: Settler Colonialism, Antiblackness, and the Grounded Relationalities of Resistance,'" *Critical Ethnic Studies*, Vol. 5, No. 1–2 (Spring 2019): p. 223.
41. Morgensen, "Settler Homonationalism," p. 106.
42. See Marlon M. Bailey and Rashad Shabazz, "Gender and Sexual Geographies of Blackness: Anti-Black Heterotopias (Part 1)," *Gender, Place & Culture*, Vol. 21, No. 3 (2014): pp. 316–321; Bailey and Shabazz, "Gender and Sexual Geographies of Blackness (Part 2), pp. 449–452.
43. Banks, *Is Marriage for White People?*; Katrina Bell McDonald and Caitlin Cross-Barnett, *Marriage in Black: The Pursuit of Married Life among American-born and Immigrant Blacks* (New York: Routledge Press, 2018).
44. Daniel Barnes, *Raising the Race*, p. 4.
45. Ibid., p. 10.
46. Ibid., p. 11.
47. Ibid., p. 173.
48. Dianne M. Stewart, *Black Women, Black Love: America's War on African American Marriage* (New York: Seal Press, 2020), p. 11.

49. Ibid., p. 3.
50. Ibid., p. 10.
51. David Harvey, *A Brief History of Neoliberalism* (Oxford: Oxford University Press, 2005), p. 2.
52. U.S. Government Accountability Office, "Defense of Marriage Act: Update to Prior Report," January 23, 2004.
53. Robin D. G. Kelley, *Freedom Dreams: The Black Radical Imagination* (Boston: Beacon Press, 2002), p. 154.
54. Ibid.
55. Linda La Rue, "The Black Movement and Women's Liberation," in *Words of Fire: An Anthology of African-American Feminist Thought*, ed. Beverly Guy-Sheftall (New York: The New Press, [1970], 1995), p. 171.
56. Ibid.
57. E. Frances White, "Africa on My Mind: Gender, Counter Discourse and African-American Nationalism," *Journal of Women's History*, Vol. 2, No. 1 (1990): pp. 76–77.
58. Ibid., p. 77.
59. June Jordan, *Some of Us Did Not Die: New and Selected Essays of June Jordan* (New York: Basic Books, 2002), p. 133.
60. Keeanga-Yamahtta Taylor, *How We Get Free: Black Feminism and the Combahee River Collective* (Chicago: Haymarket Books, 2017), p. 60.
61. The Combahee River Collective (1977), "A Black Feminist Statement," in *Words of Fire: An Anthology of African-American Feminist Thought*, ed. Beverly Guy-Sheftall (New York: The New Press, 1995), pp. 232–240.
62. Taylor, *How We Get Free*, p. 8.
63. Ibid.
64. Ibid., p. 9.
65. Andrea J. Ritchie, *Invisible No More: Police Violence against Black Women and Women of Color* (Boston: Beacon Press, 2017).
66. Loretta J. Ross and Rickie Solinger, *Reproductive Justice: An Introduction* (Oakland: University of California Press, 2017).
67. L. H. Stallings, *Funk the Erotic: Transaesthetics and Black Sexual Cultures* (Urbana: University of Illinois Press, 2015), p. 122.
68. Ibid.
69. Ibid., p. 125.
70. Ibid., p. 128.
71. Lewis Gordon, *An Introduction to Africana Philosophy* (New York: Cambridge University Press, 2008).
72. Lewis R. Gordon, ed., *Existence in Black*: An Anthology of Black Existential Philosophy (New York: Routledge, 1997); Denise James, "Pragmatism and Radical Social Justice: John Dewey, W. E. B. Du Bois, and Angela Davis," in *Pragmatism and Justice*, ed. Susan Dieleman, David Rondel, and Christopher Voparil (New York: Oxford University Press, 2017); Howard McGary and Bill E. Lawson, *Between Slavery and Freedom: Philosophy and American Slavery* (Bloomington: Indiana University Press, 1992); Tommy Lott, ed., *African-American Philosophy: Selected Readings* (Upper Saddle River: Prentice Hall, 2002); Ronald R. Sundstrom, *The Browning of America and the Evasion of Social Justice* (Albany: State University of New York Press, 2008); Joy James, *Seeking the Beloved Community: A Feminist Race Reader* (Albany: State University of New York Press, 2013).
73. One notable exception is found in the work of Justin L. Clardy. See Justin L. Clardy, *Why It's Ok to Not be Monogamous* (New York: Routledge, 2023).
74. See Anita L. Allen, "Interracial Marriage: Folk Ethics in Contemporary Philosophy," in *Women of Color and Philosophy: A Critical Reader*, ed. Naomi Zack (Malden: Blackwell Publishers, 2000); Isaac Ehaleoye Ukpokolo, "What Is This

Thing Called Love? A Gender Implication of the Ontologico-Epistemic Status of Love in an African Traditional Marriage System," *Human Affairs*, Vol. 22 (2012): pp. 79-88. Ronald Sundstrom considers sexual and romantic intimacy in *The Browning of America and the Evasion of Social Justice* (Albany: State University of New York Press, 2008). See also Roderick A. Ferguson, "A Question of Personhood: Black Marriage, Gay Marriage, and the Contraction of the Human," *philoSophia: A Journal of Continental Feminism*, Vol. 9, No. 2 (Spring 2019): pp. 1-19.
75. Allen, "Interracial Marriage, p. 182.
76. Ibid., p. 186.
77. Ibid., p. 183.
78. Ibid.
79. Charles W. Mills, *The Racial Contract* (Ithaca: Cornell University Press, 1997); Charles W. Mills, *Blackness Visible: Essays on Philosophy and Race* (Ithaca: Cornell University Press, 1998); Charles W. Mills, *Black Rights/White Wrongs: The Critique of Racial Liberalism* (New York: Oxford University Press, 2017). In *Black Rights, White Wrongs*, Mills defines racial liberalism as "a liberalism in which key terms have been written by race and the discursive logic shaped accordingly" (p. xv). He asserts that liberalism has been penetrated by racism; thus, it is not the case that liberalism itself is constitutive of racism. He hopes to redeem liberalism "by self-consciously taking this history into account" in order to recognize "the historic racialization of liberalism *so as to better deracialize it*" (p. xv).
80. In a footnote to this article, Mills acknowledges that he may be accused of utilizing a heterosexist framework. The accusation he imagines would be that he failed to consider that Black women could forego relationships with Black men and engage in lesbian relationships. The construction of this alleged counterargument is quite curious. Critical interrogation of the morality of interracial relationships is an endeavor that is applicable to all relationships across the sexuality spectrum. Thus, the heterosexist accusation is not that Mills failed to consider the possibility of sexual fluidity among heterosexual Black women but rather that the only relationship type included within the discussion is heterosexual. Charles W. Mills, "Do Black Men Have a Moral Duty to Marry Black Women," *Journal of Social Philosophy*, 25th Anniversary Special Issue (1994): p. 152.
81. Mills, "Do Black Men Have a Moral Duty to Marry Black Women," p. 147.
82. My usage of the term "whiteliness" is influenced by Paul C. Taylor's interpretation. I engage whiteliness in greater detail in Chapter 4. Paul C. Taylor, "Silence and Sympathy: Dewey's Whiteness," in *What White Looks Like*, ed. George Yancy (New York: Routledge, 2004).
83. Mills, *Blackness Visible*, p. 228.
84. Ibid., p. 6.
85. Ibid., p. 17.
86. Ibid., pp. 17-18.
87. Mills, *The Racial Contract*.
88. Ibid., p. 5.
89. Ibid., p. 27.
90. Kathryn T. Gines, "Black Feminist Reflections on Charles Mills's 'Intersecting Contracts,'" *Critical Philosophy of Race*, Vol. 5, No. 1 (2017): pp. 19-28; Kristie Dotson, "Word to the Wise: Notes on a Black Feminist Metaphilosophy of Race," *Philosophy Compass*, Vol. 11, No. 2 (2016): pp. 69-74.
91. Mills, *The Racial Contract*, p. 57.
92. Angela Davis, "Reflections on the Black Woman's Role in the Community of Slaves," in *The Angela Y. Davis Reader*, ed. Joy James (Malden: Blackwell Publishers, [1971], 1998), pp. 111-128.
93. Mills, *The Racial Contract*, p. 137.

94. Ibid., p. 49.
95. Ibid., p. 50.
96. Ibid.
97. Ibid., p. 51.
98. Christina Sharpe, *In the Wake: On Blackness and Being* (Durham: Duke University Press, 2016), p. 13. While I do not share Sharpe's afro-pessimist stance, I do share in the experience of psychic violence that she finds in the work of Black scholars working with our enslaved past through the imposition of colonial methodologies.
99. Sharpe, *In the Wake*, p. 13.
100. Ibid.
101. Kristie Dotson, "How Is This Paper Philosophy?" *Comparative Philosophy*, Vol. 3, No. 1 (2012): pp. 3–29.
102. Ibid., p. 26.
103. Ibid., p. 19.
104. Evelynn Hammonds, "Black (W)holes and the Geometry of Black female Sexuality," *Differences: A Journal of Feminist Cultural Studies*, Vol. 6, No. 2–3 (Summer–Fall 1994).
105. Joanne Barker, ed., *Critically Sovereign: Indigenous Gender, Sexuality, and Feminist Studies* (Durham: Duke University Press, 2017), p. 6.
106. Ibid.
107. Jeffrey Q. McCune Jr., "The Queerness of Blackness," *QED: A Journal in GLBTQ Worldmaking*, Vol. 2, No. 2 (2015): p. 173–176. *Project MUSE* muse.jhu.edu/article/585660; Amber Johnson, "Trans Identity as Embodied Afrofuturism," in *African American Arts: Activism, Aesthetics, and Futurity*, ed. Sharrell D. Luckett (Lewisburg: Bucknell University Press, 2019).
108. Jafari S. Allen, "Black/Queer/Diaspora at the Current Conjuncture," *GLQ: A Journal of Lesbian and Gay Studies*, Vol. 18, No. 2–3 (2012): p. 222.
109. McCune, "The Queerness of Blackness," p. 173.
110. Ibid.
111. Ibid., p. 174.
112. Ariela R. Dubler, "In the Shadow of Marriage: Single Women and the Legal Construction of the Family and the State," *The Yale Law Journal*, Vol. 112, No. 7 (2003): pp. 1641–1715. Accessed December 30, 2020.
113. Ibid., p. 1646.
114. *Obergefell v. Hodges*, 135 S. Ct. 2584 (2015).
115. Courtney G. Joslin, "The Gay Rights Canon and the Right to Nonmarriage," *Boston University Law Review*, Vol. 97, No. 425 (2017): pp. 425–488; Nancy D. Polikoff, "We Will Get What We Ask for: Why Legalizing Gay and Lesbian Marriage Will Not 'Dismantle the Legal Structure of Gender in Every Marriage,'" *Virginia Law Review*, Vol. 79, No. 7, Symposium on Sexual Orientation and the Law (October 1993): pp. 1535–1550; Tamara Metz, *Untying the Knot: Marriage, the State, and the Case for Their Divorce* (Princeton: Princeton University Press, 2010).

Chapter 2

1. Michelle Obama, *Becoming* (New York: Crown Publishing Group/Penguin Random House, 2018).
2. Adam Chandler, "A Eulogy in Charleston," *The Atlantic*, June 26, 2015, https://www.theatlantic.com/national/archive/2015/06/a-eulogy-in-charleston/396998/.

3. *Obergefell v. Hodges*, 135 S. Ct. 2584 (2015).
4. Obama, *Becoming*, p. 398.
5. Melissa Murray, "Obergefell v. Hodges and Nonmarriage Inequality," *California Law Review*, Vol. 104 (2016).
6. *Obergefell v. Hodges*, p. 3.
7. See Stephanie Coontz, *The Way We Never Were: American Families and The Nostalgia Trap* (New York, NY: BasicBooks, 1992); Peter Wallenstein, *Tell the Court I Love My Wife: Race, Marriage, and Law—An American History* (New York, NY: Palgrave Macmillan, 2002).
8. In the opinion, Kennedy uses the terms "gays" and "lesbians." I am intentionally using the acronym LGBTQ+ to acknowledge the broad expanse of queer individuals implicated by this judicial decision.
9. Justice Kennedy has significantly influenced LGBTQ+ jurisprudence as author of the majority opinions for pivotal cases, including *Lawrence v. Texas*, 539 U.S. 558 (2003); *United States v. Windsor*, 570 U.S. 744 (2013); and *Obergefell v. Hodges*.
10. See Clare Huntington, "Obergefell's Conservatism: Reifying Familial Fronts," *Fordham Law Review*, Vol. 84 (2015); R. A. Lenhardt, "Race, Dignity, and the Right to Marry," 84 *Fordham Law Review* 1 (2015).
11. Some scholars reject the notion that *Obergefell* marks a setback for the protections of nonmarital unions. See Joslin, "The Gay Rights Canon and the Right to Nonmarriage"; Douglas NeJaime, "Before Marriage: The Unexplored History of Nonmarital Recognition and Its Relationship to Marriage," *California Law Review*, Vol. 102 (2014).
12. Murray, "Obergefell v. Hodges and Nonmarriage Inequality," p. 1210.
13. Ibid., p. 1240. Some family law scholars refute the pessimistic outlook concerning the implications of *Obergefell* upon nonmarital families. See Serena Mayeri, "Marriage (In)equality and the Historical Legacies of Feminism," *The Circuit* (2015). Mayeri views *Obergefell* as a fulfillment of second-wave feminism values. She remains optimistic in the face of a decision that "provides no generalizable theory of equality based on sex or sexual orientation" that could be applicable in cases of discrimination in housing, employment, etc." (135). If the Court can evolve to recognize same-sex marriage, then, she reasons, "perhaps the status of marriage as legally superior to all other family forms need not remain frozen in time" (136).
14. Huntington, "Obergefell's Conservatism." Her worries are evident within the current rise of anti-LGBTQ+ legislation, including religious exemption clauses and the repeal of protections. See also Clare Huntington, "Staging the Family," *New York University Law Review*, Vol. 88 (2013): p. 589.
15. Claudia Rankine, Citizen: An American Lyric, (Minneapolis: Graywolf Press, 2014), pp. 61, 63.
16. See Jelani Cobb, "Murders in Charleston," *The New Yorker*, June 18, 2015, https://www.newyorker.com/news/news-desk/church-shooting-charleston-south-carolina.
17. See "Violent History: Attacks on Black Churches," *The New York Times*, June 18, 2015, https://www.nytimes.com/interactive/2015/06/18/us/19blackchurch.html. See also Taryn Finley and Hilary Fung, "There Have Been At Least 100 Attacks on Black Churches Since 1956," *HuffPost*, October 21, 2015, https://www.huffpost.com/entry/there-have-been-at-least-100-attacks-on-black-churches-since-1956_n_5627d677e4b0bce347039ef6.
18. There is a longstanding history of sexism, homophobia, and transphobia within the "Black church." I am not claiming that this religious institution has been a site of refuge for all Black people in need. Rather, I am acknowledging that it is a target for white supremacist violence. Sandra L. Barnes, "Black Megachurches and Gender Inclusivity," *Women, Gender, and Families of Color*, Vol. 3, No. 2 (2015): p. 115. The

CERCL Writing Collective, "Black Churches, Hip-Hop, and Sexuality," in *Breaking Bread, Breaking Beats: Churches and Hip-Hop—A Basic Guide to Key Issues* (Minneapolis: Augsburg Fortress, 2014), pp. 123–138.
19. Charles Lemert and Esme Bhan, eds., *The Voice of Anna Julia Cooper: Including a Voice from the South and Other Important Essays, Papers, and Letters* (Legacies of Social Thought Series) (Lanham: Rowman & Littlefield Publishers, 1998). While Cooper did hold questionable views regarding Victorian principles that were common in this historical period, I maintain that her reference to "mothers" is neither solely defined by biology nor a consignment of women to childbearing. Cooper herself never bore children, though she did adopt as a single woman late in her life. In 1915, she gained custody of her nephew's five children, ranging in age from six months to 12 years. At the age of 55, she purchased a home for herself and the children, which would later, in 1931, also house Frelinghuysen University, of which she was president from 1930 to 1941.
20. Cooper, *A Voice from the South*, p. 63.
21. See Katherine Franke's account of the racialization of the marriage equality movement to the detriment of communities of color by "equating homosexuality with whiteness" in Franke, *Wedlocked: The Perils of Marriage Equality* (New York: New York University Press, 2015), p. 12.
22. Lenhardt, "Race, Dignity, and the Right to Marry," p. 60.
23. Courtney G. Joslin, "Discrimination In and Out of Marriage," *Boston University Law Review*, Vol. 98 (2018): p. 2019.
24. Lenhardt, "Race, Dignity, and the Right to Marry," p. 60.
25. Ibid. p. 53.
26. Ibid., p. 65.
27. Alys Eve Weinbaum, "Reproducing Racial Capitalism," *Boston Review*, 10 (Spring 2019): p. 95. My understanding of neoliberalism draws upon David Harvey's definition. He describes neoliberalism as a "theory of political economic practices that proposes that human well-being can best be advanced by liberating individual entrepreneurial freedoms and skills within an institutional framework characterized by strong private property rights, free markets, and free trade." David Harvey, *A Brief History of Neoliberalism* (Oxford: Oxford University Press, 2005), p. 7.
28. *Lawrence v. Texas*, 539 U. S. 558, 575.
29. For example, *Griswold v. Connecticut*, 381 U.S. 479, 484–486 (1965), which upheld the married couple's rights to use contraception; *Loving v. Virginia*, 388 U.S. 1, 12 (1967), which struck down bans on interracial marital unions; *Zablocki v. Redhail*, 434 U.S. 374, 384 (1978), which allowed fathers behind in child support to marry; and *Turner v. Safley*, 482 U.S. 78, 95 (1987), which granted prisoners the right to marry.
30. *Obergefell v. Hodges*, p. 14.
31. See Kai M. Green, "In the Life: On Black Queer Kinship," *Women, Gender, and Families of Color*, Vol. 7, No. 1 (2019): p. 98.
32. Hortense Spillers, "Interstises: A Small Drama of Words," in *Pleasure and Danger: Exploring Sexuality*, ed. Carol Vance (Boston, MA: Routledge, 1984), pp. 73–100; Joy James, "Black Feminism: Liberation Limbos and Existence in Gray," in *Existence in Black: An Anthology of Black Existential Philosophy*, ed. Lewis R. Gordon (New York, NY: Routledge, 1996), pp. 215–224; Kristie Dotson, "Theorizing Jane Crow, Theorizing Unknowability," *Social Epistemology*, Vol. 31, No. 5 (2017): pp. 417–430; Anika Simpson and Paul C. Taylor, "Marital Shade: Studies in Intersectional Invisibility," *Philosophical Topics*, Vol. 49, No. 1 (Spring 2021): pp. 45–59.
33. Jennifer L. Morgan, "*Partus sequitur ventrem*: Law, Race, and Reproduction in Colonial Slavery," *Small Axe*, Vol. 22, No. 1 (2018): p. 2.
34. Ibid., p. 16.

35. Cedric Robinson, *Black Marxism: The Making of the Black Radical Tradition* (Chapel Hill: University of North Carolina Press, 1983/2000).
36. "Racialism" is Robinson's term.
37. Robinson, *Black Marxism*, p. 2.
38. See Deborah Gray White, *Ar'n't I a Woman? Female Slaves in the Plantation South* (New York: Norton, 1985); Darlene Clark Hine, *Hine Sight: Black Women and the Reconstruction of American History* (Bloomington: Indiana University Press, 1994); Thavolia Glymph, *Out of the House of Bondage: The Transformation of the Plantation Household* (New York: Cambridge University Press, 2003).
39. Amy Dru Stanley, *From Bondage to Contract: Wage Labor, Marriage, and the Market in the Age of Slave Emancipation* (Cambridge: Cambridge University Press, 1998).
40. Saidiya Hartman, *Lose Your Mother: A Journey Along the Atlantic Slave Route* (New York: Farrar, Straus and Giroux, 2007), p. 80.
41. Hunter, *Bound in Wedlock*, pp. 143–147.
42. Ibid., p. 147.
43. One aspect of the Congressional debate was the explicit concern that the conferral of marital rights might be construed as elevating Black women to the moral regard of white women. Congressional leaders made it expressly clear that they vehemently opposed moral and social equivalences between Black and white women.
44. Amy Dru Stanley, "Instead of Waiting for the Thirteenth Amendment: The War Power, Slave Marriage, and Inviolate Human Rights," *The American Historical Review*, Vol. 115, No. 3 (2010): p. 773.
45. A seminal account of enslavement and social death is found in Orlando Patterson's *Slavery and Social Death: A Comparative Study* (Cambridge, MA: Harvard University Press, 1982). I will take up the racial and gendered implications of civil and social death in more detail in Chapter 4. My account of the performance of illegibility is grounded by the scholarship of feminists of color who address the polyvalent experience of hypervisibility and invisibility. See Judith A. Clair, Joy E. Beatty, and Tammy L. MacLean, "Out of Sight but Not Out of Mind: Managing Invisible Social Identities in the Workplace," *Academy of Management Review*, Vol. 30, No. 1 (2005); Isis H. Settles, NiCole T. Buchanan, and Kristie Dotson, "Scrutinized but Not Recognized: (In)visibility and Hypervisiblity Experiences of Faculty of Color," *Journal of Vocational Behavior*, Vol. 113 (2019).
46. The successes and failures of the Bureau were enumerated and analyzed by W. E. B. Du Bois in *Black Reconstruction: An Essay Toward a History of the Part Which Black Folk Played in the Attempt to Reconstruct Democracy in America, 1860–1880* (New York: Harcourt, Brace and Company, 1935). See also Mary Farmer-Kaiser, *Freedwomen and the Freedmen's Bureau: Race, Gender, and Public Policy in the Age of Emancipation* (New York, NY: Fordham University Press, 2010).
47. Saidiya Hartman, *Scenes of Subjection* (New York, NY: Oxford University Press, 1997), p. 116.
48. Farmer-Kaiser, *Freedwomen and the Freedmen's Bureau*, p. 9.
49. Ibid., p. 27. See also Nancy Cott, *Public Vows*, p. 93; Hunter, *Bound in Wedlock*.
50. The Civil Rights Act of 1866 granted Freedmen the right of household rule.
51. Farmer-Kaiser, *Freedwomen and the Freedmen's Bureau*, p. 49.
52. This deprivation was evident before emancipation in free Northern states. Free Black women were closely surveilled and were often run out of towns if they could not show their marriage certificates or provide the name of the officiant at their wedding. As Tera Hunter puts it, this scrutiny was a method to "weed out poor black women and children" so that towns were not responsible for their care. Marriage certificates became an alternative form of freedom papers and dissuaded

unmarried women from residing in the town of their choosing. Hunter, *Bound in Wedlock*, p. 105.
53. Hunter, *Bound in Wedlock*, p. 152.
54. Ibid., pp. 142–143.
55. James, *Seeking the Beloved Community*, p. 121, emphasis is in the original text.
56. Emancipation Proclamation, January 1, 1863; Presidential Proclamations, 1791–1991; Record Group 11; General Records of the United States Government; National Archives; U.S. Const. amend. XIII.
57. Maryland Act of February 6, 1879; Virginia Cohabitation Act of 1866.
58. James, *Seeking the Beloved Community*, p. 120.
59. In Northern states, Hunter writes, "Free people of color were questioned publicly and punished disproportionately for failure to provide proof of legal marriages, legitimacy of children, and legal residency as gradual laws increasingly manumitted slaves." This exemplifies a form of state punishment against single Black mothers, regardless of whether they were truly single, or simply left their marriage certificate at home. Hunter, *Bound in Wedlock*, p. 105.
60. This was not unique to Black people in this era. Jennifer Denetdale argues that "indigenous feminist and queer analysis demonstrates how the spaces of the domestic and intimate are also sites of colonial surveillance and control, thereby gendering settler colonialism." At the Bosque Redondo prison camp (1863–1868), "Navajo prisoners were subjected to American policies intended to transform them into the image of White American citizens... These efforts, now known as ethnic cleansing, coerced Navajos into conformity with American heterosexuality, in which patriarchy was privileged." Denetdale writes, "the processes of colonialism have meant the remaking of the Diné in the image of the white man, but without the full benefits and entitlements accorded white male citizens. The imposition of U.S. authority over the Diné not only included efforts to remake Navajo individuals into citizens who embrace heterosexual patriarchy; it also resulted in the creation of a Navajo Nation that was formed to privilege heterosexual patriarchy as normative." Jennifer Nez Denetdale, "Return to 'The Uprising at Beautiful Mountain in 1913': Marriage and Sexuality in the Making of the Modern Navajo Nation," in *Critically Sovereign: Indigenous Gender, Sexuality and Feminist Studies*, ed. Joanne Barker (North Carolina: Duke University Press, 2017), pp. 72, 75, 91.
61. Cott, *Public Vows*, p. 89.
62. Act of February 20, 1865, 1865 Mo. Laws 68 (concerning marital rights and children of colored persons); Clements, 42 Tex. at 223; Cumby, 25 S.W. at 677. *Williams v. Kimball*, 16 So. 783, 784–85 (Fla. 1895); *Allen v. Allen*, 71 Ky. (8 Bush) 490, 490–92 (Ky. 1871).
63. Act of March 9, 1866, 1866 Ga. Laws 240; Act of December 13, 1866, 1867 Ga. Laws 156; *Pascal v. Jones*, 41 Ga. 220, 221 (1870).
64. These states included Missouri, Maryland, Tennessee, North Carolina, South Carolina, Virginia, Texas, and Alabama. See Act of February 20, 1865, 1865 Mo. Laws 68; Karst, supra note 26; *Thomas v. Holtzman*, 18 D.C. (7 Mackey) 62, 67 (1888); Act of May 26, 1866, 1866 Tenn. Pub. Acts 65; TENN. CODE §§ 3303, 3304 (Milliken & Vertrees 1884); *Brown v. Cheatham*, 17 S.W. 1033, 1034 (Tenn. 1892); Act of February 27, 1879, 1879 N.C. Sess. Laws 136; *Spaugh v. Hartman*, 64 S.E. 198, 199 (N.C. 1909); *Tucker v. Tucker* 13 S.E. 5, 6 (N.C. 1891); *Jones v. Hoggard*, 12 S.E. 906, 906–07 (N.C. 1891); *Tucker v. Bellamy*, 4 S.E. 34, 35 (N.C. 1887); Act of December 21, 1865, 1866 S.C. Acts 291; Cohabitation Act of 1866, 1866 Va. Acts 85; TEX. CONST. of 1869, art. XII, § 27; TEX. REV. CIV. STAT. art. 1656 (1879); *Clements v. Crawford*, 42 Tex. 601, 603 (1874); *Hill v. Fairfax*, 38 Tex. 220, 222–23 (1873); *Cumby v. Garland*, 25 S.W. 673, 674 (Tex. Civ. App. 1894); *Stikes v. Swanson*, 44 Ala. 633, 635 (1870).

65. *Livingston v. Williams*, 13 S.W. 173, 173 (Tex. 1890).
66. Teri A. McMurtry-Chubb, "'Burn This Bitch Down!': Mike Brown, Emmett Till, and the Gendered Politics of Black Parenthood," *Nevada Law Journal*, Vol. 17 (2016): p. 626.
67. See *Comas v. Reddish*, 35 Ga. (1866) and *Timmins v. Lacy*, 30 Tex. (1867).
68. Hunter, *Bound in Wedlock*, p. 20.
69. Ibid., p. 20.
70. Cott, *Public Vows*, p. 93.
71. Montesquieu, Charles de Secondat, baron de, 1689–1755. *The Spirit of Laws* (London: Printed for J. Collingwood, 1823).
72. Hartman, *Lose Your Mother*, p. 133.
73. See R. A. Lenhardt, "Marriage as Black Citizenship?" 66 *Hastings Law Journal* 1317 (2015).
74. *Obergefell v. Hodges*, p. 12.
75. See Claudia Card, "Against Marriage and Motherhood," *Hypatia: A Journal of Feminist Philosophy*, August 1996. Card cites the coercive nature of the marital institution that may compel her to marry her partner against their personal preferences in order to access necessary benefits.
76. Harvey, *A Brief History of Neoliberalism*, p. 7.
77. June Carbone and Naomi Cahn, *Marriage Markets: How Inequality Is Remaking the American Family* (Oxford: Oxford University Press, 2014).
78. Carbone and Cahn define class as a social construct that is most often associated with one's income.
79. Carbone and Cahn, *Marriage Markets*, p. 22.
80. Daniel Patrick Moynihan and U.S. Department of Labor, *The Moynihan Report: The Negro Family—The Case for National Action* (New York: Cosimo Reports, 2018), pp. 29, 47.
81. Ibid., p. 29.
82. Ibid., p. 30.
83. Ibid., p. 47.
84. Ibid., p. 29.
85. Ibid., p. 48.
86. Linda M. Burton and M. Belinda Tucker, "Romantic Unions in an Era of Uncertainty: A Post-Moynihan Perspective on African American Women and Marriage," *The Annals of the American Academy of Political and Social Science*, Vol. 621 (January 2009), pp. 132–148; Serena Mayeri, "Historicizing the 'End of Men': The Politics of Reaction(s)," *Boston University Law Review*, Vol. 93 (2013): 729–744; Sara McLanahan, "Fragile Families and the Reproduction of Poverty," *The Annals of the American Academy of Political and Social Science*, Vol. 621 (January 2009), pp. 111–131.
87. Carbone and Cahn, *Marriage Markets*, p. 27.
88. Ibid., p. 27.
89. Richard Herrnstein and Charles Murray, *The Bell Curve: Intelligence and Class Structure in American Life* (New York: Simon & Schuster, 1996).
90. Betty Friedan, *The Feminine Mystique* (New York: Norton, 1963); Toni Morrison gives voice to the positive aspects of the financial contributions of Black mothers and wives to their households, in contradistinction to the specter of the emasculating Black matriarch heralded by Moynihan. See Morrison, "What the Black Woman Thinks about Women's Lib," *The New York Times Magazine*, August 22, 1971, p. 64.
91. *Obergefell v. Hodges*, p. 13.
92. Ibid., p. 16.
93. Ibid., p. 17.

94. Ibid., p. 16.
95. Marxist feminism contributed to the development of racial capitalism. See Michéle Barret, *Women's Oppression Today: The Marxist/Feminist Encounter* (London: Verso, 1980/2014).
96. Jodi Melamed, "Racial Capitalism," *Critical Ethnic Studies*, Vol. 1, No. 1 (Spring 2015): p. 77.
97. Jodi Melamed, *Represent and Destroy: Rationalizing Violence in the New Racial Capitalism* (Minneapolis: University of Minnesota Press, 2011), p. 140.
98. Ibid.
99. Melamed, "Racial Capitalism," p. 78. Melamed augments David Harvey's depiction of a "state-finance nexus" with a racial analysis provided by Chandan Reddy to put forward her notion of a state-finance-racial violence nexus. See David Harvey, *The Enigma of Capital: And the Crisis of Capitalism* (Oxford: Oxford University Press, 2010); Chandan Reddy, *Freedom with Violence: Race, Sexuality, and the U.S. State* (Durham: Duke University Press, 2011).
100. Melamed, "Racial Capitalism," p. 78.
101. *Obergefell v. Hodges*, p. 14. Emphasizing the importance of parenthood within the marital institution has a significant history within the fight for the legal recognition of same-sex marital unions. "LGBT advocates would ultimately emphasize the relationship between marriage and childrearing to support same-sex couples' claims to marriage—and Justice Kennedy made much of this childrearing aspect of marriage in *Windsor*." NeJaime, "Before Marriage," p. 169.
102. *Obergefell v. Hodges*, p. 15.
103. Ibid. Kennedy expressed this sentiment in *Windsor*, stating that "it humiliates tens of thousands of children now being raised by same-sex couples. The law in question makes it even more difficult for the children to understand the integrity and closeness of their own family and its concord with other families in their community and in their daily lives," *United States v. Windsor*, 570 *U.S.* 744 (2013), p. 23.
104. Huntington, "Obergefell's Conservatism," p. 23.
105. Ibid.
106. Huntington's account of social fronts is based on the work of sociologist Erving Goffman. See Erving Goffman, *The Presentation of Self in Everyday Life* (New York: Anchor, 1959). Faculty Scholarship at Penn Law, paper 1593 (2015): p. 1277.
107. Huntington, "Obergefell's Conservatism," p. 28.
108. Jodi Byrd, "*Loving* Unbecoming: The Queer Politics of the Transitive Native," in *Critically Sovereign: Indigenous Gender, Sexuality and Feminist Studies*, ed. Joanne Barker (North Carolina: Duke University Press, 2017), p. 208.
109. *Obergefell v. Hodges*, p. 16.
110. Murray, "Obergefell v. Hodges and Nonmarriage Inequality," p. 1244.
111. I will address the invisibility of nonnormative families in Chapter 3 with examination of *Moore v. City of East Cleveland* (1977).
112. See Dale Carpenter, *Flagrant Conduct: The Story of* Lawrence v. Texas (New York: W. W. Norton, 2012).
113. *Lawrence v. Texas*, 539 U.S. 558, 567 (2003). Murray notes that "in *Griswold v. Connecticut* (1965), the Court referenced marriage in similar terms." Murray, "Obergefell v. Hodges and Nonmarriage Inequality," p. 1228.
114. Cott, *Public Vows*.
115. Amy L. Brandzel, "Queering Citizenship? Same-Sex Marriage and the State," *GLQ*, Vol 11, No. 2 (2005): p. 177.
116. Ibid., p. 176.

117. Mignon Moore, "Marriage Equality and the African American Case: Intersections of Race and LGBT Sexuality," *Differences: A Journal of Feminist Cultural Studies*, Vol. 29, No. 2 (2018): p. 198.
118. In her sociological study, Siobhan Brooks also argues that "for lesbian and bisexual Black women, gay marriage does not represent state-sponsored benefits, but rather recognition in Black civil society." Her research subjects "use marriage as a vehicle for visibility and acceptance within their religious community." Siobhan Brooks, "Black on Black Love: Black Lesbian and Bisexual Women, Marriage, and Symbolic Meaning," *The Black Scholar*, Vol. 47, No. 4 (2017): pp. 33, 42.
119. Moore, "Marriage Equality and the African American Case," p. 202.

Chapter 3

1. To be sure, queer, Black scholar-activists have questioned the prioritization of legalizing same-sex marriage in light of the severe inequities facing Black LGBTQ+ communities. However, this questioning has not prompted scholarship or advocacy that calls for marital reform or abolishment.
2. Card, "Marriage and Motherhood," p. 6.
3. For instance, references to single motherhood are found within Hip Hop, including Tupac Shakur's "Dear Mama," Shawn Carter's (Jay-Z) "Blueprint (Momma Loves Me)" (2001), and Kanye West's "Hey Mama" (2005). See also Frazier, *The Negro Family in the United* States; McDonald and Cross-Barnett, *Marriage in Black*; Banks, *Is Marriage for White People?*; Patricia Hill Collins, *Black Feminist Thought* (New York: Routledge, 2000).
4. C. Riley Snorton, *Black on Both Sides: A Racial History of Trans Identity* (Minneapolis: University of Minnesota Press, 2017), p. 104.
5. Ibid.
6. Ibid., p. 107.
7. Linda Martín Alcoff, *Visible Identities: Race, Gender, and the Self* (New York: Oxford University Press, 2006), p. 126.
8. Hans-Georg Gadamer, *Truth and Method* (New York: Bloomsbury, 2013), p. 312.
9. Ibid., p. 313.
10. Alcoff, *Visible Identities*, p. 96.
11. Ibid., p. 114.
12. Ibid., p. 102.
13. Ibid., p. 113.
14. Ibid., p. 111.
15. Ibid., p. 113.
16. Ibid., p. 106.
17. Ibid., p. 111.
18. Ibid., p. 110.
19. Toni Morrison, *What Moves at the Margin: Selected Nonfiction* (Jackson: University of Mississippi, 2008), p. 70.
20. Ibid., p. 71.
21. Alcoff, *Visible Identities*, p. 110.
22. Kristie Dotson, "On Intellectual Diversity and Differences That May Not Make a Difference," *Ethics and Education*, Vol. 13, No. 1 (2018): p. 128.

23. Scott Lauria Morgensen, *Spaces Between Us: Queer Settler Colonialism and Indigenous Decolonization* (Minneapolis: University of Minnesota Press, 2011), p. 35. Morgensen encourages future scholarship that explores the "triangulated histories of Native peoples, African diasporic peoples, and white settlers in the United States" that links Saidiya V. Hartman's account of sexual terror of slavery "with the colonial education of desire under white settler colonialization of Native peoples." A longer exploration focused on the legacies of these historical relationships is beyond the scope of this particular project. Saidiya V. Hartman, *Scenes of Subjection: Terror, Slavery, and Self-Making in Nineteenth-Century America* (New York: Oxford University Press, 1997).
24. Denetdale, "Return to 'The Uprising at Beautiful Mountain in 1913,'" p. 85.
25. Ibid., p. 77.
26. Ibid., p. 76.
27. Ibid., p. 91.
28. Ibid., p. 90.
29. See Higginbotham, *Righteous Discontent*; Darlene Clark Hine, *Hine Sight: Black Women and the Re-Construction of American History* (Brooklyn: Carlson Publishing, 1994); Jenkins, *Private Lives, Proper Relations*.
30. Brittney C. Cooper, *Beyond Respectability: The Intellectual Thought of Race Women* (Urbana: University of Illinois Press, 2017), p. 15.
31. Curwood, *Stormy Weather*, p. 15.
32. Ibid.
33. Ibid., p. 23.
34. Ibid.
35. See *My Name Is Pauli Murray*, Betsy West and Julie Cohen, Directors (Amazon Studios, 2021); *Pauli*, National Public Radio podcast (North Carolina Public Radio, 2021).
36. Cooper, *Beyond Respectability*, p. 88. For an epistemological analysis, see Dotson, "Theorizing Jane Crow," pp. 417–430.
37. In contemporary queer culture, Pauli Murray's gender identity would most likely be considered as gender expansive or transgender, accompanied by an array of pronoun possibilities (e.g., she/they, he/they, they/them). However, I will use the pronouns that Murray selected for herself in this chapter.
38. See Doreen Marie Drury, "'Experimentation on the Male Side:' Race, Class, Gender, and Sexuality in Pauli Murray's Quest for Love and Identity, 1910-1960," Dissertation (Boston College: Department of History, 2000).
39. Rosalind Rosenberg, *Jane Crow: The Life of Pauli Murray* (New York: Oxford University Press, 2017), p. 127.
40. Cooper, *Beyond Respectability*, p. 106.
41. Rosenberg, *Jane Crow*, p. 172. Murray married William "Billy" Roy Wynn on November 30, 1930, under the duress of dire financial conditions when she was a student at Hunter College. They married in secret to avoid the loss of her YWCA. During this period, Murray admitted having negative feelings about sexual intimacy with men, and she left Wynn after one weekend. She was still legally married to Wynn at the time of the article's publication and sought an annulment in 1948. Their marriage was annulled in 1949.
42. Pauli Murray, "Why Negro Girls Stay Single," *Negro Digest*, Vol. 5, No. 9 (1947): p. 8. Murray addressed sexuality in a sermon years later.
43. Angela Davis, *Blues Legacies and Black Feminism* (New York: Random House, 1999), p. 333.
44. This dynamic is exemplified in popular culture through the music of Beyoncé Knowles. Her commercially successful album Lemonade (2016) chronicles the emotional consequences stemming from her husband's infidelity. The album ends

on a note of reconciliation between Mr. and Mrs. Shawn Carter, which serves to safeguard the image of the Black married maternal.
45. Davis, *Blues Legacies and Black Feminism*, p. 15.
46. Ibid., p. 201.
47. Ibid., p. 39.
48. Ibid., p. 238.
49. Ibid., p. 38.
50. Ibid., p. 44.
51. Ibid., p. 9.
52. See Sissy Blues (Thomas Dorsey). In this song, Ma Rainey sings, "Woke up and found my man in a sissy's arms ... My man's got a sissy, his name is Miss Kate/He shook that thing like jelly on a plate. Davis, *Blues Legacies and Black Feminism*, p. 243.
53. Cornel West, *Keeping Faith: Philosophy and Race in America* (New York: Routledge, 1993).
54. For instance, Anna Julia Cooper, Mary Church Terrell, Ida B. Wells, and Fannie Barrier Williams.
55. While oral traditions are not beholden to the written word, I contend that these traditions are as important to the phenomenological study of consciousness as Gadamer's hermeneutical study.
56. Gadamer, *Truth and Method*, p. 87.
57. Ibid.
58. Ibid., p. 88.
59. Ibid., p. 89.
60. Keeanga-Yamahtta Taylor, *From #BlackLivesMatter to Black Liberation* (Chicago: Haymarket Books, 2016), p. 103.
61. Ibid., p. 26.
62. Ibid., p. 47.
63. President Barack Obama continues to push this narrative through My Brother's Keeper and The Obama Foundation. See Derecka Purnell, "Why Does Obama Scold Black Boys?" *The New York Times*, February 23, 2019, https://www.nytimes.com/2019/02/23/opinion/my-brothers-keeper-obama.html. Purnell is critical of President Obama's remarks to an audience of young Black men at a My Brother's Keeper town hall. Noting his allusions to toxic masculinity, Purnell writes, "In the town hall, there was no black feminism, nothing that recognized the ordinary humanity of black girls and women; they were either on a pedestal or on the floor."
64. McMurty-Chubb, "'Burn This Bitch Down!.'"
65. https://www.cnn.com/2014/11/25/us/michael-brown-stepfather-video/index.html.
66. McMurty-Chubb, "'Burn This Bitch Down!,'" p. 644.
67. Ibid.
68. Ibid., p. 645.
69. https://www.washingtonpost.com/news/morning-mix/wp/2016/11/18/fla-loud-music-murder-firing-into-car-full-of-teens-playing-rap-music-not-self-defense-court-rules/.
70. Erica S. Lawson, "Bereaved Black Mothers and Maternal Activism in the Racial State," *Feminist Studies*, Vol. 44, No. 3 (2018): p. 730.
71. https://www.theatlantic.com/politics/archive/2014/02/i-am-still-called-by-the-god-i-serve-to-walk-this-out/284064/.
72. See Ariane Cruz, *The Color of Kink: Black Women, BDSM, and Pornography* (New York: New York University Press, 2016); Mireille Miller-Young, *A Taste for Brown Sugar: Black Women in* Pornography (Durham: Duke University Press, 2014); Jennifer C. Nash, *The Black Body in Ecstasy: Reading Race, Reading Pornography* (Durham: Duke University Press, 2014); Stallings, *Funk the Erotic*.

73. Cathy Cohen, "Deviance as Resistance: A New Research Agenda for the Study of Black Politics," *DuBois Review*, Vol. 1, No. 1 (2014): p. 29.
74. Ibid.
75. Ibid., p. 30.
76. Ibid.
77. Ibid., p. 33.
78. Ibid.
79. Ibid., p. 32.
80. Ibid., p. 117.
81. Ibid., p. 108.
82. L. H. Stallings, *Mutha' Is Half a Word: Intersections of Folklore, Vernacular Myth, and Queerness in Black Female Culture* (Columbus: The Ohio State University Press, 2007), p. 2.
83. Ibid.
84. Lewis R. Gordon, "Re-Imagining Liberations," *International Journal of Critical Diversity Studies*, Vol. 1, No. 1 (2018): p. 15.
85. Ibid.
86. Ibid.
87. Tommie Shelby, *Dark Ghettos: Injustice, Dissent, and Reform* (Cambridge: The Belknap Press of Harvard University Press, 2016), p. 5.
88. Ibid.
89. Ibid., p. 170.
90. Ibid., p. 125.
91. The pledges of support offered by American corporations and Congress have not yielded significant positive impact upon the lives of Black people. See https://www.washingtonpost.com/business/interactive/2021/george-floyd-corporate-america-racial-justice/ and https://www.washingtonpost.com/politics/immigration-reconciliation-democrats-agenda/2021/09/20/bee98da2-1a29-11ec-a99a-5fea2b2da34b_story.html.
92. Shatema Threadcraft, "Believe Black Women," *Political Theory*, Vol. 47, No. 4 (2019): p. 535.
93. Ibid.
94. Bailey and Shabazz, "Gender and Sexual Geographies of Blackness (Part 1)," p. 318.
95. Marlon M. Bailey, "Gender/Racial Realness: Theorizing the Gender System in Ballroom Culture," *Feminist Studies*, Vol. 37, No. 2 (2011): p. 366.
96. Shelby, *Dark Ghettos*, p. 123.
97. Christopher Lebron, "Race, Affect, and Contract," *Political Theory*, Vol. 47, No. 4 (2019): p. 548.
98. Shelby, *Dark Ghettos*, p. 139.
99. Ibid., p. 140.
100. Mink, *The Wages of Motherhood*. Roberts, *Killing the Black Body: Race, Reproduction, and the Meaning of Liberty* (New York: Pantheon Books, 1997).
101. Jael Silliman et al., *Undivided Rights: Women of Color Organize for Reproductive Justice* (Chicago: Haymarket Books, 2004).
102. Roberts, *Killing the Black Body*, p. 305.
103. Ibid.
104. Ibid., p. 295.
105. Ibid., p. 213. Roberts recounts an earlier instance of limiting excess based on the introduction of a bill into the 1958 Mississippi state legislature mandating the sterilization of any unmarried mothers who give birth to additional children. Mississippi state representative David H. Glass explicitly referenced the number of Black children born outside of the marital institution as justification for the

bill. Roberts states that this bill was a tactic to force unemployed Blacks on welfare to migrate to the north. The state legislature did not wish to bear the economic "burden" of supporting impoverished Black mothers and children.
106. Roberts, *Killing the Black Body*, p. 225.
107. Murray, "Obergefell v. Hodges and Nonmarriage Inequality."
108. *Moore v. City of East Cleveland* 431 U.S. 494 (1977).
109. Angela Onwuachi-Willig, "Extending the Normativity of the Extended Family: Reflections on Moore v. City of East Cleveland," *Fordham Law Review* 2655, Vol. 85 (2017): p. 2657.
110. *Moore v. City of East Cleveland*.
111. Ibid.
112. Ibid.
113. Ibid.
114. Ibid.
115. Ibid.
116. Ibid.
117. Ibid.
118. Onwuachi-Willig, "Extending the Normativity of the Extended Family," p. 2656.
119. Ibid., p. 2661.
120. Ibid., p. 2662.
121. Ibid., p. 2663.
122. Ibid.
123. Paul C. Taylor, "The Unjustly Disadvantaged: African American Life and Political Life (Review of Shelby's Dark Ghettos," *Black Perspectives blog*, African American Intellectual History Society), July 1, 2017.
124. David L. Eng, *The Feeling of Kinship: Queer Liberalism and the Racialization of Intimacy* (Durham: Duke University Press, 2010), p. 4.
125. Ibid.
126. Alcoff, *Visible Identities*, p. 113.
127. Lewis R. Gordon, "Phenomenology and Race," in *The Oxford Handbook of Philosophy and Race*, ed. Naomi Zack (New York: Oxford University Press, 2017), p. 2. See Gordon's *An Introduction to Africana Philosophy* for a more in-depth exploration of African philosophers' engagement with phenomenology.
128. Gordon, "Phenomenology and Race," p. 10.
129. Sara Ahmed, *Queer Phenomenology: Orientations, Objects, Others* (Durham: Duke University Press, 2006), p. 3.
130. Ibid., pp. 19–20.
131. Ibid., p. 161.
132. Ibid., p. 21.
133. José Esteban Muñoz, *Cruising Utopia: The Then and There of Queer Futurity* (New York: New York University Press, 2009), p. 1.
134. Ibid.

Chapter 4

1. Geraldine Pratt and Victoria Rosner, *The Global and the Intimate: Feminism in Our Time*, edited by Geraldine Pratt and Victoria Rosner (New York: Columbia University Press, 2012), p. 8.
2. Ibid., p. 3.
3. Ibid.

4. Ferguson, "A Question of Personhood," p. 3.
5. Ibid.
6. There are many feminist critiques of the marital institution, ranging from advocacy for its abolition to call for significant reform. Critics include, but are not limited to, the following, listed in chronological order of first publication: Mary Wollstonecraft, *A Vindication of the Rights of Woman* (London: Constable and Company, 1996 [1792]); John Stuart Mill, *On Liberty and the Subjection of Women* (Ware: Wordsworth, 1996 [1859 and 1869]); Emma Goldman, "Marriage and Love," *Anarchism and Other Essays* (Mineola: Dover Publications, 1969 [1910]); Simone de Beauvoir, *The Second Sex* (London: Vintage, 1997 [1949]); Friedan, *The Feminine Mystique*; Sheila Cronan, "Marriage," in *Radical Feminism*, ed. Anne Koedt, Ellen Levine, and Anita Rapone (New York: Times Books, 1973 [1970]); Shulamith Firestone, *The Dialectic of Sex* (London: The Women's Press, 1979); Marjorie M. Shultz, "Contractual Ordering of Marriage: A New Model for State Policy," *California Law Review*, Vol. 70, No. 204 (1982); Lenore J. Weitzman, *The Marriage Contract: Spouses, Lovers and the Law* (London: Free Press, 1983); Carole Pateman, *The Sexual Contract* (Cambridge: Polity Press, 1988); Paula L. Ettelbrick, "Since When Is Marriage a Path to Liberation," *We Are Everywhere: A Historical Sourcebook of Gay and Lesbian Politics*, ed. Mark Blasius and Shane Phelan (London: Routledge, 1997 [1989]); Susan Moller Okin, *Justice, Gender, and the Family* (New York: Basic Books, 1989); Martha Albertson Fineman, *The Neutered Mother, The Sexual Family, and Other Twentieth Century Tragedies* (London: Routledge, 1995); Card, "Against Marriage and Motherhood"; Jane Lewis, *The End of Marriage? Individualism and Intimate Relations* (Cheltenham: Edward Elgar, 2001); Janet C. Gornick, "Reconcilable Differences," *The American Prospect Online* (March 25, 2002), http://prospect.org/article/reconcilable-differences; Petra Boynton, "Abiding by The Rules: Instructing Women in Relationships," *Feminism & Psychology*, Vol. 13, No. 2 (2003); Virginia Braun, "Thanks to my Mother . . . A Personal Commentary on Heterosexual Marriage," *Feminism & Psychology*, Vol. 13, No. 4 (2003); Sarah-Jane Finlay and Victoria Clarke, '"A Marriage of Inconvenience?' Feminist Perspectives on Marriage," *Feminism & Psychology*, Vol. 13, No. 4 (2003); Merran Toerien and Andrew Williams, "In Knots: Dilemmas of a Feminist Couple Contemplating Marriage," *Feminism & Psychology*, Vol. 13, No. 1 (2003); Maria Bevacqua, "Feminist Theory and the Question of Lesbian and Gay Marriage," *Feminism & Psychology*, Vol. 14, No. 1 (2004); Anne Kingston, *The Meaning of Wife* (London: Piatkus, 2004); Martha Albertson Fineman, "The Meaning of Marriage," in *Marriage Proposals: Questioning a Legal Status*, ed. Anita Bernstein (New York: New York University Press, 2006); Nancy D. Polikoff, *Beyond (Straight and Gay) Marriage: Valuing All Families Under the Law* (Beacon Press, 2008); Brook J. Sadler, "Re-Thinking Civil Unions and Same-Sex Marriage," *The Monist*, Vol. 91, No. 3/4 (2008); Metz, *Untying the Knot*; Elizabeth Brake, *Minimizing Marriage: Marriage, Morality, and the Law* (Oxford: Oxford University Press, 2012).
7. Discourses centering on intimacy have been explored within queer, feminist, and anticolonial scholarship. See Elizabeth Bernstein, *Temporarily Yours: Intimacy, Authenticity, and the Commerce of Sex* (Chicago: University of Chicago Press, 2007); Anthony Giddens, *The Transformation of Intimacy: Sexuality, Love, and Eroticism in Modern Societies* (Stanford: Stanford University Press, 1992); Phil Hubbard, "Sex Zones: Intimacy, Citizenship, and Public Space," *Sexualities*, Vol. 4, No. 1 (February 2001): pp. 51–71; Mark B. Padilla, "Love and Globalization: Transformations of Intimacy in the Contemporary World," ed. Mark B. Padilla et al. (Nashville: Vanderbilt University Press, 2007); Ann Laura Stoler, ed., *Haunted by Empire: Geographies of Intimacy in North American History* (Durham: Duke University Press, 2006).

8. Elizabeth A. Povinelli, *Empire of Love: Toward a Theory of Intimacy, Genealogy, and Carnality* (Durham: Duke University Press, 2006), p. 13.
9. The appearance of female performers in minstrel shows was rare.
10. Eric Lott, *Love & Theft: Blackface Minstrelsy and the American Working Class* (New York: Oxford University Press, 2013), p. 141.
11. Ibid., p. 142. This performativity is also evident among white women writers. See Rachel Dolezal, a former instructor in Africana Studies at Eastern Washington University in Spokane, Washington (https://www.npr.org/sections/codeswitch/2015/06/12/413887930/making-sense-of-rachel-dolezal-the-alleged-white-woman-who-passed-as-Black). Jessica Krug, George Washington University professor of African and Latin Studies; Lauren Michele Jackson, "The Layered Deceptions of Jessica Krug, The Black-Studies Professor Who Hid that She Is White," *New Yorker*, September 12, 2020. Author Margaret Seltzer penned a widely acclaimed, yet fabricated, memoir in which she alleged having Indigenous ancestry and being raised by a Black foster mother (https://www.latimes.com/archives/la-xpm-2008-mar-04-me-author4-story.html).
12. Cott, *Public Vows*, p. 57.
13. The sexual violence perpetrated against enslaved Africans was neither exclusively heterosexual nor directed solely against enslaved women. See Thomas A. Foster, *Rethinking Rufus: Sexual Violations of Enslaved Men* (Athens: University of Georgia Press, 2019).
14. Cott, *Public Vows*, p. 61. Stephanie McCurry, *Masters of Small Worlds: Yeoman Households, Gender Relations, and the Political Culture of the Antebellum South Carolina Low Country* (New York: Oxford University Press, 1995); Stephanie McCurry, "The Two Faces of Republicanism: Gender and Proslavery Politics in Antebellum South Carolina," *The Journal of American History*, Vol. 78, No. 4 (March 1992): pp. 1245–1264.
15. Cott, *Public Vows*, p. 65.
16. Ann D. Gordon, "Stanton and the Right to Vote: On Account of Race or Sex," in *Elizabeth Cady Stanton, Feminist as Thinker: A Reader in Documents and Essays*, ed. Ellen Carol DuBois and Richard Cándida Smith (New York: New York University Press, 2007), pp. 111–127; Jen McDaneld, "White Suffragist Dis/Entitlement: The *Revolution* and the Rhetoric of Racism," *Legacy*, Vol. 30, No. 2 (2013): pp. 243–264.
17. Ann duCille, "Blacks of the Marrying Kind: Marriage Rites and the Right to Marry in the Time of Slavery," *Differences: A Journal of Feminist Cultural Studies*, Vol. 29, No. 2 (2018): p. 29.
18. Stephanie E. Jones-Rogers, *They Were Her Property: White Women as Slave Owners in the American South* (New Haven: Yale University Press, 2019), p. xv.
19. Ibid., p. xiii.
20. Ibid.
21. Ibid., p. xvii.
22. Ibid.
23. Elizabeth McRae, *Mothers of Massive Resistance: White Women and the Politics of White Supremacy* (New York: Oxford University Press, 2018), p. 5.
24. Ibid.
25. Ibid., p. 8.
26. The Virginia Racial Integrity Act of 1924 states, "4. No marriage license shall be granted until the clerk or deputy clerk has reasonable assurance that the statements as to color of both man and woman are correct. If there is reasonable cause to disbelieve that applicants are of pure white race, when that fact is stated, the clerk or deputy clerk shall withhold the granting of the license until satisfactory proof is produced that both applicants are 'white persons' as provided for in this act. The clerk or deputy clerk shall use the same care to assure himself that both applicants

are colored, when that fact is claimed. 5. It shall hereafter be unlawful for any white person in this State to marry any save a white person, or a person with no other admixture of blood than white and American Indian. For the purpose of this act, the term 'white person' shall apply only to the person who has no trace whatsoever of any blood other than Caucasian; but persons who have one-sixteenth or less of the blood of the American Indian and have no other non-Caucasic blood shall be deemed to be white persons. All laws heretofore passed and now in effect regarding the intermarriage of white and colored persons shall apply to marriages prohibited by this act," http://www2.vcdh.virginia.edu/lewisandclark/students/projects/monacans/Contemporary_Monacans/racial.html, accessed on July 18, 2023.

27. McRae, *Mothers of Massive Resistance*, p. 5.
28. Ibid., p. 9. A century later, this work continues, as evidenced by the wave of white supremacist political activity within national school boards, to include book bans and curricular changes. Odette Yousef, "Moms for Liberty among Conservative Groups Named 'Extremist' by Civil Rights Watchdog," National Public Radio, June 7, 2023; Samanth R. Foran, "Parents' Rights or Parents' Wrongs?: The Political Weaponization of Parental Rights to Control Public Education, *Wisconsin Law Review*, Vol. 1513 (2022): pp. 1514–1547.
29. Toni Morrison, *Playing in the Dark: Whiteness and the Literary Imagination* (New York: Vintage Books, 1992), p. 6.
30. Ibid., p. 11.
31. Ibid., p. 12.
32. Pateman, *The Sexual Contract*, p. 221, emphasis in original. Charles Mills furthers Pateman's engagement with contract theory in *The Racial Contract*, in which he argues that whiteness is interwoven in the original contract alongside the sexual contract. However, in both iterations of the original contract offered by Mills and Pateman, the anti-Black racism of white women is lost. The appearance of white female absolution is maintained from Pateman's *Sexual Contract* to her cowritten work with Mills, *Contract and Domination*. In *Contract and Domination*, she does not assume the position of Black women as evident in the *Sexual Contract*. Rather, when asked to confront the implications of white supremacy in the context of contract, Pateman evades the whiteness of her womanhood. She writes, "my discussion here is not about racism. My interest is in the development of the idea of race as part of the structure of a modern state." Carole Pateman and Charles Mills, *Contract and Domination* (Cambridge: Polity Press, 2007), p. 135, Kindle Edition. Charles Mills, *The Racial Contract* (Ithaca: Cornell University Press, 1997).
33. References to a false equivalency between white wives and Black slaves is not exclusive to female critics of the marital institution. John Stuart Mill, for example, made this comparison in *The Subjection of Women*, published in 1869. He writes, "no slave is a slave to the same lengths, and in so full a sense of the word, as a wife is . . . 'Uncle Tom' under his first master had his own life in his 'cabin,' almost as much as any man whose work takes him away from home, is able to have in his own family. But it cannot be so with the wife." John Stuart Mill, *The Subjection of Women* (State College: The Pennsylvania State University, 2006), p. 37. He states further, "now that negro slavery has been abolished . . . Marriage is the only actual bondage known to our law. There remain no legal slaves, except the mistress of every house," Mill, *The Subjection of Women*, p. 89. A sustained examination of the racial implications within the theoretical contributions of men to marriage abolition and reform offers a fruitful line of future inquiry. My focus, however, lies within my curiosity about how the marital regime sustains impediments to platonic intimacies between Black and white women.
34. Pateman, *The Sexual Contract*, p. 118.
35. Ibid., p. 60.

36. Ibid., p. 121.
37. Ibid.
38. Ibid., p. 64; Orlando Patterson Slavery and Social Death: A Comparative Study (Cambridge, Harvard University Press, 1982).
39. David Eltis and David Richardson, eds., "Trans-Atlantic Slave Trade Database," https://www.slavevoyages.org/voyage/database.
40. Pateman, *The Sexual Contract*, p. 122.
41. Ibid., p. 124.
42. Beverly Guy-Sheftall, ed., *Words of Fire: An Anthology of African-American Feminist Thought* (New York: The New Press, 1995).
43. Ann Petry, "What's Wrong with Negro Men," *Negro Digest* (March 1947), p. 4.
44. Gwendolyn Brooks, "Why Negro Women Leave Home," *Negro Digest* (March 1951), p. 27.
45. This erasure coexists with Black Women's hypervisibility such that the very inclusion of Black women in their texts serves to make them disappear. Evelynn M. Hammonds, "Toward a Genealogy of Black Female Sexuality: The Problematic of Silence," in *Feminist Genealogies, Colonial Legacies, Democratic Futures*, ed. M. Jacqui Alexander and Chandra Talpade Mohanty (New York: Routledge, 1996); Settles, Buchanan, and Dotson, "Scrutinized but Not Recognized," pp. 62–74.
46. Card, "Against Marriage and Motherhood," p. 2. Throughout my discussion of Card's article, I will use the terms she employs, namely "lesbian" and "gay," in lieu of the more expansive terminology used today.
47. She cites Nel Noddings, *Caring: A Feminine Approach to Ethics and Moral Education* (Berkeley: University of California Press, 1984); Sara Ruddick, *Maternal Thinking: Toward a Politics of Peace* (Boston: Beacon Press, 1989); Virginia Held, *Feminist Morality: Transforming Culture, Society, and Politics* (Chicago: University of Chicago Press, 1993); and Annette C. Baier, *Moral Prejudices: Essays on Ethics* (Cambridge: Harvard University Press, 1994).
48. Card, "Against Marriage and Motherhood," p. 3.
49. Ibid., p. 5.
50. Chandan Reddy, "Race and the Critique of Marriage," *South Atlantic Quarterly*, Vol. 115, No. 2 (2016): pp. 424–432; Meg Wesling, "The Unequal Promise of Marriage Equality," *American Quarterly*, Vol. 66, No. 1 (March 2014): pp. 171–179.
51. Card, "Against Marriage and Motherhood," p. 11.
52. Ibid.
53. Ibid.
54. Ibid.
55. Julie Melin, "Desperate Choices: Why Black Women Join the U.S. Military at Higher Rates than Men and All Other Racial and Ethnic Groups," *New England Journal of Public Policy*, Vol. 28, No. 2 (2016); Wendy M. Christensen, "The Black Citizen-Subject: Black Single Mothers in US Military Recruitment Material, *Ethnic and Racial Studies*, Vol. 39, No. 14 (2016); Kimberley L. Phillips, *War! What Is It Good For?: Black Freedom Struggles and the U.S. Military From World War II to Iraq* (Chapel Hill: The University of North Carolina Press, 2012).
56. Card, "Against Marriage and Motherhood," p. 6.
57. Ibid., p. 9.
58. Taylor, "Silence and Sympathy," p. 230. For more on "whitely" perspectives, see Marilyn Frye, "White Woman Feminist," in *Moral Issues in Global Perspective Volume 2: Human Diversity and Equality*, ed. Christine Koggel (Ontario: Broadview Press, 2006).
59. Card, "Against Marriage and Motherhood," p. 16.
60. Ibid.
61. Ibid., p. 17.

62. Cheshire Calhoun, *Feminism, The Family, and the Politics of the Closet: Lesbian and Gay Displacement* (New York: Oxford University Press, 2000), p. 76.
63. Ibid., p. 1.
64. Ibid., p. 11.
65. Ibid., p. 4, emphasis in original.
66. Ibid.
67. Written in 2000, Calhoun's research ignores the abundance of queer Black feminist scholarship available at the time. This includes Combahee River Collective, "The Combahee River Collective Statement (1974)," in *How We Get Free: Black Feminism and the Combahee River Collective*, ed. Keeanga-Yamahtta Taylor (Chicago: Haymarket Books, 2017); Audre Lorde, *Sister Outsider* (Freedom: The Crossing Press, 1984); Cathy J. Cohen, "Punks, Bulldaggers, and Welfare Queens: The Radical Potential of Queer Politics?" *GLQ*, Vol. 3 (1997).
68. Charles Lemert and Esme Bhan, eds., *The Voice of Anna Julia Cooper* (Lanham: Rowman and Littlefield, 1998), p. 112. In his introduction, Lemert states that Cooper's text was "the first *systematic* working out of the insistence that no one social category can capture the reality of the colored woman." Lemert and Bhan, eds., *The Voice of Anna Julia Cooper*, p. 14.
69. Elizabeth Alexander writes that Cooper understands experience to be "crucial to the theorization of a race- and gender-based critique of America . . . Anna Julia Cooper posits an African-American woman's lived experience as evidentiary, just as are the written words of the many white male writers with whom she engages in *A Voice*," Elizabeth Alexander, "'We Must Be about Our Father's Business': Anna Julia Cooper and the Incorporation of the Nineteenth-Century African-American Woman Intellectual," *Signs*, Vol. 20, No. 2 (1995): p. 343.
70. Lemert and Bhan, eds., *The Voice of Anna Julia Cooper*, p. 95.
71. Patricia Hill Collins, *Black Feminist Thought: Knowledge, Consciousness, and the Politics of Empowerment* (New York: Routledge Classics, 2009), p. 76.
72. Ibid.
73. Ibid.
74. Ibid., p. 77.
75. Calhoun, *Feminism, The Family, and the Politics of the Closet*, p. 11.
76. Ibid.
77. I would like to thank one of the readers of this manuscript for encouraging me to clarify my critique of Calhoun.
78. Micki McElya, *Clinging to Mammy: The Faithful Slave in Twentieth-Century America* (Cambridge: Harvard University Press, 2007); Kimberly Wallace-Sanders, *Mammy: A Century of Race, Gender, and Southern Memory* (Ann Arbor: University of Michigan Press, 2008); and Charlotte Hawkins Brown, Mammy: An Appeal to the Heart of the South (Boston: Pilgrim, 1919).
79. Stedman, Charles Manly, 1841–1930, A Monument in Commemoration of the Faithful Colored Mammies of the South: Speech of Hon. Charles M. Stedman of North Carolina on H.R. 13672 in the House of Representatives, January 9, 1923. Washington: G.P.O., 1923.
80. See https://www.nytimes.com/2020/02/06/opinion/sunday/confederate-monuments-mammy.html.
81. Raquel Kennon, "Subtle Resistance: On Sugar and the Mammy Figure in Kara Walker's A Subtlety and Sherley Anne Williams's Dessa Rose," *African American Review*, Vol. 52, No. 2 (Summer 2019): p. 144.
82. Ibid.
83. McElya, *Clinging to Mammy*, p. 7.
84. Ibid.
85. Ibid.

86. Ibid., p. 9.
87. Ibid, p. 8.
88. Ibid, p. 10.
89. Ibid, p. 3.
90. Ibid.
91. Kennon cites the many Black artists who sought "to reclaim, repurpose, or radicalize Mammy . . . in the intervening decades between 1923 and 2014, a rich archive of artistic production flourishes, most notably during the Black Arts Movement." Kennon, "Subtle Resistance," p. 144.
92. It was not until 2020 and 2021, respectively, that the mammy images of Mrs. Butterworth and Aunt Jemima featured on breakfast goods were removed. See https://www.nytimes.com/2020/06/17/business/aunt-jemima-mrs-butterworth-uncle-ben.html.
93. Calhoun, *Feminism, The Family, and the Politics of the Closet*, p. 76, emphasis in original.
94. Ibid.
95. Ibid, p. 76.
96. Ibid, p. 77.
97. Ibid, p. 106.
98. Ibid, p. 79.
99. Ibid, p. 80.
100. Lord, *Sister Outsider*, p. 138.
101. Ibid.
102. Cohen, "Punks, Bulldaggers, and Welfare Queens," p. 453.
103. Paul Hemez and Chanell Washington, "Children of Same-Sex Parents More Likely to Be Adopted Than Those Living with a Parent in an Opposite-Sex Relationship," United States Census Bureau, July 13, 2022, https://www.census.gov/library/stories/2022/07/most-kids-with-parent-in-same-sex-relationship-live-with-female-couple.html.
104. Ibid.
105. https://williamsinstitute.law.ucla.edu/publications/Black-lgbt-adults-in-the-us/.
106. M. V. L. Badgett et al., eds., *LGBT Poverty in the United States: A Study of Differences Between Sexual Orientation and Gender Identity Groups* (Los Angeles, CA: The Williams Institute, October 2019).
107. Calhoun, *Feminism, The Family, and the Politics of the Closet*, p. 123.
108. Ibid., p. 129.
109. Ibid.
110. Ibid., p. 139.
111. Ibid.
112. Ibid., p. 160.
113. Paget Henry, "Whiteness and Africana Phenomenology," in *What White Looks Like*, ed. George Yancy (New York: Routledge, 2004), p. 196.
114. Ibid.
115. Ibid.
116. Ibid.
117. Brake, *Minimizing Marriage*, pp. 88–89.
118. Ibid., p. 156. The phrase "minimal marriage" is a nod to Robert Nozick's minimal state. Robert Nozick, *Anarchy, State, and Utopia* (New York: Basic Books, 1974).
119. Brake, *Minimizing Marriage*, p. 165.
120. Ibid.
121. Charles W. Mills, *Black Rights, White Wrongs: The Critique of Racial Liberalism* (New York: Oxford University Press, 2017), p. 34.
122. Ibid.

123. This peril is evident in the activist efforts of the UndocuBlack network, which addresses the needs of currently and formerly undocumented Black people.
124. Clare Chambers, *Against Marriage: An Egalitarian Defence of the Marriage-Free State* (Oxford: Oxford University Press, 2017), p. 2.
125. Ibid., p. 7.
126. José Medina, *The Epistemology of Resistance: Gender and Racial Oppression, Epistemic Injustice, and Resistant Imaginations* (New York: Oxford University Press, 2013), p. 256.
127. Ibid., p. 252.

Chapter 5

1. See Chapter 2 for detailed treatment of *partus ventrem sequitur* and chattel slavery.
2. Kelley, *Freedom Dreams*, p. 12.
3. Frantz Fanon, *Black Skin, White Masks* (New York: Grove Press, 1967), p. 41.
4. Ibid., p. 43.
5. Fanon observes that any interested individual "can amass references and quotations to prove that 'color prejudice' is indeed an imbecility and an iniquity that must be eliminated." Fanon, *Black Skin, White Masks*, p. 29.
6. Fanon, *Black Skin, White Masks*, p. 9.
7. See Chapter 1 for a more detailed explication of ballroom's queer origins.
8. W. E. B. DuBois, *Black Reconstruction in America* (New York: Harcourt, Brace and Company, 1935).
9. Angela Davis, "From the Prison of Slavery to the Slavery of Prison: Frederick Douglass and the Convict Lease System," in *The Angela Y. Davis Reader*, ed. Joy James (Malden, MA: Blackwell Publishers, 1998), pp. 74–95.
10. Jeffrey Paris, "Abolition Democracy and the Ultimate Carceral Threat," *Radical Philosophy Today*, Vol. 5 (2007): p. 238.
11. Michelle Alexander, *The New Jim Crow: Mass Incarceration in the Age of Colorblindness* (New York: The New Press, 2010); Ritchie, *Invisible No More*; Joy James, ed., *The New Abolitionists: (Neo)slave Narratives and Contemporary Prison Writings* (Albany: State University of New York Press, 2005).
12. Beth E. Richie, "Reimagining the Movement to End Gender Violence: Antiracism, Prison Abolition, Women of Color Feminisms, and Other Radical Visions of Justice (Transcript)," *University of Miami Race & Social Justice Law Review* 257, Vol. 5, No. 2 (2015): p. 264.
13. Angela Davis et al., *Abolition. Feminism. Now* (Chicago: Haymarket Books, 2022), p. 82. In solidarity with the sentiments expressed by the coauthors, my articulation of *throwing marital shade* is "unthinkable without feminism" just as "feminism is unimaginable" without abolition (p. 168).
14. For instance, see Ahmed, *Queer Phenomenology*; Bailey and Shabazz, "Gender and Sexual Geographies of Blackness (Part 2)," pp. 449–452; Cohen, "Punks, Bulldaggers, and Welfare Queens," pp. 437–465; Kara Keeling, *Queer Times, Black Futures* (New York: New York University Press, 2019).
15. Comedic outlets have served as a consistent site of refuge for Black people seeking temporary relief from stress owing to anti-Black racism. This refuge has been corrupted by the comedic star Dave Chappelle, who has launched sustained attacks upon the transgender community in his stand-up routines. While his remarks have been met with severe criticism from LGBTQ+ communities, he has also garnered significant support within Black communities. Julian Mark, "Dave

Chappelle Told His Audience He Has Been Canceled. A Transgender Activist Says He Continues 'Mocking Us,'" *The Washington Post*, October 26, 2021. https://www.washingtonpost.com/nation/2021/10/26/chappelle-response-transgender-criticism-video/.
16. Alexis Pauline Gumbs, "'We Can Learn to Mother Ourselves:' A Dialogically Produced Audience and Black Feminist Publishing 1979 to the 'Present,'" *Gender Forum: An Internet Journal for Gender Studies* No. 22 (2008): p. 40.
17. Ibid., p. 42.
18. *Obergefell v. Hodges*, 135 S. Ct. 2584 (2015), p. 14.
19. Ibid., p. 15. Justice Anthony Kennedy expressed this sentiment in Windsor, stating "it humiliates tens of thousands of children now being raised by same-sex couples. The law in question makes it even more difficult for the children to understand the integrity and closeness of their own family and its concord with other families in their community and in their daily lives." *United States v. Windsor*, 570 U.S. 744 (2013), p. 23.
20. Grace Kyungwon Hong, *Death beyond Disavowal: The Impossible Politics of Difference* (Minneapolis University of Minnesota Press, 2015), p. 98.
21. See Chapters 2 and 3 for further discussion.
22. https://www.cnn.com/2021/03/11/politics/stacey-plaskett-responds-house-gop-black-lives-matter-cnntv/index.html.
23. https://www.cnn.com/2021/03/11/politics/stacey-plaskett-responds-house-gop-black-lives-matter-cnntv/index.html.
24. Jayden Donahue and Miss Major Griffin-Gracy, "Making It Happen, Mama: A Conversation with Miss Major," in *Captive Genders: Trans Embodiment and the Prison Industrial Complex*, second edition, ed. Eric A. Stanley and Nat Smith (Oakland: AK Press, 2015), p. 311.
25. Kaila Adia Story, "On the Cusp of Deviance: Respectability Politics and the Cultural Marketplace of Sameness," in *No Tea, No Shade*, ed. E. Patrick Johnson (Durham: Duke University Press, 2018), p. 364.
26. "Dobbs v. Jackson Women's Health Organization," (2022).
27. Ibid., p. 3.
28. The Respect for Marriage Act was signed into law in December 2022.
29. Amy L. Brandzel, "Queering Citizenship? Same-Sex Marriage and the State," *GLQ: A Journal of Lesbian and Gay Studies*, Vol. 11, No. 2 (2005): p. 198.
30. Ibid.
31. Ibid.
32. Eng, *The Feeling of Kinship*, p. 10.
33. Ibid.
34. See Chapter 2 for further discussion on the porous aspects of the public and private spheres in relation to single Black motherhood.
35. Davis et al., *Abolition. Feminism. Now.*, p. 70.
36. The cumulative effect of the privileging of marital unions is captured in the Pew Research Center's 2021 analysis of census data pertaining to partnered and unpartnered adults. According to the Pew Research Center, "Unpartnered adults have lower earnings, on average, than partnered adults and are less likely to be employed or economically independent. They also have lower educational attainment and are more likely to live with their parents. Other research suggests that married and cohabiting adults fare better than those who are unpartnered when it comes to some health outcomes ... Cohabiting adults tend to fare better than unpartnered adults, and married adults fare better still." Pew Research Center, "Rising Share of U.S. Adults Are Living Without a Spouse or Partner.".
37. Understanding Federal Estate and Gift Taxes, Congressional Budget Office, June 2021. https://www.cbo.gov/publication/57272.

38. Topic No. 701, Sale of Your Home, https://www.irs.gov/taxtopics/tc701.
39. These barriers are discussed at length in Chapter 2.
40. See Chapter 3 for discussion of *Moore v. East Cleveland* (1977). See https://www.washingtonpost.com/magazine/interactive/2022/family-zoning-moore-city-east-cleveland/ for contemporary treatment of zoning ordinances.
41. Eng, *The Feeling of Kinship*, p. 10.
42. Ibid.
43. I discuss the analogous relationship between the marital institution and the conception of citizenship referenced during the founding of the United States in Chapter 2.
44. This particular form of racialized violence was captured in the poignant essay by poet Caroline Randall Williams entitled "You Want a Confederate Monument? My Body Is a Confederate Monument," https://www.nytimes.com/2020/06/26/opinion/confederate-monuments-racism.html.
45. Hortense Spillers and Ann Ducille, "Expostulations and Replies," *Differences: A Journal of Feminist Cultural Studies*, Vol. 29, No. 2 (2018): pp. 7–8.
46. Ibid., p. 7.
47. Ibid.
48. Ibid.
49. Ibid., p. 8.
50. Eve Tuck and K. Wayne Yang, "Decolonization Is not a Metaphor," *Decolonization: Indigeneity, Education & Society*, Vol. 1, No. 1 (2012): pp. 1–40.
51. Lewis R. Gordon, "Decolonizing Philosophy," *The Southern Journal of Philosophy*, Vol. 57, Spindel Supplement (2019): pp. 16–36.
52. Ibid., p. 25.
53. Nelson Maldonado-Torres, "The Decolonial Turn," in *New Approaches to Latin American Studies*, ed. Juan Poblete (New York: Routledge, 2017), p. 111. Mignolo and Walsh note that "Coloniality is constitutive, not derivative, of modernity. That is to say, there is no modernity without coloniality, thus the compound expression: modernity/coloniality . . . the colonial matrix of power was constituted, managed, and transformed from its historical foundation in the sixteenth century to the present." See W. D. Mignolo and C. E. Walsh, *On Decoloniality: Concepts, Analytics, Praxis* (Durham: Duke University Press, 2018), p. 4.
54. Mignolo and Walsh, *On Decoloniality*, p. 4.
55. Cohen, "Deviance as Resistance," pp. 27–45.
56. This phrase is a nod to Krista Benson's call for "decolonial prison abolitionist praxis." Krista L. Benson, "Carrying Stories of Incarcerated Indigenous Women as Tools for Prison Abolition," *Frontiers: A Journal of Women Studies*, Vol. 41, No. 2 (2020): pp. 143–167.
57. Mignolo and Walsh, *On Decoloniality*, p. 17.
58. Ibid.
59. Donahue and Griffin-Gracy, "Making It Happen, Mama," p. 311.
60. Maldonado-Torres, "The Decolonial Turn," p. 112.
61. Ibid.
62. Jennifer Nez Denetdale, "Return to 'The Uprising at Beautiful Mountain in 1913:' Marriage and Sexuality in the Making of the Modern Navajo Nation," in *Critically Sovereign: Indigenous Gender, Sexuality, and Feminist Studies*, ed. Joanne Barker (Durham: Duke University Press, 2017), p. 92. Attitudes and policies regarding sexual orientation and same-sex marriage with Native American nations are not monolithic. See Steven J. Alagna, "Why Obergefell Should Not Impact American Indian Tribal Marriage Laws," *Washington University Law Review*, Vol. 93, No. 6 (2016): pp. 1577–1612; Ann E. Tweedy, "Tribal Laws & Same-Sex Marriage: Theory, Process, and Content," *Columbia Human Rights Law*

Review, Vol. 46, No. 3 (Spring 2015): pp. 104–162; M. Alexander Pearl and Kyle Velte, "Indigenizing Equality," *Yale Law & Policy Review*, Vol. 35, No. 2 (Spring 2017): pp. 461–498.
63. Gordon, "Decolonizing Philosophy," p. 25.
64. Ibid.
65. Ahmed, *Queer Phenomenology*; Keeling, *Queer Times*.
66. Lyndon K. Gill, "In the Realm of Our Lorde: Eros and the Poet Philosopher," *Feminist Studies*, Vol. 40, No. 1 (2014): p. 173.
67. Ibid.
68. Tiffany Lethabo King, *The Black Shoals: Offshore Formations of Black and Native Studies* (Durham: Duke University Press, 2019).
69. Amadahy and Lawrence, "Indigenous Peoples and Black People in Canada," p. 107.
70. Byrd, "Weather with You," p. 213.
71. Harris, "Of Blackness and Indigeneity," p. 223. Harris is drawing upon the analysis of Aileen Moreton-Robinson, *The White Possessive: Property, Power and Indigenous Sovereignty* (Minneapolis: University of Minnesota Press, 2015).
72. Harris, "Of Blackness and Indigeneity," p. 223.
73. See Chapter 3 for a discussion of *Moore v. East Cleveland*, which demonstrates the cost of violating this normative principle concerning property and family.
74. Jodi A. Byrd, "Follow the Typical Signs: Settler Sovereignty and its Discontents," *Settler Colonial Studies*, Vol. 4, No. 2 (2014): p. 153.
75. Kristie Dotson, "On the Way to Decolonization in a Settler Colony: Re-introducing Black Feminist Identity Politics," *Alternative: An International Journal of Indigenous Peoples*, Vol. 14, No. 3 (2018): p. 2.
76. Ibid., p. 1.
77. Katherine McKittrick offers significant insight into the relationship between geographies of domination and Black women's geographies. For McKittrick, Toni Morrison's site of memory provides "a way to reaffirm contemporary geopolitical possibilities." McKittrick declares that "the site of memory displays and utters new sites of being, and a different sense of place," which reveal that "there are new histories, and new memories, and new historical geographies we can engage with, now." Katherine McKittrick, *Demonic Grounds: Black women and the Cartographies of Struggle* (Minneapolis: University of Minnesota Press, 2006), p. 33. Retrieved from http://ebookcentral.proquest.com.
78. King et al., "Beyond Incommensurability toward an Otherwise Stance on Black and Indigenous Relationality," p. 8.
79. Ibid.
80. These two approaches are evident in both Elizabeth Brake's argument for marriage reform and Tommie Shelby's depiction of the political ethics of the oppressed as untheorized. Brake, *Minimizing Marriage*; Shelby, *Dark Ghettos*.
81. Mignolo and Walsh, *On Decoloniality*, p. 7.
82. Ibid.
83. Quashie observes that Black studies serves to "expose the human ... as a category and method of analysis that reveals much about the structures of the modern world." Kevin Quashie, *Black Aliveness, or a Poetics of Being* (Durham: Duke University Press, 2021), p. 16. See also Gordon, *An Introduction to Africana Philosophy*.
84. Leanne Betasamosake Simpson, "Land as Pedagogy: Nishnaabeg Intelligence and Rebellious Transformation," *Decolonization: Indigeneity, Education & Society*, Vol. 3, No. 3 (2014): p. 16.
85. Ibid., p. 8.
86. McKittrick, *Demonic Grounds*, p. x. Retrieved from http://ebookcentral.proquest.com.

87. Ibid.
88. Dotson, "On the Way to Decolonization in a Settler Colony."
89. McKittrick, *Demonic Grounds*.
90. Ibid., p. xi. Retrieved from http://ebookcentral.proquest.com.
91. Ibid.
92. Ibid., p. xix. Retrieved from http://ebookcentral.proquest.com.
93. Ibid, p. 5. Retrieved from http://ebookcentral.proquest.com.
94. Quashie, *Black Aliveness*, p. 5.
95. Ibid.
96. Ibid., p. 11.
97. C. Riley Snorton, *Black on Both Sides: A Racial History of Trans Identity* (Minneapolis: University of Minnesota Press, 2017), p. 104.
98. Gordon, "Phenomenology and Race," p. 300.
99. Ibid.
100. Ibid.
101. Ibid.
102. James Baldwin, *The Fire Next Time* (New York: The Dial Press, 1963), p. 112.
103. Ibid.
104. Audre Lorde, *Sister Outsider* (Freedom: The Crossing Press, 1984), p. 101.
105. Ibid., p. 146.
106. Donahue and Griffin-Gracy, "Making It Happen, Mama," p. 311. This specific terror is evidenced in the statistics chronicling the murder of Black trans women. C Mandler, "Murders of trans people nearly doubled over past 4 years, and Black trans women are most at risk, report finds," CBS News, October 13, 2022. https://www.cbsnews.com/news/transgender-community-murder-rates-everytown-for-gun-safety-report/.
107. Lorde, *Sister Outsider* (Freedom: The Crossing Press, 1984), p. 36.
108. Ibid., p. 38.
109. Ahmed, *Queer Phenomenology*, p. 19.
110. Keeling, *Queer Times*.
111. Kara Keeling, "Looking for M—Queer Temporality, Black Political Possibility, and Poetry from the Future," *GLQ: A Journal of Lesbian and Gay Studies*, Vol. 15, No. 4 (2009): pp. 566–567.
112. Ibid., p. 565. Keeling draws upon Frantz Fanon's exploration of temporality, colonization, and liberation in *Black Skin, White Masks*, with specific reference to his quotation of Karl Marx from *The Eighteenth Brumaire of Louis Bonaparte*, in which Marx references poetry from the future. Fanon, *Black Skin*.
113. Keeling, "Looking for M," pp. 566–567. According to Keeling, Marx's phrase "poetry from the future" serves as a marker for "just such an impossible possibility"; Keeling, "Looking for M," p. 567.
114. Lorde, *Sister Outsider*, p. 37.
115. Ibid.
116. Ibid., p. 101. Lest we unfairly criticize her for biological reductionism, we must acknowledge that for Lorde the poeticism of the Black maternal "exists in every one of us." The "Black mother who is the poet" exceeds not only contrived binaries of sex and gender but also racialization.
117. E. Patrick Johnson, "A Revelatory Distillation of Experience," *WSQ: Women's Studies Quarterly*, Vol. 40, No. 3 and 4 (Fall/Winter 2012), p. 311.
118. Quashie, *Black Aliveness*, p. 22.
119. Lorde, *Sister Outsider*, p. 38.
120. Ibid.
121. Ibid.
122. Ibid., p. 39.

123. Ibid., p. 100.
124. Ibid., p. 36.
125. Inspired from the "Dharma of Audre Lorde and James Baldwin course taught by Dr. Rima Fled, Barre Center for Buddhist Studies, Summer 2021."
126. Roderick A. Ferguson, "Of Sensual Matters: On Audre Lorde's 'Poetry Is Not a Luxury' and 'Uses of the Erotic,'" *WSQ: Women's Studies Quarterly*, Vol. 40, No. 3 and 4 (Fall/Winter 2012): p. 296.
127. Lorde, *Sister Outsider*, p. 39.

Index

For the benefit of digital users, indexed terms that span two pages (e.g., 52–53) may, on occasion, appear on only one of those pages.

Africana philosophy, 15, 20, 67–68, 84, 127
   Black philosophers, 15, 17, 19–20
Ahmed, Sara, 81, 132–33
Alcoff, Linda, 54–56
Allen, Anita L., 15–16
anti-Black racism, 1–2, 7–8, 13, 26–27, 41–42, 43–44, 53–54, 71–72, 76, 80, 83–85, 86, 89, 90–91, 96, 97–98, 100–1, 110, 113, 120, 127

Baldwin, James, 131–32
Barnes, Riché J. Daniel, 9–10
Black liberation, 2, 16–17
Black matriarch, 2–3, 5, 6, 12, 42–43, 99, 128–29
Black women's club movement, 3–4, 58–59
blues feminism/women, 58, 61–62, 63–64, 65, 70–71, 77
Brake, Elizabeth, 107–8

Cahn, Naomi, 42, 43–45, 47
Calhoun, Cheshire, 91–92, 97–98, 99–102, 103–4, 105–6
Carbone, June, 42, 43–45, 47
Card, Claudia, 53, 91–97
Chambers, Clare, 107–8, 109
citizenship, 40–41, 42–43, 51
   settler sexual citizenship, 6–7, 8–9, 11–12, 15, 65–66, 73, 111–12, 113–14, 115–18, 121, 122–23, 124, 126–27, 128, 130, 132, 134–35
   sexual citizenship, 7, 57, 59, 60, 70–71, 77, 78–79, 83–84, 85, 91–92, 95, 97–98, 103, 105–6, 107–8, 120, 122

Cohen, Cathy, 67–68, 69–70, 80–81, 104–5, 122–23
Collins, Patricia Hill, 18–19, 92, 99–100
Combahee River Collective, 13
Cooper, Anna Julia, 27, 98–99
Cooper, Brittney, 58–59, 60
Cott, Nancy, 7–8, 38, 40, 51
coverture, 84–85, 87–88
Curwood, Anastasia, 5–6, 59

Davis, Angela, 2–3, 18, 61–64, 112
Denetdale, Jennifer Nez, 57–58
deviation, 65, 70–71, 81–82
Dobbs v. Jackson Women's Health Organization, 116–17
Dotson, Kristie, 19–20, 57, 125–26
Dubler, Ariela, 22
Du Bois, W. E. B., 3–6, 54, 112, 130

emancipation, 6, 22–23, 27, 31, 33, 35–37, 40, 58, 88, 112, 128
Eng, David L., 80, 118, 119–20

Fanon, Frantz, 110–11
feminism
   abolition feminism, 2, 112, 113
   Black feminism, 1–3, 12, 91, 98, 129
   Black radical feminism, 8, 11–12, 13, 113–14
   liberal feminism, 2
Freedmen's Bureau, 22–23, 33–35, 36, 37–38

Gadamer, Hans-Georg, 55, 65
Gordon, Lewis, 70, 122, 123–24, 130–31
Griffin-Gracy, Miss Major, 115–17, 123

INDEX

Hammonds, Evelyn, 20
Higginbotham, Evelyn Brooks, 9–10
hooks, bell, 92, 96
Hunter, Tera, 1, 32
Huntington, Clare, 48–50

Indigenous, 7–9, 124–25
intimacy, 84–85, 86, 97–98

James, Joy, 36–37
Jones-Rogers, Stephanie E., 87–88
Jordan, June, 12

Keeling, Kara, 133
Kennedy, Justice Anthony, 26, 27, 29, 41–42, 45–46, 47–51, 114

Lawrence v Texas, 29, 50–51
Lenhardt, Robin, 27–29
liberalism, 3, 83, 109
 neoliberalism, 10–11, 42
Lincoln, Abraham, 32, 33
Livingston v. Williams, 38–39
Lorde, Audre, 92, 104, 130, 132, 133–35

mammy, 96, 100–3
marital shade, 22
 Black married maternal, 23, 54–55, 58, 62, 74
 performance of illegibility, 22–23, 29–30, 33, 35, 36, 41, 51
 theoretical blackface, 2, 85–86
 throwing marital shade, 1, 111–12
marriage
 marriage abolition, 12, 24, 36–37, 52, 59, 84, 85, 95–96, 107–8, 109, 113, 122–23, 125–26, 130
 marriage contract, 18–19, 22–23, 33, 34–35, 37, 89–90
McElya, Micki, 101–2
McKittrick, Katherine, 127–29
McMurtry-Chubb, Teri A., 39, 66–67
McRae, Elizabeth, 88
Melamed, Jodi, 46
Merleau-Ponty, Maurice, 55–56, 80
Mignolo, Walter, 122–23, 126
Mills, Charles, 16–19, 108–9

Moore, Mignon, 52
Moore v. East Cleveland, 77–78, 119
Morrison, Toni, 56–57, 64, 88–89
Moynihan Report, 42–43, 114
Murray, Pauli, 60–61, 65

Obama, Michelle, 25–26
Obergefell v. Hodges, 22–23, 25–28, 41, 42, 47, 52, 92–93, 106, 114, 117–18
Onwuachi-Willig, Angela, 78–80

partus sequitur ventrem, 30–31, 32, 54, 56, 110, 132
Pateman, Carol, 89–91
phenomenology, 80–82

Quashie, Kevin, 129
queerness, 20–22, 64, 74–75, 80, 81–82

racial capitalism, 31, 34, 41, 43–44, 46, 47, 87, 95, 97–98
racial contract, 17–19
racial justice, 5–6, 16, 18–19, 22–23, 36–37, 52, 54, 65–66, 76–77, 95–96, 108–9, 113, 124–25
Rainey, Gertrude "Ma", 61–62, 63, 64–65
respectability politics, 9–10, 58–59, 68–69, 95–96
Roberts, Dorothy, 76–77
Robinson, Cedric, 31

settler colonialism, 5–6, 7–9, 122, 125–26
settler sexuality, 7, 9–10, 12, 62–63, 67–68, 69–70, 127
Shelby, Tommie, 67–68, 70–76, 77, 79–81
slavery, 6, 33, 34
Smith, Bessie, 61–63, 64
Snorton, C. Riley, 54, 130
Spillers, Hortense, 120–21
Stallings, L. H., 14–15, 69–70
Stewart, Dianne M., 10–11

Taylor, Keeanga-Yamahtta, 65–66, 73
Taylor, Paul C., 4, 79–80, 95–96
Threadcraft, Shatema, 74

Walsh, Catherine, 122–23, 126